The Porning of America

The Porning of America

The Rise of Porn Culture,
What It Means, and
Where We Go from Here

Carmine Sarracino and Kevin M. Scott

BEACON PRESS
BOSTON

Beacon Press
25 Beacon Street
Boston, Massachusetts 02108-2892
www.beacon.org

Beacon Press books
are published under the auspices of
the Unitarian Universalist Association of Congregations.

11 10 09 08   8 7 6 5 4 3 2 1

This book is printed on acid-free paper that meets the uncoated paper
ANSI/NISO specifications for permanence as revised in 1992.

Text design and composition by
Wilsted & Taylor Publishing Services

Library of Congress Cataloging-in-Publication Data

Sarracino, Carmine
 The porning of America : the rise of porn culture, what it means, and where we
go from here / Carmine Sarracino and Kevin M. Scott.
    p. cm.
 Includes index.
 ISBN 978-0-8070-6153-4
 1. Pornography in popular culture—United States. 2. Pornography—Social
aspects—United States. 3. Sex in popular culture—United States. I. Scott,
Kevin M. II. Title.

 HQ472.U6S37 2008
 306.77—dc22   2008008099

To Tamara, Dante, and Carina Sarracino
and
Mary Ann, Connor, and Maisie Scott—
for their patience, support, and encouragement.

Contents

Introduction

As college professors, we usually write about subjects that we hold at arm's length: objective, intellectual, dispassionate. But not so in this book.

We are very much part of—involved in, living through—the phenomenon we describe as the porning of America. We are American males, husbands, and parents of small children, each of us the father of a girl and a boy. Strolling in the mall last week, one of us came upon something we had before only read about: thong underwear for little girls.

The other recently saw his four-year-old daughter, enrapt, watching a television ad for Bratz dolls, which look remarkably like prostitutes.[1] Our sons, eight and ten, pretend indifference when such ads appear on their cartoon stations, but we have seen them stealing glimpses, and even ogling, eyes riveted, when they didn't know they were being watched.

How can we, as fathers who are ourselves sexual males, blame them? We too appreciate the allure of the female form and of sex. And we are thankful that our children will grow up in an atmosphere of sexual freedom that will spare them most of the ignorance, hypocrisy, and repression of earlier times. If guilt is disappearing from sensuality and sex, along with shame about the human body, we happily wave goodbye to all that. But what is coming in its place?

What has in fact already arrived is a culture increasingly being shaped by the dominant influence: porn. Porn has so thoroughly been absorbed into every aspect of our everyday lives—language, fashion, advertisements, movies, the Internet, music, magazines, television, video games—that it has almost ceased to exist as something separate from the mainstream culture, something "out there." That is, we no longer have to go to porn in order to get it. It is filtered to us, in some form, regardless of whether we want it or are even aware of it.

If we want porn, the Playboy Channel brings it right into our living rooms. But even if we don't want it, Paris Hilton, for one, brings it into our living rooms via, for example, a television ad for the fast food chain Carl's Jr. in which Hilton—it can only be described this way—performs oral sex on a hamburger. (Shortly after the ad aired, the comedian David Spade remarked that while watching TV he saw a hamburger get to second base with Paris Hilton.) The Internet offers literally millions of porn sites to anyone who wants a peek. But it also offers peeks if you don't want them. For example, one of us, in the weeks before Christmas a few years ago, with an eager kid on each knee, made the mistake of Googling "toys." (And that was in the days when, as is less common now, a closed porn screen automatically launched one or two new porn screens, creating an impromptu video game in which one must click closed pop-ups faster than new ones can open—*flashing butts and breasts!*—while simultaneously elbowing kids off one's knees and shouting, "Daddy needs a minute here!")

For that matter, toys themselves have been, if not rendered pornographic, drafted into pornography's service. Consider again the Bratz doll. The doll pictured here belongs to a line called Bratz Play Sportz, but it is difficult to imagine any sport—outside of a pornographic video—that dresses young women in uniforms of thigh-high fishnets and stiletto heels (popularly called fuck-me

Bratz doll.   *Kevin M. Scott*

pumps). Bratz dolls fundamentally redefine girlhood—and lead many parents to feel as if porn is *hunting* their daughters.

Porn is everywhere in ordinary American life in 2008; indeed, in this book we show that porn is a cultural trend affecting all age groups, all races, and all classes, and that virtually every aspect of ordinary day-to-day life is being shaped by porn. It's not, then, so much that porn has become mainstream, which we often hear, as that the mainstream has become porned. Increasingly in America, we live porn in our daily lives.

What are we to make of this development? Are we worse off, for instance, than we were in earlier times, when pornography was consigned to the back alleys of our culture? The question is far from simple. In fact, it serves as a good entry point into the complexity of the porning phenomenon.

For one thing, those earlier times, sometimes known as the good old days in America, are often sentimentalized. We forget, for instance, that in the nineteenth century boys were commonly told by trusted elders—ministers, fathers, grandfathers—that the sin of "self-pollution" would bring not only eternal damnation in the next world, but physical debility and even insanity in this one. They often sat through blood-chilling lectures that were part of antimasturbation moralist campaigns. Girls, for their part, were informed by their mothers, grandmothers, and aunts that women took no pleasure from sexual intercourse and bore with it simply to produce children. The only women who were exceptions to this rule were prostitutes, whose supposed abnormal sensuality led them to a disgraced life on the streets.

Suffering resulted from such sexual ignorance, repression, and hypocrisy. In 1856 Walt Whitman wrote the first poem in American literature dealing with masturbation, "Spontaneous Me," trying to reassure young men and women that such irrepressible urges were completely natural.

Porn has always existed in some form in America, and it can be found in all the cultures of the world, ancient and modern. If nothing else, the universality of porn forces us to acknowledge a fundamental reality: men and women are, in fact, sexual creatures. And the more that porn has emerged from the shadows and back alleys, the more directly and honestly we as a culture have had to face our own sexuality and decide what we will make of it.

In America today, porn has blown away most of the old dodges and blinders. There are certainly exceptions depending on where one lives and whether one identifies with a religious faith, but it is more difficult now than ever before, for instance, to maintain that pubescent boys and girls should never masturbate. Or that we experience sexual desire only with our "one true love," so that having sex ("making love") becomes the proof positive of having found the chosen one we were destined to marry. Or that normal women have no sexual urges, a falsehood that has been falling away piecemeal over time—the sexual double standard being one of the last vestiges to begin to totter in our own day. Or, to cite another bit of sexual ignorance only now (when the elderly figure prominently on many porn websites) beginning to crumble: that past a certain age, perhaps sixty or seventy, men and women cease to exist as sexual beings. For all the minuses that exist, then, there is clearly a positive side to porn as well.

But it's difficult to make an overall, blanket judgment about porn because the word itself is so imprecise, so vague, that two people arguing on opposite sides of the question might in fact not even be talking about the same thing. Studying porn for the past few years in preparation for this book, we realized almost immediately that porn is not one thing. Porn is not, to put it this way, a single color but rather a whole spectrum. Therefore, its influences on the culture are similarly varied and complex. Some porn is clearly, unequivocally damaging, such as child pornography. As parents, we wish we could consign it not just to the back alleys, but to the back alleys of some distant planet.

And along with child pornography, a good deal of porn can be labeled cultural toxic waste, such as the very dark porn eerily gaining popularity on the Internet, featuring physical abuse, violence, and torture. But there is another side of the spectrum. Some porn movies, especially those produced and directed by women, as well as some amateur homemade adult videos posted on websites, celebrate sensuality and a joyful, mutually shared, playful and affectionate sexuality. It seems mistaken, then, to group these celebratory movies with, say, films depicting sexual torture, as if the two were the same, or equivalent.

To put it simply, there's a whole lot of stuff out there, dramatically varied but all called porn. We need, first of all, to sort through the various types of material and indicate the important differences among them. But in preparing to sort through material referred to as *porn* and *pornography*, it's enlightening first of all to consider that the words have different associations and can convey different things.

Porn is the grandchild of pornography. Porn may share the same gene pool, more or less, as pornography, but it is much younger and hipper, and far more varied. The word *pornography* was invented (from the Greek roots *porne* + *graphien,* or "depicting the acts of prostitutes") by nineteenth-century European art historians who were abashed and flummoxed by what they regarded as obscene paintings, sculptures, and frescoes. The National Museum of Naples was the focal point for this problem, as it held extensive materials from excavations at Pompeii. The excavations had begun in the mid-eighteenth century and almost immediately unearthed shockingly sexual artifacts: a representation of the god Priapus, for instance, with an enormously exaggerated erect phallus, along with frescoes depicting couples copulating.

What to do with this Roman art? As art historians, their aesthetic values compelled them to respect it. But as Catholics, their religious values forbade them from publicly displaying it. How, then, to catalog and store it? To include it in the museum's holdings would have meant exposing the public, especially the young, to the corrupting, immoral influence of graphic sexuality.

So a secret room for the "Pornographic Collection," as it was officially cataloged, was created in the National Museum of Naples in 1866, a room constantly under lock and key, whose doors were guarded day and night. *Pornography* was thus created, both as a word and as a category of human sexuality. It was in a sense an assemblage, stitched together from disparate parts, a painting here, a fresco there, rather like a certain monster similarly pieced together a bit earlier in the century by a young Englishwoman with a wild imagination. And like Mary Shelley's monster, it soon slipped the locks of its secret room and began to rove among the populace, striking fear across the continent.

Pornography, then, the older of the two words, is much more heavily stigmatized. To the curators of the National Museum of Naples, *pornography* connoted "bad." Similarly, the oldest pornography in America consisted of what most of us would regard as —if not bad—undesirable, sexist, objectionable. That is, early pornography in America, from the stereoscopic slides of the Civil War soldiers through the 8 mm blue movies of the decades just after World War I, generally depicted males dominating females for their own pleasure, and often demeaning their female partners, who were usually prostitutes. American feminists generally had in mind male-dominated, exploitative sexuality when they began attacking pornography in the 1960s.

In the 1960s and 1970s the word *porn* began to replace *pornography.* Nowadays, one hears and sees *porn* far more often than *pornography.* The words differ not only in that *porn* refers to a much larger body of material that is far less homogeneous than what was covered by *pornography,* but also in that *porn* is much less stigmatized than its forerunner.

Pornography applied almost exclusively to visual images, either still photos or movies, and only occasionally to writing. On the other hand, *porn* is used loosely, especially by those under forty, to label a great variety of material, including movies, photos, and writing, as well as anime, video games, peep shows, sex toys, and

X-rated lingerie—all without the judgmental sense of "bad." The word *porn* even feels more casual and familiar than *pornography,* like the nickname of a pal.

In Chapter 1, we provide a brief history of pornography in America, showing that in order to enter the mainstream, porn stars began to imitate ordinary men and women. Then, in turn, ordinary men and women began imitating porn stars.

We open the chapter with a discussion of Timothy Greenfield-Sanders' 2004 exhibit, XXX. In this exhibit Greenfield-Sanders, a renowned photographer who has photographed presidents and the most famous celebrities, presented paired portraits of porn stars: on one panel, a nude shot as the individual is familiarly seen in porn films, and in the next, the same individual in street clothes —looking like an ordinary person, someone like you and me.

How did porn stars come to be like you and me? And, more significantly, how have we come to be like porn stars? The answers to these questions bring us to the heart of the cultural phenomenon we call the porning of America.

In Chapter 2 we look at one result of this phenomenon: universal sexualization. Increasingly, ordinary life mimics the ethic of porn, that everyone—regardless of age, profession, social rank— exists to a heightened degree as a sexual entity and therefore as a potential sex partner. The unprecedented sexualization of children (we look closely in Chapter 1 at the Olsen twins) is one manifestation of this phenomenon. But the elderly too are sexualized as never before. Indeed, whatever one's public identity—athlete, politician, schoolteacher—everyone is sexualized in a way and to a degree historically unprecedented before the last quarter of the twentieth century.

Chapter 3 again takes a historical perspective, examining a time often idealized for its supposed dramatic contrast with contemporary times, the 1950s. It was precisely in this "innocent" era of the postwar 1940s and 1950s, however, that pornography began slipping out of the alleys and back rooms of American society and into mainstream culture, especially in comics and men's magazines. Bettie Page, for example, regularly appeared nude in leather and lingerie. But she also appeared in bondage and domination photos that express the struggle to contain the rising social threat —to many men, a threat—of female economic and sexual independence.

The porning of America involves so many important figures that it is impossible to consider them all. In Chapter 4 we have selected (from a possible multitude including Ralph Ginzburg, Henry Miller, Hugh Hefner, Larry Flynt, and Seka) six figures we regard as porn exemplars: Russ Meyer, Al Goldstein, Madonna, Jenna Jameson, Snoop Dogg, and Paris Hilton. We present short portraits of each, focusing on what these individuals brought to the process of furthering the normalization of porn.

Advertising has played a vital role in America's porning, and this is the topic of Chapter 5. We look first at the advertising industry's use of porn to sell all sorts of products, some quite directly linked to sex, but others sexualized only through the porn-derived context of the ad. Hamburgers, for instance, are inherently nonsexual but were presented sexually in the Paris Hilton television commercial for Carl's Jr. Every ad that uses porn to sell a product is at the same time an advertisement for porn. In this chapter we also look at the way thinking about our bodies and sexuality as commodities (an attitude derived from porn) finds popular expression on such websites as Craigslist, MySpace, and Stickam.

In Chapter 6 we examine what might become a major direction for porn, for it is growing in popularity on the Internet, and perhaps in our culture as well: violent sex that emphasizes debasement, humiliation, and the infliction of serious pain. We regard the mistreatment of detainees at the Iraqi prison Abu Ghraib as a watershed in the connection between degradation porn and violence.

So, is this a pro- or anti-porn book? Before addressing that important question directly, in Chapter 7 we look at women's responses to porn. We discuss the first assaults on porn made by feminists such as Andrea Dworkin and Catharine MacKinnon in the 1960s and 1970s, and the often heated debate over porn that continues to the present day. We review the current research surrounding such important questions as whether porn causes violence against women, and we discuss women's influence on the industry as both consumers and producers of porn.

In the last chapter, thinking about where we go from here, we stake out our own position. We would reframe the question of whether our book is anti- or pro-porn and say that it is unequivocally pro-sex. We regard sexuality as a great good in human life, not only for the taking of one's own pleasure, but also for the giving of pleasure—that is, for the enhanced joy of both receiving and imparting a surpassingly ecstatic experience. Of all the ways in which we interact with others in this world, the back-and-forth exchange of sensual pleasure is one of the most satisfying and blissful of all possibilities.

Being wholeheartedly pro-sex, then, we have to say that porn is often *not* pro-sex, and sometimes even anti-sex. Women's porn (produced and directed by women and intended for a female audience), and true amateur porn, consisting mostly of video clips posted on host sites by ordinary men and women, are the most pro-sex porn we have seen.

Typically, in true amateur porn, the sex partners, who are not paid, engage in passionate, playful, personalized sex: they seem to know and like each other and to want to please each other sexually. Their bodies might not be perfect—in fact are sometimes far from perfect—but their sensual excitement and pleasure is undiminished. Contributor blurbs, on sites that include them, often indicate committed relationships—"me and my boyfriend," or even "me and my husband." Often, the sex partners look into each other's eyes, as almost never happens in professional porn, sometimes grin or giggle. For all the lust, in other words, there is also affection and an evident desire to please the partner.

Early in our final chapter we present a critique of porn. An important part of our critique consists of considering alternatives to the anti-sex porn, exploring directions that would remove from porn its—surprising, perhaps—vestiges of Puritanism. For to surf through websites is to revisit, in an odd way, American Puritanism: the sex these sites offer is *nasty, bad, dirty,* the women *sluts* and *whores.* The pornographers and the Puritans start from the same premises. The main difference between them is that the porn sites revel in what the Puritans fled. But there are alternatives to sex rooted in sin and shame. Tantra, which we briefly discuss, is one tangible example of a sensual, ecstatic approach to sexuality that is completely absent the stigma and guilt, and consequent degradation and humiliation, characterizing so much porn.

In thinking about where we go from here, we identify sexualization—which is rampant in our culture—as the root problem underlying the damaging and dangerous practice of turning individuals, especially girls and young women, into sexual objects. Through sexualization individuals are seen as having no value beyond their sexuality. In this regard, we look to the landmark *Report of the American Psychological Association Task Force on the Sexualization of Girls* (2007) for our analysis of the problem, and also for ways to counteract and combat it. Sex without sexualization is an ideal to be pursued.

Porn, then, as the word is used in 2008, ranges from the liberating to the objectionable. The title of our book, *The Porning of America,* simply recognizes that the whole range of possibilities is active now in shaping American culture—in some ways for the better, but in many ways for the worse.

We enjoy enormous sexual freedom in America. As individuals we can explore our own sexuality and make choices about appearance, dress, behavior, identity—about what is broadly called *lifestyle*—as never before in this country. The walls of restriction, limitation, taboo, are everywhere toppling.

In *The Brothers Karamazov*, a main character, Ivan, thinking about the general decline of traditional codes of right and wrong, says, "Now everything is permitted!" Ivan is thrilled at the prospect of unlimited freedom. But he is also deeply troubled.

For *everything is permitted* is as daunting a realization as it is exhilarating. There are, after all, no built-in guarantees, and with unlimited options, we can choose badly as easily as choose well. Violent sexuality, for instance, is gaining in popularity on the Internet and even in Hollywood movies. The abuse and torture at Abu Ghraib alert us to the dangers posed to our very humanity by pornography that is based on sexual humiliation and degradation.

The Porning of America, then, will help you understand clearly what is going on in our culture. And, more than that, it will help you make the most, and not the worst, of our hard-won sexual freedom.

1. Normalizing the Marginal

On a cool Saturday night in New York City, October 30, 2004, a much-anticipated show at a Fifth Avenue art gallery, the Mary Boone, is drawing the bright and the beautiful. The exhibition will eventually travel across the country to other galleries, but this is the opening, and it is part of an intricately choreographed rollout involving book, documentary, and music releases that will get much of elite America talking about its subject: porn.

Ben Stiller and his wife, Christine Taylor, wander the gallery, bumping into the likes of movie directors Barry Levinson and Darren Aronofsky. Calvin Klein, Rachel Weisz, and, of all people, television handyman Bob Vila are present and chat casually with the artist, Timothy Greenfield-Sanders.

Greenfield-Sanders is one of the most famous photographers in America. He has photographed a number of recent tenants of the White House, including President George W. Bush and First Lady Laura Bush, George H. W. and Barbara Bush, Jimmy and Rosalind Carter, Hillary Clinton, and Vice President Al Gore and several Supreme Court justices. He has photographed world-famous actors, musicians, artists, and writers. Like appearing on the cover of *Time* as a politician, or reaching the $20-million-per-movie level as an actor, to be photographed by Greenfield-Sanders is to be recognized as having made it. Big time.

At the gallery, however, neither the glitterati nor the renowned photographer are suns around which the planets orbit. Rather, attention goes to the subjects of several of Greenfield-Sanders's exhibited portraits who are present in the room: Gina Lynn, Nina Hartley, Tera Patrick, Savanna Sampson, and Chad Hunt. Together, they have starred in well over a thousand porn films.

Greenfield-Sanders was inspired to create this exhibition, XXX, after he watched the 1997 Paul Thomas Anderson film *Boogie Nights,* which explores the lives of porn stars. If there is a plot at all to *Boogie Nights,* it is the growth of the porn industry: its increasing awareness of what popular audiences want and, in response, its imitation of Hollywood. (The fictional director, played by Burt Reynolds, finally realizes his great dream of making porn —*With a plot! Like a real movie!*)

Similarly, Greenfield-Sanders's exhibition attempts to show porn as mainstream. The exhibit is a series of thirty diptychs, each depicting side-by-side portraits of an individual in identical poses, except that in one the porn star is clothed, and in the other, naked. The portraits are large, about five by four feet, and placed high on the wall, so the viewer must look up at the faces (and chests) of the figures. Several are slightly larger than life size, yet each figure stares straight out from the photo. With a few exceptions, the figures exude confidence and ease, especially in the nude photos.

To most Americans, the names of those pictured would be unfamiliar, but a few figures have achieved a kind of fame that breaks through the old barriers against pornography. Ron Jeremy, the porn everyman, portly and unthreatening, regularly takes cameos in movies and television shows. Nina Hartley has become an intellectual critic of porn, and of culture in general. Most famous of all, certainly, is Jenna Jameson, a voluptuous blonde who looks back at the viewer with a gaze both sexual and challenging—a Marilyn Monroe with attitude.

It is a purposely provocative show. Greenfield-Sanders has said that his intention for the exhibit is to start a discussion about who these people are and what they do. Who, indeed, are they, then? And what do they do?

The back-and-forth visual transference from the clothed, average-looking person (as most of them are) to the naked, sexual one, breaks down the difference between the two. On one side is the portrait of an apparently ordinary man or woman, dressed in a sweater and jeans or some other casual outfit. On the other side, we see the same person in almost the identical pose, but wearing not a stitch. The overall effect of these side-by-side presentations, clothed/naked, clothed/naked, one after another, is to fuse the ordinary and the normal with the world of porn.

Who are these people? People like you and me. What do they do? They make a living naked, having sex in front of a camera.

The XXX exhibit was an artistic expression of a truth about American life: porn had found its way into mainstream culture. How many of the exhibit viewers, though, exiting into the chilly New York City night, thought about the other side of the equation of porn stars and themselves? The side of the equation dealing with porn's transformative impact on the way people live. That is, if porn stars have become like us, how have we in turn become like porn stars?

When we ask the question in terms of how porn has changed us, we get to the heart of the matter. We are then asking not how porn has become mainstream but, much more important, how the mainstream has become porned. A host of further questions then arise: How has porn changed the way we see one another and ourselves? How has it altered our personal relationships and our sexual behavior? How has it changed the social order? How has it shaped our individual identities, and our national identity? To begin to answer these questions, we need to have some understanding of the development of pornography in America.

GROWTH OF THE PORN RUNT

Nathaniel Philbrick's *In the Heart of the Sea: The Tragedy of the Whaleship Essex* (2000) tells about a surprisingly sexually active religious sect in colonial America: the Quakers living off the coast of Massachusetts on Nantucket Island. In this community, where men were at sea hunting whales for long periods of time, sometimes even years, it was an open secret that the women had learned to pleasure themselves. Their journals contain opaque references to their masturbatory activities, including code words for dildos, such as *he's at homes*. In 1979, homeowners remodeling a house in the historic district of Nantucket found a six-inch dildo made of clay.

Still, examples of what might be considered porn from seventeenth- and eighteenth-century America are rare, and consist mainly of cheaply printed pamphlets, called chapbooks, containing smutty jokes, lewd drawings, and cartoons.[1] The chapbooks were produced surreptitiously, bought for a penny or two, and passed around among males.

Unlike the Nantucket Quakers, the Puritans, the largest group of earliest settlers, kept their secret sex lives, if they had them, secret. And yet, as we will show, the Puritans figure importantly in the construction of the American idea of pornography.

Despite the stereotype of them as austere and sexually repressed, the Puritans were quite sexually active. Recent scholars, for instance, have examined the records of births, deaths, and marriages in various colonies and discovered that quite often the date of a first child's birth was less than nine months from the time of the parents' marriage. This may well have been a result of the practice of bundling, in which prospective couples were allowed to sleep in the same bed, typically in the home of the young woman's parents, provided they were individually restrained in garments or separated by a board. Unsurprisingly, many young people found their way around these obstacles and into each other's embrace. Also, remarriage after the death of a spouse often happened quickly, without the observance of what many today would consider a proper period of mourning. One cannot help wondering whether the later marriage had originated as a liaison of some sort.[2]

But the reason we connect the Puritans with pornography has to do with their religious condemnation of sexuality as sinful and satanic, and the denial (whether hypocritical or not) of their own sensual nature, which they constantly tried to hold in check.

One of the first things that the Puritans built in the New World were high walls separating their settlements from the natural world, which they feared for both rational and irrational reasons. Rationally, there were of course beasts and hostile Indians to fear. But reading their journals and letters, it quickly becomes clear that their fear of "the howling wilderness," as one eminent Puritan, William Bradford, repeatedly described the American landscape in his journals, had more to do with their phobia regarding wildness than with any actual threat. The term so came to describe the new continent for the Puritans that Josias Winslow used it in his elegy of Bradford as a man who, if God bade him, would again follow God into "a howling wilderness."

The beasts *out there* and the Indians *out there*...on the other side of the wall, in the dark woods...were *wild!* They gave in to all sorts of base and lewd desires. But within the settlement walls the Puritans could hold themselves apart from lawless, godless, unchecked impulses. They could remain focused on Scripture and under control, no matter how white-knuckled and tight-lipped.

Pornography, as it grows and strides across America over the mid-nineteenth and twentieth centuries, and then dominates American culture at the turn of the new millennium, typically has an essentially Puritan point of view on sensuality and sex. The vocabulary of the typical Internet porn site could be written by one of Nathaniel Hawthorne's *Scarlet Letter* Puritans: Sex is *sinful! Nasty! Naughty!* The only difference in this regard between the Puritans and the pornographers is that from the same starting point they go not merely in different, but in opposite, directions. Porn revels in what Puritanism rejects.

In the world of porn, sex is dirty, the women are sluts—but unlike what happens in the world of Puritanism, in porn all restraints are off. The walls are down. The Puritan wilderness becomes the porn playground. The immensely popular contemporary series of porn films called Girls Gone Wild is a Puritan nightmare come horribly, horribly true.[3]

FROM THE CIVIL WAR TO CELEBRITY CULTURE: PORN COMES INTO ITS OWN

In all the changes wrought by the Civil War, from the earthshaking to the trivial, the oddest may be this: the War Between the States marked the beginning of the pornography industry in America.[4]

In the middle of the nineteenth century, for the first time, it became technologically possible to cheaply and quickly produce multiple prints of a photograph. And just when this happened, the Civil War separated hundreds of thousands of men and boys from their wives and sweethearts. For most of them it was their first time away from home. They were lonely and bored in camps. The words *horny* and *hooker* came into widespread usage.[5]

Photographs of all kinds were important to the soldiers. In the pockets of their frock coats they carried ambrotypes of their loved ones. They mailed home small calling cards, called *cartes de visite,* showing themselves photographed in uniform, wielding Colt revolvers and bowie knives. And deep down in their haversacks, or under the straw mattresses of their winter quarters, they hid stereoscopic photos of seductive women. When viewed through a special holder, two side-by-side photographic images transformed into the three-dimensional form of a girl clad only in see-through gauze, or brazenly lying with her legs spread. The popular *carte de visite* had a prurient incarnation: a prostitute's nude form occupied the space normally reserved for the image of the gallant soldier.

It did not take long for some to spot a market opportunity, however illicit. Young men may have been horny before the war, but they were spread thinly across a nation of farms. Now they were amassed in camps, by the thousands and tens of thousands, away from the prying eyes at home that would certainly have prevented them from trafficking in pornography via the mail. Companies such as G. S. Hoskins and Co. and Richards & Roche in New York City sent out flyers and catalogs to the soldiers, detailing their offerings: photographs of Parisian prostitutes; condoms and dildos; even miniaturized photographs that could be concealed in jewelry such as stickpins, and that, when held close to the eye, revealed a couple engaged in a sex act.

Despite the sea of catalogs that were printed, only a handful survive. From time to time field commanders "cleaned up camp" and built bonfires with the copious material. No doubt countless more after the war fell victim to former soldiers' pangs of conscience or to the fear that a family member might happen upon them. In *The Story the Soldiers Wouldn't Tell: Sex in the Civil War,* Thomas P. Lowry reviews five catalogs, including one that ended up in the National Archives because a Capt. M. G. Tousley wrote to President Lincoln complaining of the obscene catalogs and thought to include a sample. We don't know whether Lincoln ever saw the catalog, but it is droll to imagine him, in those darkly serious days, paging through "mermaids wearing only mist and foam," and "The Temptation of St. Anthony," showing the "naked charms" of the seductresses, and "Storming the Enemy's Breastworks," in which a Northern soldier quite literally assaults the breasts of a Southern belle.

A new industry had been created, and a lot of money was changing hands. So much obscene material was passing through the mail that the Customs Act of 1842, which contained the first federal antiobscenity legislation, was strengthened in 1857. In

1865, in an attempt to check the flood of pornography triggered by the Civil War, a federal statute prohibited the use of the mail to ship obscene books and pictures. After the war, alarmed moralists led by the zealous crusader Anthony Comstock, who was truly obsessed with stamping out smut, passed the Comstock Act of 1873, making it illegal to trade in "obscene literature and articles of immoral use." As Walter Kendrick notes in *The Secret Museum: Pornography in Modern Culture*, Comstock himself, in 1874, reported seizing and destroying in a two-year period 134,000 pounds of "books of improper character" as well as 194,000 pictures and 60,300 "sundries" such as "rubber articles."

Those who today look to legislation, or to a moral crusade, as the best means to limit if not eliminate pornography, would do well to recall Comstock's relentless, but ultimately futile, efforts. Attorney General Edwin Meese and his Commission on Pornography, convened about a hundred years after Comstock's campaign (the commission's final report was issued, and almost immediately ignored, in 1986), could have saved time and energy had it recalled that earlier zealot's failure.

And zealot he certainly was. Comstock, who was not above using false names and even disguises to investigate obscene materials, pursued wrongdoers with the tenacity of a pit bull. He drove one offender, W. Haines, a surgeon by training who became rich producing more than three hundred obscene books, to suicide.

Before Haines, an Irishman, appeared on the scene, America had only imported from Europe, but not produced, obscene books. Haines changed all that. By 1871 he was selling one hundred thousand such books a year. The night before he killed himself, Haines received a message: "Get out of the way. Comstock is after you. Damn fool won't look at money." In later years Comstock, who would blush at an indelicate photograph, boasted about the suicide, which he regarded as a victory over the forces of evil.

But neither the criminalization of obscenity in 1865 nor Comstock's obsessive crusade killed off pornography. Another war, the Great War, was not far on the horizon, and it would once again concentrate huge numbers of lonely, horny men—and with photographic and printing technologies further advanced, offer them an improved, more enticing product.

Porn's birth weight had been low, and the runt was pushed into the dark alleys of American life. But there it thrived. By the end of the twentieth century, it had emerged mature and powerful—son of the European curators' Frankenstein. Widely known if not respected, it had corporate offices in New York, Chicago, and Los Angeles. Its annual earnings at the turn of the twenty-first century were estimated at $10 billion to $14 billion.

But the financial success of the pornography industry, including its close ties to Fortune 500 corporations, is not our principal interest. As teachers and scholars, we have been drawn to culture studies. One of us has for many years taught a college course called Growing Up in America. The other has written and lectured on twentieth-century popular culture, such as comic books, men's magazines, and video games. Along such lines of interest, we have turned our attention to pornography.

Why would we do so? Because porn increasingly dominates American life in 2008, shaping our entertainments, influencing the way we dress and talk, the way we see one another, and the way we behave sexually. If we want to know who we are now—as individuals and as a nation—we must recognize and come to understand the phenomenon that we call the porning of America.

From the Civil War until recent times, pornography was marginalized and stigmatized. Lately, though, it has moved from the edges to the mainstream of American culture. But more than that—and far more importantly—it has now become the dominant influence shaping our culture.

Porn spread beyond a particular segment of the population— soldiers at war—and began to enter the mainstream of American culture via early porn films variously known as blue movies, stag movies, and smokers. These were typically anonymous productions, and the participants were often, like outlaws, masked. Not only were they not like us, they were, visually, the opposite of us: we show our faces and hide our genitals; they hid their faces and showed their genitals.

Further, the individuals who appeared in these short movies (fifteen to twenty minutes long) were not "acting" in any sense. The women were usually prostitutes, photographed performing sexual acts with their johns.

But by the turn of the twenty-first century the outlaws had become entertainers, celebrities even, acting in scripted movies. Many of these porn stars were so familiar to so many Americans that a sophisticated and highly regarded exhibit of their portraits, the XXX exhibit, could be shown in a major art gallery. Rather than misfits and deviants, then, they had become, in about a hundred and fifty years, people like you and me. They had become like us and we in turn had come to imitate the way they dressed, talked, and behaved sexually. Our identities merged to such a degree that what had been marginalized and stigmatized became instead the norm.

"SHE'S GONNA LOOK JUST LIKE A PORN STAR!"

Dr. 90210 is a reality television show on the E! network featuring patients undergoing plastic surgery. A recent show was typical of the offerings.

"Heather Ann," an attractive, self-employed beautician in her twenties, was about to receive breast implants. As she was sedated in preparation, she expressed anxiety about undergoing surgery to her mother and boyfriend.

Then the cameras followed Dr. Robert Rey, a Harvard Medical School graduate, as he deftly inserted implants to enlarge Heather Ann's breasts. Camera cutaways showed the patient's mother and

boyfriend fidgeting and chatting nervously throughout the proce-
dure. Finished, Dr. Rey cleaned up and went to the waiting room.
He assured Heather's mother and boyfriend that everything had
gone very well, adding: "She's gonna look just like a porn star!"
They beamed back at him.

Even as a joke—a lighthearted comment to break the tension
—we cannot imagine anything comparable from a doctor speaking to a patient's family members much before the mid-1990s, by
which time porn had been destigmatized for most Americans. Dr.
Rey did not know the mother and boyfriend well, but well enough
to surmise that neither was, say, a Christian fundamentalist. For
the most part, only religious extremists and the elderly (who tend to
think of porn in terms of its earlier, stigmatized incarnations)
would now take offense at the easygoing comparison of a daughter
or girlfriend with a porn star.

Porn stars, like celebrities in general, had become not only culturally accepted but even objects of emulation, as exemplified by
popular books published in 2004 and 2005, *How to Make Love Like
a Porn Star*, by Jenna Jameson, and *How to Have a XXX Sex Life*,
by "the Vivid Video stars," eight performers well known in the
industry—all functioning now as educators of a public eager to
learn their sex secrets. So destigmatized had the term become that
girls and young women playfully sported T-shirts emblazoned with
the words PORN STAR.

The release of the porn film *Deep Throat* in 1972 would be
a pivotal event in the cultural changes that permitted Dr. Rey
his icebreaker. But the mainstreaming of porn actually began in
those innocent days of the 1950s, with Hugh Hefner and *Playboy*
magazine.

Before *Playboy* started publication in 1953, porn was low-rent.
As we have seen, the earliest pornography in seventeenth- and
eighteenth-century America consisted of ribald tales badly printed
and shabbily bound. Through the nineteenth century and most of

the twentieth, pornography was typically printed on cheap paper, featuring grainy photographs of prostitutes and their johns. Prostitutes were depicted as desperate women—alcoholics and drug addicts, victimized by brutal pimps. The marginalization of the women and men in the photographs was evident in the illegal, seedy-looking presentations of porn and the underground nature of the porn industry.

The communications theorist Marshall McLuhan famously said, "The medium is the message." On its simplest level this complex understanding may be applied to *Playboy*'s presentation of soft-core pornography. The "message" in the medium of the cheap catalogs sold to Civil War soldiers, for instance, was: *Here are deviants, losers, engaged in sinful, taboo, illicit—but tempting! exciting! —sexual behavior. Want to take a peek?* (While of course allowing the partaker to remain on the other side of the line separating darkness from light.)

Shame—the shame of poverty, of transgression, the shame of the outsider—was in a sense encoded into the early presentations of pornography. Shame inhibits identification. We don't want to see as "ourselves" those who are socially, morally, and legally stigmatized.

Hefner, however, imitated prestigious magazines such as *The Saturday Evening Post* and *The New Yorker* in the quality of paper and sophisticated formatting and graphics he used, publishing only the best writers and photographers. Most importantly, he featured seminude and nude photographs of "the girl next door"—an All-American girl who, in a typical profile, enjoyed long walks on the beach, playing the guitar, and sharing a candlelit bottle of wine with a special someone.

The principal element in the mainstreaming of porn is that it enters the world that the readers/viewers themselves inhabit or would like to inhabit. It must enter their actual or desired reality in order for them to identify with it. In the case of *Playboy*, readers hefted the slick pages of stunning photographs of wholesome, beautiful girls, intermixed with images of and information about high-end stereo equipment, hip apartments, and sports cars, and thought, consciously or not: *This is me! This is who I am—or who I want to be!* Interviews with luminaries (McLuhan himself was featured in March 1969) added the element of intellectual attainment to material acquisition.

Were the *Playboy* playmates actually "like" the readers of the magazine? Were they the girl next door? Only if the girl next door happened to be an anatomically perfect aspiring or established model or actress who mingled with celebrities in a certain Chicago mansion. The playmates were, in their own way, as distant from the men and women who read *Playboy* as the catalog hookers were from the farm boy soldiers marching to Gettysburg.

Through *Playboy*, however, pornography (albeit soft core) not only detached itself from the negative associations of earlier porn, but also in fact attached itself to the polar opposite of those negatives. If earlier porn inhibited individuals' readiness to identify with losers, *Playboy*, on the contrary, made them feel like the affluent, smart, informed winners they aspired to be.

Within this elevation of the social context of pornography, in 1972 *Deep Throat* took porn movies in an entirely new direction, much as *Playboy* had done for print porn. *Deep Throat* abandoned the stag movie format, and instead starred an actress, billed as Linda Lovelace, along with a supporting cast. Instead of the twenty-minute length of the traditional 8 mm stag movie, it ran about an hour and a half. And—wonder of wonders—it was actually scripted, with characters and a plot (of sorts), as well as all the sex expected of a blue movie. It was, in other words, in all its basic elements a Hollywood movie, but with the added feature of plenty of graphic sex.

To say that the movie is a cultural milestone (as has become fashionable since the release of the 2005 documentary *Inside Deep*

Throat) does not exaggerate its significance. Top celebrities—the likes of Frank Sinatra, Mike Nichols, and Sammy Davis Jr.—not only admitted watching the film, but raved about it. (The documentary features such intellectual luminaries as Gore Vidal, Norman Mailer, and Camille Paglia, with cameos by the political satirist Bill Maher and Hugh Hefner.) From a financial point of view, the movie was an unprecedented blockbuster: shot for around $24 thousand, it has grossed perhaps as much as $600 million in worldwide revenues from an audience estimated at 10 million viewers. In the industry of pornography, nothing like it had ever been seen—or probably even imagined.

What explains *Deep Throat's* acceptance and cultural assimilation? Although not billed as a porn comedy, the film adopts a goofy comic tone right from the outset. The camera follows Linda Lovelace walking along the docks in Miami, and getting into her car as credits roll and a sound track plays. For a couple of minutes the camera watches over her shoulder from the backseat as she drives (a somewhat eerie shot for those who know that the actress was involved in three serious car wrecks, the third fatal in 2002, when she was fifty-three. In fact, camera angles were carefully planned in *Deep Throat* to avoid showing a scar on her abdomen that had resulted from an earlier accident.)

When Linda arrives home, she finds her mother in the living room, legs spread over a chair, enjoying cunnilingus. Well, sort of enjoying: in addition to its silliness, a tone of ennui pervades the film. Her mother, for instance, languidly lights a cigarette, tilts up the head of her busy partner, and asks, "Mind if I smoke while you're eating?" The sound track plays "Taking a Break from the Mundane."

The structure of the film is simple, consisting of typical 8 mm sex loops, without dialogue but with musical accompaniment, interspersed with a plot based on a nutty premise: Linda learns from a Dr. Young, a psychiatrist, that the reason she cannot achieve orgasm is that her clitoris is in her throat. Concluding her gynecological examination, he announces, "No wonder you hear no bells, you have no tinkler!" During the exam, the sound track consists of a dirty version of Mickey and Sylvia's well-known "Love Is Strange."

One more example of the slapstick humor that characterizes the film: Dr. Young consoles Linda, "Having a clitoris deep down in the bottom of your throat is better than having no clitoris at all." "That's easy for you to say," she objects. "Suppose your balls were in your ear?" He is momentarily flummoxed, until a lightbulb pops on over his head: "Well, then I could hear myself coming!"

Humor, even lame humor, is disarming. From a propagandistic point of view, the makers of *Deep Throat* had stumbled onto a mass-market presentation of porn that would assist its acceptance, its normalization.

First, the opening credits announced, "Introducing Linda Lovelace As Herself." We had an actress, then, rather than the prostitute of a typical 8 mm stag movie, but she was "playing herself" —an ordinary, attractive young woman—someone we might know. Once the movie begins, the humor takes over and in effect tells us to lighten up, not to take it seriously. It's just entertainment, dizzy and raunchy, like some weird, X-rated *I Love Lucy*.

It worked. The star, Linda Lovelace, appeared in an extensive photo layout by Richard Fegley in *Playboy* in April 1973, and the next month on the cover of *Esquire* magazine dressed in a polkadot dress modestly buttoned to the white wing collar and wearing white gloves—a send-up of the girl next door, but the girl next door nevertheless.

Hidden beneath the appearance of an ordinary young woman starring in a new kind of porn film, however, lay an altogether different reality—one representative, in fact, of "old porn." Linda Susan Boreman, "Linda Lovelace," was a former prostitute who had appeared in such 8 mm stag movies as *Dogarama* (also known

Linda Lovelace, May 1973.
Anthony Edgeworth for Esquire.

as *Dog Fucker*) in 1969, and *Piss Orgy* in 1971. Her husband/
manager, Chuck Traynor, had forced her—often at gunpoint, she
later claimed—to perform in the stag movies and in *Deep Throat*.
Add to this submerged reality the heavy use of hard drugs by
Linda, her husband, and others in the movie, along with mob involvement (mainly financial, but some theaters were reportedly
strong-armed into featuring *Deep Throat*), and the film seems
quite far afield indeed from mainstream American culture's notions of acceptability.

Still, the crucial step had been taken: Linda Lovelace presented
herself in some important ways as "one of us." She was, after all, the

star of a kind of movie we recognize as legitimate: one that plays in theaters, not in the back rooms of smoky men's clubs, features attractive actors in a narrative that defused its illicit subject matter with a comic outlandishness, had a sound track and rolled credits, and was viewed and praised by well-known and respected figures. As film critic Richard Corliss pointed out in a March 29, 2005, *Time* online article, "That Old Feeling: When Porno Was Chic," even comics such as Johnny Carson and Bob Hope, cultural icons in 1972, made jokes about *Deep Throat,* conferring a kind of blessing on the film, tacitly legitimatizing it and its place in the world.

The film was quickly followed by another in 1972, *Behind the Green Door.* In it, Marilyn Chambers was in fact billed as "the All-American Girl." Chambers (who would in 1975 marry Chuck Traynor, divorced from Linda Lovelace) was indeed so all-American looking that just as *Behind the Green Door* was released, Ivory Snow soap flakes put out a newly designed box featuring a photo of a mother holding her baby. The mother was none other than Marilyn Ann Briggs, otherwise known as Marilyn Chambers, the suddenly famous porn star. Procter and Gamble abashedly withdrew the box design.

Like *Deep Throat, Behind the Green Door* imitated the Hollywood movie and contained a hip sound track, an important element in getting the audience to identify with the characters in the film. Again, to paraphrase McLuhan, an audience does not so much listen to a sound track as put it on, bathe in it. A sound track of hits feels familiar and comfortable, making everything associated with it more familiar and comfortable.

These two movies from 1972 launched the porn movie industry as we know it today, catapulting its stars to celebrity status and playing to larger and larger audiences of men and women, especially through the addition of video (and later DVD) rentals and sales.

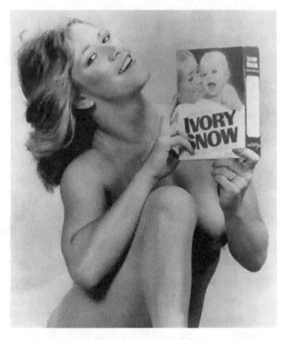

Marilyn Chambers, holding the box of Ivory Snow for
which she posed as the mother.

Beginning in the early 1970s, then, it became increasingly easy
to acquire porn without buying it under the counter or from a
shady character on a street corner. One could simply go to the
neighborhood theater or, beginning in the 1980s, to a hotel or mo-
tel with in-room pay-per-view. In the 1990s, of course, porn would
come right to your home through cable offerings such as Vivid, the
Spice Channel, and the Playboy Channel. In these ways, the acquisition of porn has become quick and easy, a critical step in its des-
tigmatization.

But the story of the mainstreaming of pornography, with its
shaping influence on American life and culture, is more complex
and subtle than simply the evolution of the pornographic movie industry. If *Deep Throat* took porn films in a totally new direction by

imitating Hollywood, and by drawing on girl-next-door and all-American stereotypes, soon enough Hollywood and ordinary people would in turn begin imitating porn.

In the same year as *Deep Throat* and *Behind the Green Door,* Marlon Brando starred in Bernardo Bertolucci's *Last Tango in Paris,* which transgressed the limits of traditional Hollywood treatments of sex, even containing an infamous "butter scene" of anal penetration. But the film was controversial, and not in any sense mainstream. It was originally unrated, then later rated NC-17.

Fast-forward to the mid-1990s, however, and a Hollywood movie could now deal with explicit sex, including such taboos as anal sex. The celebrated film *Leaving Las Vegas* (1995), for instance, contained these lines delivered by the prostitute Sera (played by Elisabeth Shue) to Ben Sanderson (Nicholas Cage): "So for five hundred bucks you can do pretty much whatever you want. You can fuck my ass. You can come on my face—whatever you wanna do. Just keep it outta my hair, I just washed it."

It is impossible to imagine those lines ever finding their way into a Hollywood movie without the decades of porn films preceding it. Later in the movie, Sera is anally gang-raped, and we see her nude in the shower (an overhead shot) with blood washing down her legs and into the drain. The film was regarded as somewhat risqué, but not seriously controversial. It was rated R. In fact, Elisabeth Shue was nominated that year for an Academy Award for Best Actress for her role as Sera, and Nicholas Cage won the Oscar for Best Actor.

If Hollywood had been transformed by porn (a character like Sera could not have existed in a movie of the 1950s, 1960s, or even the 1970s), so had the audience. Only an audience in a sense made ready by the kind of porn films that *Deep Throat* pioneered would accept such language and images in a Hollywood movie.

SOFTENING THE CONTOURS

Two films from the 1970s and early 1980s—*Pretty Baby* (1978) and *Blame It on Rio* (1984)—are instructive in showing the major role that Hollywood played in normalizing pornography, thereby increasing its power to influence and eventually dominate American culture.

In his review of *Pretty Baby* in the *New York Times,* Vincent Canby remarked that the filmmakers (Louis Malle directed and cowrote the screenplay) had "softened the contours of what was probably a very sordid history by making a film of dazzling physical beauty."

In much the same way that Hugh Hefner glamorized soft-core pornography through the sophistication of *Playboy* as a physical artifact, Louis Malle took on a subject that had only been dealt with in the most taboo kinds of hard-core pornography—child pornography and child prostitution—and made his treatment not only acceptable but admirable.

A good part of the physical beauty that Canby found in the film was provided by a young Brooke Shields, in the role of Violet, the "trick baby" of New Orleans prostitute Hattie (Susan Sarandon). In the film, Hattie auctions off her preteen daughter's virginity.

Canby does not mention in his review that the film includes nude scenes of the twelve-year-old Shields, photographed in ways that are provocative and enticing. (He does assert, however, that the film is "neither about child prostitution nor is it pornographic.")

Although the film is indeed about a misfit photographer (whom Canby takes as the "real" subject of the movie), it nevertheless also plays to the prurience of the audience, which is viewing what would in other less-normalized contexts be regarded (and perhaps even prosecuted) as child pornography. But the film distances itself from child pornography by first of all being *about* child prostitution, and then further distances itself because it clearly does not in any sense endorse prostitution, and in fact presents us with the pathos of a prostitute who is sexy, savvy, and also enjoys playing with her very first doll.

Perhaps most important of all, it distances itself from what Canby rightly notes is a sordid history by virtue of the film's style— not only its cinematic aesthetic but the glamour of the Hollywood celebrities the movie features (Keith Carradine, Susan Sarandon) and the allure of the child star Shields.

So *Pretty Baby*, in 1978, after the era of *Deep Throat* and other Hollywood-like porn movies, could present the topic of child-as-sex-object in candid and graphic ways that, by contrast, Stanley Kubrick's *Lolita* could not dare in 1962. In Kubrick's movie, a nude scene of Sue Lyon as Lolita was so unthinkable it was never even proposed by Vladimir Nabokov, who wrote the screenplay, or Stanley Kubrick, who directed. Lolita and Humbert Humbert (James Mason) were not allowed even to kiss, let alone display any kind of sexuality—as later they would in the 1997 remake of *Lolita* starring Jeremy Irons and Dominique Swain.

Two years after *Pretty Baby*, Brooke Shields was back on the screen in *The Blue Lagoon*, again nude, now as an early teen (both fictionally and in fact). Just as *Deep Throat* opened a door for other porn movies to crowd through, so *Pretty Baby* opened a farther door for the unabashed portrayal of children as sex objects, frequently partnered with adults.

Blame It on Rio, for example, another star-studded movie (Michael Caine, Valerie Harper, Demi Moore), dealt with two older men, best friends, who vacation in Rio with their teenage daughters. One of them, Matthew (played by Michael Caine) winds up in a sexual relationship with the other's daughter (Jennifer, played by Michelle Johnson). Johnson was not yet eighteen when the movie was filmed. Caine was fifty-one.

Age in this film—Jennifer's and, for that matter, Matthew's—is treated in comic, and even titillating, ways, not as something truly problematic or disturbing. Consider the following exchanges.

MATTHEW: I'm twenty years older than you.
JENNIFER: Twenty-eight.
MATTHEW: Twenty-five.

A bit later, Jennifer comes in while Matthew is shaving and asks for a kiss.

MATTHEW: Kiss you? I'll spank you!
JENNIFER: Ooooooo, please! And bite me too!

In 1980 Brooke Shields moved offscreen to star in ads for Calvin Klein jeans. The most famous of these showed Shields slightly bent over (presumably having just pulled on a pair of jeans) beginning to button her enticingly open blouse, with the tag line: "Nothing comes between me and my Calvins." She was now fifteen years old and a familiar sex symbol in America and overseas as well. A teenager functioning as a sex symbol had by now become, culturally speaking, accepted as normal—thanks in large part to the barrier-breaking influence of pornography (such as *Deep Throat*) on Hollywood mainstream movies.

The contours of the taboo had been sufficiently softened that, by the 1990s, children as sex objects had become culturally familiar in movies, on television, and in advertisements—with all sorts of offshoots. For instance, beauty pageants for very little girls—five or six, and even younger—swelled into a multimillion-dollar industry of local, regional, and national competitions involving highly paid consultants and coaches, clothing designers, makeup specialists, and so on. Arguably, the winner of these pageants is the child who most successfully combines adult sexuality with childlike innocence. (The most well known of such child beauty queens, of course, is JonBenét Ramsey, who was murdered in 1996.)

Calvin Klein's use of children as sex objects continued in the 1990s with an ad campaign featuring children in highly sexualized situations. When rumors began circulating that he was being investigated on charges of the sexual exploitation of children, he began pulling the ads in August 1995. Sexualized children, however, continued to appear in ads, movies, and on television. Consider, for instance, the Olsen twins.

Mary-Kate and Ashley Olsen have become a brand name. After the twins turned eighteen, in June 2004, they took over control of their corporation, Dualstar Entertainment Group, a company that brings in over a billion dollars a year and has made each of the twins worth a reported $137 million. The twins first gained fame as the character Michelle Tanner on the sitcom *Full House,* starting their acting careers at less than a year old. The show ran for eight years, so the country watched them grow up nearly from their birth. The public's attachment to the girls was clearly a significant component in the popularity of the series, and the twins' manager parents quickly took advantage of their daughters' popularity by getting the girls involved in making movies and music designed, at first, for the children's market, and later for the increasingly important "tween" market of eight-to-twelve-year-olds.

Like Martha Stewart, the twins themselves became the product their company sold, and it sold them hard. Dualstar continues to produce the Olsen twins' movies and music, but also their makeup, perfume, dolls, books, furniture, and, most importantly, a profitable clothing line available at Wal-Mart. More than any other single popular-culture figure, the twins, for over a decade, determined what tweeners could aspire to. And while Dualstar has always marketed the twins as wholesome American girls, their popularity has grown, in significant part, due to the steady porning of Mary-Kate and Ashley. Whether the marketing of the twins intentionally adopted the imagery of porn or whether the online porn community merely appropriated the twins, they became the fuel for an online porn engine that combined pedophilia and kiddie porn with twin and sister porn.

From the beginning, much of the charm of each sister has been the fact that she is half of a set, and as the girls evolved from being twin actresses to a business phenomenon, their twin-ness was the focus of the marketing campaign. Today, dozens of websites are dedicated to the twins as children, and many more include photographs of the girls at ages two, three, four, etc. . . . The most common kind of image pictures Mary-Kate with her arms around Ashley, or vice versa, faces close together and both smiling widely into the camera.

Theorists have long studied the fascination with twins, generally suggesting that the dual nature of twins is so provocative because it underscores the singleness most of us experience as lone and separate entities. Pornography, of course, has always found ways to sexualize such fascinations.

An ad from shoe designer Steve Madden's so-called big-headed-girl campaign finds a marketing use for the twins fascination. The twins pictured in the ad display more than their shoes here, and their handholding, their gazes, and their overt sexuality invite the viewer to imagine them together, without their shoes on or any other clothing. The ad hardly strives for subtlety, however, as every business on the street has the word *twins* in its name.

Until 2005, the Steve Madden brand openly targeted women in their teens and early twenties, and the big-headed-girl ads captured the precise mixture of attitude and sexuality that would make the midpriced brand popular. It also captured the self-sexualization trend that girls and young women are increasingly expected to adopt. The twins in the ad—who look suspiciously like the Olsen twins—possess the bodies of Bratz dolls and strike the same pose as well, right down to their cocked wrists. With their massive

Steve Madden ad.

heads and extra-large eyes, Bratz dolls have roughly the same pro-portions as toddlers and combine come-hither sexuality with child-like vulnerability.

This, of course, is the same strategy apparent in the selling of the Olsen twins. (No wonder, then, that bloggers and discussion board posts have long described the Olsen twins as living Bratz dolls.) The imagery of the Olsens began to change as they entered puberty. With increasing frequency, they were photographed in clothing that was tight and revealing but still maintained, if only marginally, their persona as sweet and wholesome girls. As they moved through their teen years, these photographs steadily grew more sensual, culminating in photo shoots for *Allure* and *Rolling Stone* in the spring of 2004, before their eighteenth birthdays.

The increasing sexuality of the twins and their marketing during their teen years paralleled their increased presence online. "Olsen twins" became a phrase that, if Googled, led to cloaked porn sites. The porn community was so aware of the sexual allure of the twins that it used their names as a "Google-beater," including the words "Olsen twins" on their sites, which otherwise had no Olsen content, simply to increase hits—a strategy that assumes that a high percentage of people looking for Olsen twin information would be happy to find themselves landing on a porn site. Other porn sites, many of them dedicated to celebrity shots, have entry sites that simply list the names of the most famous female celebrities intermixed with keywords like "boobs naked nude sex hot" in order to capture web searches. "Olsen twins" is always on the list.

"Twin tracker" websites were sprinkled throughout the Internet in the years leading up to the twins' eighteenth birthdays, with reverse clocks counting down to the very minute when they would be "legal." The twins were such a porn commodity that they became the subject of a porn community debate online—is it okay to Photoshop the heads of underage women onto the bodies of performing porn stars, as was common? The community was split on the issue, but the simple fact of the discussion demonstrates the unspoken assumption that the Olsen twins were fit subjects of sexual interest.

Though the porn community was undeniably fascinated with the Olsen twins, it is not clear whether the twins, or their management company, were colluding in their online porn popularity in order to heighten their mainstream popularity or profitability. Yet it is hard to imagine that their agent or manager could have been unaware of the uses to which the online porn community was putting the twins' images. *Playboy*'s "Twins and Sisters" site includes women in trademark Olsen poses, though the Olsens appear clothed. In shot after shot, the public was presented with images of the twins leaning in toward each other, faces and mouths close, as if about to kiss. Caught by paparazzi on red carpets, the twins would snap into their standard pose, Mary-Kate's arm around Ashley's hip, Ashley's arm around Mary-Kate's neck (or vice versa). It is a pose that forces their torsos tantalizingly close, and the ease with which they assumed their positions showed how well coached and practiced they were.

The porning of the Olsen twins reached its height in the *Allure* and *Rolling Stone* articles, which essentially announced their legal status—a "Hey, we'll be legitimate sex objects next month!" message. The *Rolling Stone* article, which acknowledged the latent pedophilia of their marketing campaign by headlining them as "America's Favorite Fantasy," included images of the twins draped over each other in clearly erotic poses. The cover showed them leaning toward each other, their hands pulling at clothing and touching in a way clearly evocative of twin porn.

The signature photo for the *Allure* article showed the twins—still underage—in an unabashed sexual embrace, breasts together, mouths open in porn-pose ecstasy, their hands sliding into each other's clothing. The article, which emphasized their essential youth and innocence, also discussed whether they would ever do nude scenes ("Probably not"), the suggestiveness of the photo shoot ("If everybody knew we were straddling each other... oy vey ...All those dirty old men out there..."), and an anecdote about Mary-Kate using her finger to "slowly, firmly" remove some excess lip gloss from Ashley's lip and "slowly smear[ing] it on her own, slightly open mouth."

On one level, certainly, the twins consented to the articles in order to ease their movement into more mature careers, but the stories were also explicit acknowledgments of the porned sexualization of children. One *Rolling Stone* photo combined both messages, their youth and their sexuality, by putting them in the clothing of little girls dressing up, but with highly sexualized makeup and hairstyles, and with Ashley pulling a pearl necklace through her puckered lips—the kind of imagery dirty old men would find fascinating.

Not only are children, such as the Olsen twins, sexualized, they are also targeted as consumers of sexually charged products. *Playboy*, for example, has marketed a *Playboy* skateboard, a *Playboy* snowboard, and a pink Bunny tracksuit. The target market for such products is supposed to be eighteen- to twenty-five-year-olds, but reportedly Playmate Pink glitter cream and Bunny Pink lipstick are big hits with preteen girls.

Sexually revealing clothing, sometimes called the stripper look or slutwear, is specifically target-marketed to children as well as adults. In 2002 Abercrombie & Fitch, for example, began selling thongs in its stores catering to children, with the words EYE CANDY and WINK WINK printed on them. Thongs are also available with Simpsons and Muppets characters.

Elle, Cosmopolitan, and many other women's magazines have begun publishing versions for teens and preteens, with names like *ElleGIRL* and *CosmoGIRL!* Still other such magazines, such as *Twist,* complete with sex-advice columns, are exclusively for children, with the target group ten to fourteen.

In June 2005 a spokesperson for Sony Computer Entertainment announced that it "could not stop" software makers from producing and marketing pornographic discs for the PlayStation Portable game console, most of whose users are children. Almost 3 million of these handheld consoles, which Sony introduced in March 2005, had been delivered to Japan and the United States by June of that year. Two pornographic filmmakers had discs on the market by July, and several more followed shortly after.

At the same time, July 2005, the video game industry changed the rating of the very popular Grand Theft Auto: San Andreas, from M for mature to AO, adults only. After initial denials, Take-Two Interactive Software, makers of the game, which plays not only on PCs but also on Xbox and PlayStation 2 consoles, acknowledged that scenes of pornographic sex had indeed been programmed into the game, and could be unlocked through an Internet download, called a mod (short for *modification*) in the gaming community.

By the 1990s, not only had children become thoroughly sexualized in movies, advertisements, and marketing, but something more general had begun to occur: the sexualization of just about everyone, regardless of age or status in society.

In other words, if we ask how porn has shaped us, how it has affected how we see ourselves and one another, one answer is that we are coming to see ourselves and one another in sexual terms first and foremost, regardless of age, and regardless as well of marital, professional, or social status. Like Heather Ann with her sexier breasts—*Everyone a porn star!*

2. A Nation of Porn Stars

In 1982 Neil Postman published one of the most provocative and insightful cultural studies of our times, *The Disappearance of Childhood*. In it, Postman discusses the historical development of the concept of childhood as a separate life stage, having unique characteristics and entitling children to certain rights and privileges. Postman notes that this idea of childhood did not always exist, and that it could very well go out of existence, despite the proliferation of children among us.

According to Postman, the idea of childhood arose during the Middle Ages, just after the invention of the printing press in the mid-1400s. Before that time, people did not recognize childhood as a stage of life requiring special treatment. Children were regarded just like everybody else. They worked at the same jobs and chores as adults, though of course they were less capable. Paintings by the sixteenth-century painter Brueghel, for instance, show children engaged in laborious activities, such as carrying wood, along with adults. Careful study of the paintings also reveals that, although the artist was an excellent draftsman, he got the proportions of the bodies of children all wrong.

Children, for instance, have bigger heads, proportionally, than adults do in relation to the rest of their bodies. But Brueghel drew them the same—because he did not see children as fundamentally different from adults. You will also find beer-guzzling, drunken adults in his paintings of festivals—alongside beer-guzzling, drunken children. The ethic of medieval times, before the printing press, was *we're all in this together*. No special privileges or characteristics applied categorically to children.

Children did not, for instance, enjoy special protection from adults. The Dutch scholar Erasmus tells with some disgust about traveling to inns where drunken adults would, as a common amusement, lift a child onto the table to publicly play with his or her genitals.

A technological invention changed everything. Once Johannes Gutenberg invented the printing press, the medieval population began to differentiate: there now were those who could read and those who could not. Literacy became so important a value that convicted murderers could save themselves from hanging if in court they could demonstrate the ability to read.

It was at this time that the idea of childhood began to form. If there were literates distinct from illiterates, childhood became that special and important time of early life when one learned to read. In this way, children were recognized as a distinct group, for the first time separated out from the rest of the population.

Once children were so grouped, the concept of childhood could develop into what has become familiar to us today. Essential to the concept of childhood is innocence: it is widely accepted that children must be protected from knowledge and information that they are simply not developmentally ready to handle.

Postman refers to the means by which children have traditionally been protected from, mainly, sex and violence as "the sequence of revealed secrets." If a very young child asks where babies come from, he might be told "the cabbage patch." A bit later the same question will get a different answer: perhaps "mommy's belly." And later still the answer will be modified and amplified to include more biological and even sexual information until the answer is full and complete.

The technology of the printing press in a sense respected this sequence of revealed secrets, because a book could be written about sex in such a sophisticated vocabulary and syntax that it would simply go over the head of a child who might pick it up before she was ready for it. Therefore, in the course of the succeeding centuries, the idea of childhood grew stronger in the West.

The idea of childhood continued to develop until another technological invention appeared in the middle of the twentieth century and almost immediately began to undermine childhood —television. There is no threshold of literacy for television. It does not respect the sequence of revealed secrets. Its information goes out everywhere. It shows everything to everyone. Children with televisions in their homes could no longer be protected from knowledge they were not ready for.

By the turn of the millennium, twenty years (a blink in the scope of history) after the publication of Postman's book, children could be exposed via television to anything at all, no matter how unsuitable or even taboo. News reports of terrorist attacks feature close-ups of mangled bodies and even severed body parts. Reality television, beginning in the 1990s with programs like *Real TV*, shows surveillance-camera video of convenience store clerks being shot to death, suicidal individuals jumping off bridges, and so on. Subscription cable networks, such as the Spice Channel, show pornographic movies 24-7.

What happens to childhood innocence under such conditions? And if innocence disappears from childhood, in what sense does "childhood" continue to exist? Postman predicted—and it is hard to argue against him in light of what has transpired over the almost thirty years that have elapsed since publication of *The Disappearance of Childhood*—that our culture would soon return to the pre-Gutenberg model of a society in which children are no longer afforded the protections traditionally bestowed upon them as a special class.

WE'RE ALL IN THIS TOGETHER

If indeed the idea of childhood is disappearing, then one implication is that *adulthood* is disappearing, since these concepts depend
on each other. We can make the further generalization that former
distinctions of hierarchical status are disappearing from our society.

Robert Bly, in his *The Sibling Society* (1996), described the phenomenon of such social leveling metaphorically. It's as if, Bly says,
we are all siblings now, interacting on the level of equivalence.

He introduces his argument with a personal anecdote: When
Bly, a man well into his seventies when the book was published,
telephones his bank, the clerk asks for his account number to ver-
ify his identity. Once he provides that, the nineteen-year-old clerk,
whom he has never met, chirps, "What can I do for you, Robert?"
He informs her that the first thing she can do is address him as
"Mr. Bly."

We have lost societal distinctions in a sexual sense as well, having blurred or entirely erased earlier social signals and markers of
sexual availability in, for one thing, the way we dress. If we look at
Norman Rockwell paintings from the 1930s through the 1950s, for
instance, we see all sorts of markers of life stage and social status
reflected in clothing. Rockwell was meticulous in observing and
recording such details.

In *Missing Tooth*, his painting of three schoolgirls from 1957,
for example, we see three girls standing together, one with her
mouth open showing two missing front teeth, a slightly older girl
leaning in to have a look, and a slightly younger girl off to one side,
pouting. The oldest girl, functioning as the inspector of lost baby
teeth, publicly displays—by her appearance, especially her clothing—her place in the social pecking order. In a glance, we can determine her age (around twelve) by the way she is dressed. Her
hair is short, unlike the long hair of the younger girls, and is loose
rather than pig- or ponytailed. Moreover, she wears a blouse and a
skirt and knee socks, whereas the younger girls wear dresses and

ankle socks. There are even finer distinctions of junior status evident in the dress of the youngest girl, who stands by forlornly, not having yet lost a tooth. We also notice in the oldest, preadolescent girl just the subtlest suggestion of budding breasts under her white blouse.

And that is really what this painting is all about: a girl's journey to womanhood, through clearly marked stages. In this painting, we observe one important early stage, the rite of passage occasioned by the loss of baby teeth. Soon the youngest, pouting girl will stand in the honored place of the girl who has just lost baby teeth, and she, in turn, will move to the inspector's. The inspector will have advanced, out of this frame, into full adolescence. *And so it goes*, is the implication.

In other Rockwell paintings, older professional men are typically dressed in dark (navy or black) three-piece suits, as is invariably true of the many doctors Rockwell portrayed, as well as the grandfather in his well-known Thanksgiving painting *Freedom from Want*. Younger professional men wear lighter suits, gray or brown, but not navy or black—not until they have attained "elder" status.

In the nineteenth and early twentieth century, boys did not wear long pants until they were nine or ten years old. Girls awaited the day when their hair would come out of pigtails. Traditionally, then, in the hierarchical societies of eighteenth-, nineteenth-, and (most of) twentieth-century America, we found endless ways to signal one another about exactly where we stood in the social/developmental order at any given moment.

Contrast that, however, with the public statements that our clothes make about us today. Girls nine or ten years old, and even younger, commonly wear miniskirts or low-slung jeans, along with tank tops or midriff-baring "belly shirts," just as do adult women from the ages of twenty to fifty. Some nine- and ten-year-old girls wear thongs, just like older girls and women.

On a college campus, it is difficult to distinguish male professors from students by dress alone—except that the professors tend not to wear the ubiquitous flip-flops favored by students (although sandals are not unusual). Cotton shirts open at the neck (with no tie) or polo shirts, along with cotton pants (jeans, cargoes, or chinos) are the order of the day for both professors and students, with sweaters added (rather than sport coats) when the weather turns colder. If it's true that our clothes make a public statement, then the statement we are making today, old and young, is *we're all in this together.*

And so we are, in ways other than mere dress. In 1989, for instance, *People* magazine chose Sean Connery as its "Sexiest Man Alive." Connery was sixty at the time. In 1999, the same magazine cited Connery as the "Sexiest Man of the Century," at age sixty-nine. In that same year, Connery starred with Catherine Zeta-Jones as his love interest in a film called *Entrapment*. Connery was almost seventy and Zeta-Jones thirty.

We could make a long list of such film couplings. In *True Crime* (1999), Clint Eastwood, also almost seventy, played an over-the-hill journalist whose girlfriend, at the beginning of the movie, was a college student in her early twenties. Mary-Kate Olsen, twenty-one, whose development we traced, along with her twin sister's, in Chapter 1, and Ben Kingsley, sixty-three, star as love interests in *The Wackness*, which, the *New York Post* reported, will include a "full make out session." (The film was still in production as this book went to press, scheduled for release in early 2008.) For about two decades Americans have been watching television shows and movies dealing, in one way or another, with the sexualization of the elderly (usually elderly men) as well as children, along with the phenomenon of pairings that reach very wide across the generations.

Now, we don't mean to suggest that the elderly should not be considered sexual beings, and we aren't making a judgment about intergenerational romance; we're simply pointing out that previously recognized barriers or distinctions between the groups at either end of the age continuum are increasingly eroding.

Beginning in the 1980s, countless sitcoms featured episodes built around we're-all-in-this-together humor. A typical plot had a mother and daughter both falling for someone and, in the course of rhapsodizing to each other about the new love interest, discovering that—oh no!—*it's the same guy!*

A recent film spins this tired gag a more extreme way. In *Must Love Dogs* (2005), Sarah (Diane Lane), a forty-something recent divorcée and preschool teacher, answers an Internet personals ad and shows up to meet her date, who turns out to be—yikes!—*her own father!*

The film is replete with all-in-this-together humor. Her dad (Christopher Plummer), recently widowed, is slightly embarrassed by the turn of events, but unabashed about his Internet dating. Although he is seventy-one, a bit later in the movie Sarah happens upon him and one of his many sixty-something girlfriends deep-kissing and groping like teenagers. So highly sexed (and sexualized) is this elderly character that he has several girlfriends by his side at all times to keep up with his needs.

One of the girlfriends, Dolly (Stockard Channing), becomes Sarah's pal. One night she comes to Sarah's house distraught because one of her Internet boyfriends has just showed up to meet her—and turns out to be fifteen years old. Dolly breaks off the relationship despite the boy's desire to continue; as he explains through his braces, age is "just numbers."

Sarah adventures on in the confusing maze that the dating scene in 2005 turns out to be. One of her main love interests is the father of one of her preschool students, a forty-something hunk named Bobby (Dermot Mulroney). When she goes to his condo unexpectedly one night, she finds him with June (Julie Gonzalo), Sarah's eighteen- or nineteen-year-old teacher's assistant.

The film is ostensibly about Sarah's (and, later, her true love

Jake's) desire for a return to romantic love of the "eternal soul-mate" variety. (Jake, played by John Cusack, watches the film *Doctor Zhivago* over and over.) That sentimentality aside, the film consists of men and women, boys and girls, popping up in comically unexpected ways, as if from the opening and slamming doors of the comedy of errors that all-in-this-together America has become.

When hierarchical distinctions are blurred in a mass of social equals—a *sibling society*, in Bly's term—then all ages are sexualized. So we have beauty queens at the age of six. And male sex symbols, real and cinematic, at seventy. And pairings can occur across the spectrum of age.

So it is in the world of porn. In porn, everyone is sexualized regardless not only of age but of social position. If a porn film includes a character playing a physician, for instance, we can be sure that the good doctor will soon, like Dr. Young in *Deep Throat*, examine his patient lasciviously, and more. The mere fact that he is a doctor (a profession treated with near-reverence in the paintings of Norman Rockwell) does not elevate him above inappropriate venal behavior and sexual characterization. All barriers are broken, all lines crossed.

In the real world of America in the early years of the twenty-first century, everyone—from professional athletes to teachers to the president of the United States—is seen in sexual terms. A national online site allowing students to rate college professors, for instance, includes the possibility of adding a special symbol, a chili pepper, to the male or female professor's rating if he or she is "hot." And for those who are hot, student comments often focus more on the professor's allure and on sexual fantasies than on his or her attributes as a teacher.

The most compelling example of such universal porning occurred during the presidency of Bill Clinton. Details of the president's sex life, which were publicly revealed during his impeachment, included an initial encounter with an intern that could have come right out of a porn script. An attractive young woman snaps the waistband of her thong at the president of the United States. Like someone playing "Mister President" in a porn film, the real-life president eagerly responds to this come-on by engaging in oral sex with the young intern in the Oval Office. In one session, she masturbates with a cigar for his titillation. In another—well, we all saw the movie.

A number of polls indicated a pattern in the responses of Americans. Young people in high school and college (who view porn as entertainment and casual sexual encounters as a norm) were mainly amused by it all. Older Americans, especially those over fifty, who still attached stigma to porn, were shocked.

By 2008, however, it had become difficult to imagine anyone being truly shocked by real-life examples of "right out of a porn movie" sex. Let's consider just the most famous of recent scandals involving older male politicians and younger—sometimes very much younger—females and males.

- In 1974 Representative Wilbur Mills (D-Ark.) was found to be having an affair with a young stripper named Fanne Foxe, aka "the Argentine Firecracker," who jumped into the Tidal Basin in Washington, D.C., when police pulled over their car.
- In 1983 the House Ethics Committee censured Representatives Dan Crane (R-Ill.) and Gerry Studds (D-Mass.) for having had sexual relationships with seventeen-year-old pages, Crane with a female, Studds with a male.
- In 1988 former senator Gary Hart's relationship with actress/model Donna Rice derailed his presidential bid.
- In 1989 Stephen Gobie, the former gay lover of Barney Frank (D-Mass.), admitted having operated a male prostitution ring out of the congressman's apartment.
- In 2001 the U.S. senator Garry Condit (D-Calif.) admitted to

an affair with missing and presumed dead Chandra Levy, a young woman in her twenties, ending his political career— because of his casual response to her disappearance rather than the affair.

- In 2006 Representative Mark Foley (R-Fla.) resigned from Congress when it was revealed that he had been sending "dirty e-mails" to teenage House pages.
- In 2007 Senator Larry Craig (R-Idaho) plead guilty to disorderly conduct after being caught in a police sting operation investigating lewd acts in a Minneapolis airport men's public restroom. Craig had been widely considered a "family values" conservative.

Politics was only one source of scandals involving sex between older, more powerful adults and young partners. Religion and education were two other similarly tainted institutions.

- In 1987 Jim Bakker, a televangelist reportedly bringing in a million dollars a week in donations from followers, confessed to a sexual liaison with a young woman, Jessica Hahn (who later appeared nude in *Playboy*). That scandal was followed by a spate of similar stories involving celebrity ministers caught in sexual transgressions, the most famous of which, in the following year, 1988, was Jimmy Swaggart, who wept his confession to a national audience.
- Beginning in 2002 and extending through the next few years, reports proliferated of hundreds of Catholic priests who had molested and raped young boys and girls. Bishops who simply moved the offending priests from one diocese to another as the crimes were brought to their attention had in effect, it turned out, protected serial rapists.
- In 1996 a thirty-six-year-old schoolteacher, Mary Kay Letourneau, gained notoriety when her sexual relationship with one

of her sixth-grade students, a thirteen-year-old boy, became known. Her case was soon followed by innumerable others involving male and female high school and middle school teachers having sex (and sometimes, like Letourneau, having children) with their teenage and even preteen students.

We could go on. To see just how jaded we have become by such events, try telling someone a made-up story about having just seen a news report in which a respected individual (choose anyone in the public eye) was reported having sex with someone unlikely (make it as outlandish as you want). There may be some surprise, some heads may shake in disgust, but it's a good bet that people will accept the story as true.

Our readiness to believe almost any example of sexual pairing, however outrageous, is fueled by the fact that we are exposed not only to sensational anecdotes (which though significant are usually atypical) but also to instances of sex being infused into mainstream culture everywhere we look. Let us catalog some examples of this cultural porning, just to sample the field:

- World Wrestling Federation mixed tag team matches, which receive heavy television coverage, can only be described as soft-core porn, featuring unsubtle double entendres in the pre-match challenges and taunts ("I'm gonna slam her ass!"), and scantily clad men and women in clearly sexual positions (in their male-female and female-female pairings) during the match.

- Female athletes have become increasingly sexualized, and even marketed in soft-core formats for their sexuality rather than their athletic prowess. Anna Kournikova, for example, never a top singles professional tennis player, nevertheless became a media darling, receiving more attention than better players simply because of her sex appeal and her willingness to flaunt it. In a way, she set the pattern (seminude/nude, highly suggestive calendars and posters, advertisements, appearances in movies) that other female athletes, both professional and amateur, now must follow.

- High school cheerleaders have so dramatically sexualized their routines, often bumping and grinding like strippers, that in one recent instance, a state congressman in Texas, Representative Al Edwards, proposed legislation that would put an end to "sexually suggestive" performances at high school athletic events and other extracurricular competitions.

- Dirty dancing has gotten even dirtier. At the turn of the nineteenth century, waltz partners were thought by some alarmed moralists to be mimicking sexual intercourse. Imagine what they would make of contemporary "grinding," and "freaking," popular forms of dancing in which the female bends over and presses her buttocks against the pumping groin of her partner.

- Nude calendars have become commonplace. Beginning on a large scale in the 1990s, groups of all sorts, usually connected with charities or not-for-profit organizations, began publishing such calendars as a fund-raising ploy. One of the most well-known featured the Australian women's soccer team, the Matildas, in 1999. A dedicated website lists hundreds of nude calendars for sale, consisting of photos of amateur, volunteer models ranging in age from early twenties to senior citizens, raising money for athletic teams, theatrical companies, volunteer fire fighters, and disease research. These calendars range from depictions of naked grannies holding kittens and puppies (raising money for animal shelters) to buff male rugby players, clearly conveying the message: *Everyone a porn star!*

And the list goes on. Porn chat rooms, for example, abound on the Internet. Such spaces invite ordinary people to participate in the creation of pornography, mainly in the form of "cybering," having imagined sex, in real time, with a partner or partners in the room. The participants, who often admit that they are simultaneously masturbating, describe in detail what they are "doing" with the other (or others), how they are responding, and so on. These "performances," to describe them that way, are sometimes enhanced with webcams for one or both (or all) participants to view. Further enhanced with voice, the results can be quite complex and sophisticated, even indistinguishable from the offerings of professional porn websites.

Chatropolis, a site with both free and pay options, advertises itself as one of the largest and most active chat sites on the Web, offering about 230 chat rooms, most with a maximum capacity of twenty-five people. Not all rooms are full all the time, but if, let's say, on average, half the number of possible chatters are online, that means about three thousand are in Chatropolis at any given moment. Chatters come and go throughout the day and night, however, sometimes merely changing rooms within the site, but also logging in fresh, so the total number of chatters on this one site alone in the course of a day is huge, certainly in the thousands, perhaps even the tens of thousands.

One Chatropolis room is called "Legal Today." Another, at the other end of the age spectrum, is "Perverted Old Men." Still another links the extremes of age, "Across the Generations." Some rooms cater to phone sex, such as "Call Me." Others to sexual preferences, such as "Analopolis."

Thousands of such chat sites (free and pay, large and small) are available on the Internet. For years Yahoo, for instance, offered hundreds of rooms with cam and voice options, many exclusively pornographic—"PA Girls for Sex," for example, and many others, such as user rooms (rooms created by users) focusing on specific sex acts and fetishes, particular sexual orientations, such as bi and

lesbian, and so on.[1] Even an unscientific, thumbnail approxima-
tion, then, would conservatively find millions of Americans of all
ages in such chat rooms—all in this together—every day.

Perhaps the best—the most clear, compelling, and widespread
—behavioral example of the porning of America is the relatively
recent practice of hooking up.

HOOKING UP

The sexual practice, widespread among the young (high school
and college age), called hooking up involves two people, usually total strangers, making eye contact at a party—or in a club, a school
dance, or even at a mall—and then slipping into a room or hallway
nearby for sex. Tom Wolfe, who introduced the term to older
Americans in a recent book, says this about the practice: " 'Hooking
up' was a term known in the year 2000 to almost every American
child over the age of nine, but to only a relatively small percentage
of their parents, who, even if they heard it, thought it was being
used in the old sense of 'meeting' someone. Among the children,
hooking up was always a sexual experience."[2]

Regarding the popularity of the practice, Wolfe says: "Thirteen-
and fourteen-year-old girls were getting down on their knees and
fellating boys in corridors and stairwells during the two-minute
break between classes. One thirteen-year-old in New York, asked
by a teacher how she could do such a thing, replied: 'It's nasty, but
I need to satisfy my man.' "[3]

A related, apparently widespread, phenomenon, which Wolfe
does not mention, involves relationships in which the partners are
"fuck buddies" or "friends with benefits." Whereas the hookup
is typically a onetime occurrence, friends with benefits are pals or
associates who have an ongoing no-strings, nonromantic sexual
relationship.

Hooking up perfectly mirrors the sex that is typical in a porn
movie. It is anonymous, or nearly so, impersonal, and undertaken

without commitment. Those who hook up simply recognize the mutual sexual need of the moment, and then proceed as partners to satisfy their lust. The gag line of so many jokes about the one-night stand of earlier times—"Will you call me in the morning?"—simply does not apply in the hookup.

We might also describe it, putting aside the exchange of money for the moment, as the kind of sex typified in prostitution—remembering that the word *pornography* derives from Greek roots meaning "depicting the acts of prostitutes." In fact, one of the terms for a prostitute, *hooker,* is quite close to *hooking up. Hooker* and *hookup* then, are quite alike in suggesting a quickly made tie between two sex partners that is understood by both to be temporary and impersonal.

Let us fill out the picture of the typical hookup with details of looks and dress common in the early years of the twenty-first century.

The male might well have the kind of body common in porn movies, a body ideal painstakingly cultivated by young men all over America, referred to as buff or "cut." That is, the hours in the gym lifting free weights and working out on exercise machines are spent to achieve a *look,* not in connection with athletics or body-building. And the desired look is one we recognize from porn: the stud.

The female would almost certainly be wearing a thong, a now common article of underwear once exclusive to the porn films and strip clubs of the 1980s. (She would also have shaved her pubic hair, another style derived from strip clubs.) In fact, her glitter, heavy mascara, low-slung jeans, and midriff-baring shirt are often described (even by the companies that manufacture them) as slutwear.

If, then, this typical male and female of the new millennium—this stud of the six-pack abs and his thonged girlfriend-of-the-moment—drawn together by lust, each perhaps not even knowing the other's name, engage in a sex act without affection or commitment...who could distinguish their hookup from a scene in a porn movie?

THE AMATEURS TAKE OVER

If it is true, as we have suggested, that not only has porn become mainstream but that the mainstream has become porned, it would follow that porn produced by professionals would merge with a new kind of porn created by secretaries, bakers, nurses, auto mechanics, housewives, schoolteachers—ordinary people from the mainstream of American society who, à la Timothy Greenfield-Sanders, have come to see porn stars as like themselves, and who therefore see themselves as like porn stars. And indeed this is exactly what we do find.

Throughout the 1980s and 1990s, "amateur" porn movies were produced in great quantity, created by and large by professionals who employed unknown porn actors billed as amateur performers. Since the turn of the millennium, however, as digital video cameras and cell phones with video capability have enabled people to record their own sexual activities and post the results via their computer on a dedicated website, there has been a skyrocketing increase in true amateur porn. The number of such websites (such as Private Porn Movies, YourAmateurPorn, and Best Home Sex) is growing exponentially. Even websites that are not specifically for amateur porn become such sites de facto, because some members use their webcams on these sites to broadcast themselves masturbating or having partnered sex.

It may well be the case that true amateur porn is the future of porn in America. And to say this is perhaps to announce the end of porn. Because just as it is true that if everything in the world were blue there would be no word *blue*, when blue movies are everywhere, there are no more blue movies.

The final result of the porning of America, then, may well be the end of the recognition of porn as something separate from the mainstream. Pornography will have shrunk to porn and porn further shrunk away altogether, disappearing because it can no longer be distinguished from what we see everywhere around us on the Internet (on innumerable amateur sites, in chat rooms, on MySpace, Craigslist, Stickam, and so on), on cable television, in movies, magazines, advertisements, music videos. Porn will have become our cultural wallpaper.

3. Popping Rosie's Rivets
Porn in the Good Old Days

For many Americans, the 1950s remains hallowed ground, a version of the nation altogether healthier, saner, safer, and, most importantly, more moral than the shifting quagmire we believe ourselves to be sinking into now. This sanctification has been under fire for some time now by historians and cultural critics who have pointed out, among other things, the systemic racism and sexism of the 1950s, two dark historical facts whose submersion is necessary for the preservation of the sanitized image of white suburban life. But the 1950s was also the decade when pornography began poking its head out of the alleys and back rooms of American society and slipping into mainstream culture—unleashed, strangely enough, by that proud and determined bicep-flexing American everywoman, Rosie the Riveter.

To utter *the 1950s* is to invoke a set of images: innocent (white) teenagers jitterbugging at the hop, mothers in dresses and aprons preparing the family dinner, fathers in suits and ties arriving home from well-paying jobs. These images are historically accurate for many Americans of the times, but fail to tell the stories, all just as common, of a host of others.

Another label that encompasses the 1950s, *Cold War era,* powerfully brings to mind a very different set of images, all anxiety laden: Sputnik and the space race, the global spread of communism, rising juvenile delinquency, and the constant threat of apocalyptic nuclear war. That these vastly different, even contradictory, images apply to the same decade should reveal the dubiousness of accepting a single narrative from our complex cultural memory.

And so we need to bring some skepticism to one of the most powerful of the stories we tell ourselves about the postwar years: that the era was a paradigm of sexual conservatism. This story is in many ways true, but woefully incomplete. American cinema, despite regular challenges, still labored under the burden of the Hays Code, a set of guidelines established in 1930 to ensure that the movie industry would not be susceptible to corrupting influences and, like the "the obscene plays of Roman times," lead our nation into a similar collapse. In one of the most famous rules, if a scene included a man and a woman sitting on a bed together, one of their feet had to be on the floor. Television, increasingly the most powerful source of popular culture, had its own, similar, code.

While television and film writers and directors often included suggestive jokes that were themselves coded, the era is largely represented, on film, by married couples sleeping in separate beds, creating, in its own way, a pornography of moral purity in which the viewer is constantly aware of the potential sexuality of every situation by virtue of its assiduous suppression. Watching these films now, we wonder which type of pornography might be more destructive, the porn of moral impurity or the porn of glaring purity. When Jessie Hays divorced her husband, William, the author of the Hays Code, she cited his inability to distinguish between her navel and her clitoris.

The "innocence" of the 1950s, as represented in popular culture, is challenged by the historical reality of the postwar period. Following World War II, unexpected and stealthy social changes, mostly connected to the evolving status of women and minorities, made that innocence increasingly tenuous. Such social changes are always traumatic, and, like a neurotic patient, American culture displaced its fear and tension about gender and class roles by turning to the burgeoning world of comic books, men's magazines, and pornography.

ROSIE THE RIVETER

Most postwar social developments had their inception, of course, during the war, created largely by the removal of so many men from society and the entry of so many women into the workforce. The Rosie the Riveter phenomenon—the influx of women during the war into defense jobs and other occupations, such as ship-building, traditionally filled by men—grew out of the marriage of economic need and women's desire for self-sufficiency, with marketing officiating. By 1943, 75 percent of all adult American women were married, and 50 percent of them had jobs. Most of the Rosies (61 percent), however, had worked outside the home even before the war; only 22 percent had been full-time house-wives (now referred to as stay-at-home moms) before World War II. But the American government knew early on that this trend of women succeeding in difficult, traditionally male jobs could upset the psychology of the nation.

The propaganda arm of the war effort, the Office of War Information (OWI), dealt with this cultural threat by working with the War Advertising Council, an entity formed by advertising execu-tives, to satisfy two somewhat disparate needs: create the image of a highly competent working woman who, at the same time, sub-mitted to the ideal of male supremacy. Competent and vital in her portrayals on government war posters and in the public arena—in everything from public service announcements to advertisements for soap—Rosies were, therefore, white middle-class wives or wives-to-be.

Rosies could not, however, be portrayed as indispensable in the war effort lest the status quo of ultimate dependence on males be threatened. The solution lay in the publicized motivation of women to take up work in the first place. Entering the workplace, government propaganda suggested, was a sacrifice women made for one purpose only: to bring their men safely back from the war as soon as possible so that the women themselves could then return to their homes, and to their proper roles as wives and mothers.

The most popular image of Rosie graced the cover of *The Saturday Evening Post* in May 1943. Painted by Norman Rockwell, Rosie, clothed in coveralls and with a large, phallic rivet gun across her lap, sits on a wooden crate with a sandwich in one hand and her foot on a copy of *Mein Kampf.* It is, in many ways, a startlingly masculine image. She is confident and looks powerful with her broad shoulders, hefty biceps, and wide leather watchstrap. Yet despite the grease smudges on her cheeks, she has done up her hair attractively and wears carefully applied makeup. A compact peeks out of her hip pocket.

She is portrayed by Rockwell as a powerful woman and a source of America's economic and military strength—but also as a woman who never forgets to look good for her man. Despite all the concessions to male-dominated America, Rockwell's Rosie was, nevertheless, like her real-life counterparts, a grenade lobbed at the walls of traditional gender boundaries.

Just as women's labor was put to service in the war, so was their sexuality. War posters targeting men often highlighted both women's desirability and their sexual vulnerability. At the same time that the OWI touted American women's purity, dance hall girls served as totems of sexualized femininity, fox-trotting with men home on leave to remind them what they were fighting for. As the war drew to a close, advertisements and war posters increasingly featured narratives of redeployment, portraying relieved women who could once again return home after the sacrifices of the war.

This message of sacrifice, of women having given up something that was prized, was mostly a propaganda effort to reassure men that the status quo was intact. At the same time, the message was intended to encourage women to quit their jobs now that the war was over and such extraordinary efforts were no longer needed. Department of Labor statistics show that the large majority of women wanted to keep working after the war, including women who had been housewives before the war. And many women who believed they had recourse attempted to keep their jobs, such as female members of United Auto Workers who tried, unsuccessfully, to forestall their "demobilization." In the end, overwhelmingly, women who wanted to keep their high-paying positions could not do so and were forced back either into the kind of lower-paying jobs they had before the war or out of the workforce altogether.

It would be overstating the Rosie effect to say that the war was a watershed either with respect to women's opportunities or to attitudes about women's labor. Polls show that the idea of men as the head of the household grew dramatically after the war, and most women agreed with the notion. Indeed, in 1945, 65 percent of men and 57 percent of women believed that a married woman should not work outside the home.

Rosie did, however, have long-term effects that set the stage for the women's movement. During the war, women not only made the choice to work, but many women left entry-level jobs for better-paying positions, demonstrating their growing ambition. After the war, while most women accepted the necessity of their exit from the workforce, oral histories have shown that intense pride was the common reward for their experiences. "I never realized what I could do" was the nearly universal refrain.

And subsequent history shows that the Rosie phenomenon changed women's fundamental ideas about labor. Though the number of women working plummeted after the war, it began to creep back up within a few years. By 1960, women between forty-five and fifty-five years old led the way in returning to work, with 50 percent holding down jobs, only 10 percent less than the wartime peak. These were the same women who in their thirties had formed the largest group of Rosies.[1]

Evidently, they had not forgotten how good their wartime independence had felt. These and other aspects of women's time as Rosie the Riveter were the seeds that would eventually flower into the women's movement of the 1960s. Women's slowly building economic and social authority came to challenge the image of the strong, stoic male that had long dominated American popular culture.

FROM WAR HERO TO ORGANIZATION MAN

For decades after World War II, returning servicemen were understood as having seen and done things that they did not want to talk about except on those occasions when they gathered with other veterans. But interestingly, it is only in recent years, as we have celebrated what Tom Brokaw called "the greatest generation," that we have come more fully to fathom the depth of the former soldiers' psychological and emotional burden. After all, the images of the postwar American man had overwhelmingly emphasized virility and control. Only few postwar voices—the later works of Ernest Hemingway and movies like *The Best Years of Our Lives* (1946) and *The Man in the Gray Flannel Suit* (1956)—suggested that in fact American men were troubled.

Yet it is precisely in these images of virility and control that we can see what Arthur Schlesinger Jr. called "the crisis of American masculinity." In a November 1958 *Esquire* article, Schlesinger wrote, "Today men are more and more conscious of maleness not as a fact but as a problem. The ways by which American men affirm their masculinity are uncertain and obscure. There are multiplying signs, indeed, that something has gone badly wrong with the American male's conception of himself."

Schlesinger and other commentators saw in communism a symptom of everything that assailed American men, everything that wanted to strip America of its love of the individual and turn its men into servile automatons. Countless science fiction films of the era, such as *The Blob* and *Invasion of the Body Snatchers,* served as allegories of the fear of losing one's individuality.

Returning from World War II, white American men found a culture in which their dominant social position—and their jobs —were increasingly being challenged by white women, the former Rosies, and black men. Not only that, but the corporations for which they labored were busily developing new ideas about efficiency that would treat them much as they feared communism would, as anonymous and interchangeable parts. Having returned from war, arguably the most masculine of all endeavors, the former soldier became "the organization man" (as William H. Whyte titled a 1956 book), subsuming his own worth to that of the company.

Another work, *The Man in the Gray Flannel Suit* (both the 1955 book and the 1956 movie), follows the postwar experience of Tom Rath, a veteran who has found success in the corporate world but who has also lost there the sense of purpose he had in the war. In short, many men in the 1950s faced what they saw as a kind of social and sexual emasculation.

Much of Schlesinger's work in the postwar years was dedicated to identifying and correcting the emasculation of the American male and of American society as a whole. His star-making book, *The Vital Center: The Politics of Freedom* (1949), was, for instance, significantly responsible for the popularization of the terms *hard* and *soft,* clearly terms of male sexuality, as descriptors of attitudes about communism and the "dynamism" of American culture. American men, of course, wanted to be hard, politically and personally. It is no surprise, then, that the 1950s, despite being the era of home, family, and fidelity, also witnessed the birth of modern American pornography.

Despite our stereotypical view of the era as comparatively pure, World War II exposed American servicemen to cultures that had liberal attitudes toward sex and pornography. Servicemen fighting in France, for instance, encountered a culture with a long-standing tradition of popular pornography, much of it with a tone of mild kink. The war itself, as wars always do, created environments in which men, separated from wives and girlfriends, developed much more open attitudes about sex. Servicemen received four condoms a month, a number well short of what medical officers thought appropriate, and 80 percent of American servicemen away from home for at least two years admitted to regularly engaging in extramarital sex. In contrast, while popular culture largely gave sexually active men a free pass, it depicted women who strayed as low and unpatriotic. Nevertheless, infidelity among young married women rose during the 1940s.[2]

For men and women, then, wartime combined in powerful ways not only the concepts of love, patriotism, and sacrifice, but also sex, violence, and death. The pinup girl provides a poignant example. Brought to fame by Alberto Vargas in *Esquire* and distributed as cards and posters to servicemen with the overt purpose of reminding soldiers what they were fighting for, the pinup girl combined blushing innocence with erotic power. Taking their cue from this odd nexus of sex and war, airmen famously painted the noses of their bombers with pinups (the *Memphis Belle* is best known). Often much more explicit than the magazines and posters that inspired them, including nudity and visual jokes about penetration, nose art narrowed the gap between sex, violence, and masculinity.

Small wonder, then, that the postwar years sparked a national conversation, albeit delivered sotto voce, about sex and power. During the war, the culture had mobilized sex in much the way it had mobilized tank brigades. After the war's end, images of sex and violence would be used to negotiate the power struggle between men and women within our own borders.

THE EARLY YEARS OF ACCEPTED PORN

Pornography was hardly new to American culture. Along with France, the United States was the biggest producer of stag films, which evolved very little from the 1910s to the 1960s. These were brazenly hard-core, and generally infused with locker-room humor, sporting production credits such as A. Wise Guy, A. Prick, and Ima Cunt. Shown for audiences almost entirely of men, they presented men as dominant and assertive and the more passive women as constantly available and ready—though they too enjoyed the act. Violence, real or suggested, was nearly nonexistent.

Stags, however, generally illegal and produced secretly, were usually shown in back rooms, in brothels, or screened in traveling carnivals and other marginalized venues. A young American man could easily live his entire life without the opportunity to see one. During and after World War II, however, porn in several new forms increasingly showed its face in public.

Esquire can take much of the credit for opening the doors for what became known as girlie magazines. During the war, the Post Office Department changed the popular magazine's status from a second-class to a first-class mailing, making it much more expensive, citing as the reason for the change the pinup-style pictorials. *Esquire*'s eventual victory in 1946, in the Supreme Court, arguing that the Post Office could not effectively practice censorship, made it much easier for more explicit publications to follow. When *Playboy* debuted in 1953, it faced no such trouble.

The kinds of pornography that characterized the early postwar years tended to be what today we might view as quaint, even innocent. Indeed, the first few years of *Playboy* depicted nude women mostly in poses very familiar to men who admired the pinups of the war era. The magazine's explicit thesis, despite the glossy, retouched photographs, was that ordinary women actually enjoy sex. *Playboy* spawned hosts of copycats with titles like *Modern Man, Cabaret,* and *Mr.* For African Americans, *Ebony* fulfilled the same

role as *Esquire,* and the short-lived *Duke* offered a black *Playboy.*
The expanding world of burlesque provides an even clearer example of the relative innocence of what was then regarded as pornography.

Burlesque, and the staged striptease that became its most
famous component, had its heyday in the 1920s, after which it began to die away until the war and hosts of lonely, entertainment-
hungry men gave it a new life that would last until the late 1950s.
The burlesque striptease, like *Playboy* and the pinup, belong more
to the world of erotica than to what most people think of as pornography. Even the names of the dancers evoke not raw titillation but
a kind of jovially sexual fascination. Doe Mae Davison, who appeared under the stage names Princess Do May and the Cherokee
Half Breed, danced in headband and eagle feathers. Yvette Dare
performed "The Dance of the Sacred Parrot." Lili St. Cyr, probably
the most successful performer of the last decade of the industry,
danced a kind of sexualized ballet, and sealed her fame with a bub-
ble bath routine.

The striptease was what its name suggests, a tease. The
dancers certainly presented themselves as sexual beings, but not
as sex objects. Their distinctly individual names and their signature dances gave their acts an air of performance rather than prostitution, and there was never any question about who was in
control of the act. These were often significant productions, with
multiple costume changes and narrative arcs, and, since less flesh
was shown than we would expect today, the success of the performance depended on the relationship the dancer created with
her audience.

A successful performer like St. Cyr could play a single burlesque house for years. While some striptease artists occasionally
flashed, which they were technically forbidden to do, a customer
could pay many visits to a theater and never see it. In the late 1940s
and through the 1950s, a group of producers outside the Holly-

wood movie industry known as the Forty Thieves began making and distributing burlesque movies, spreading the aesthetic of the burlesque outside the major cities. Lili St. Cyr appeared regularly in titles like *Love Moods* and *Varietease,* as did Bettie Page, the most famous pinup girl of the era.

Page, however, was both one of the last examples of the striptease artist and one of the reasons burlesque finally faded. In the 1950s, as rules for distributing pornographic material loosened, the market for raunchier material grew, and Bettie Page tried to be in as much of it as possible, appearing in every format: cards, photographs, movies, magazines (including *Playboy*), and onstage. While much of her work, both stills and loops (films of only a few minutes), were fairly innocuous, consisting of lingerie shots less revealing than the average Victoria's Secret catalog, Page often posed nude, and eventually brought BDSM (bondage/domination/ sadomasochism) to a broad audience for the first time. Photographs and loops of her paddling bound women, and images of Page bound, gagged, and suspended by wires, brought her to national attention, including that of Senator Estes Kefauver, who subpoenaed her to appear before a Senate subcommittee holding hearings on pornography in 1955.

The bondage and S&M pornography in which Page is featured would be considered quite tame by today's standards. Any sense of threat conveyed is defused by the obvious artifice of the photographs and films. Despite the whips, handcuffs, and gags, the participants smile reassuringly, and the paddle generally never makes contact with flesh. Nevertheless, the popularity of Page's fetish images demonstrated a burgeoning interest in the intersection of sex and power.[3]

In all of these examples of midcentury pornography, including the photographs that so disturbed Senator Kefauver, in Page's bondage pictures, in burlesque and early striptease, in most stag films, and in *Playboy, Esquire,* and all of their imitators, we clearly see performance. To a degree the women are objectified, especially in photo spreads like *Playboy*'s, but Bettie Page's work, burlesque, and even stag films generally relied for a large part of their appeal on the viewer's awareness of the fully present identity and personality of the female performers. In showcasing their identities, such work opened the door to the possibility that highly stylized erotica, rather than anonymous, objectified porn, would dominate the coming sexual revolution.

There were, however, other forces gathering with a very different take on the connections between sex, identity, and power.

PORN! AND FOR KIDS!

A year before his investigation into pornography, Kefauver oversaw hearings on "Comic Books and Juvenile Delinquency." Indeed, all his hearings, including a televised Senate investigation of organized crime in 1950–51, were in his mind unified as one sustained effort to combat inextricably connected social ills. According to Kefauver and most of his witnesses, it was simple: the reading of comic books led youngsters to violence, pornography, and sexual dysfunction (including homosexuality), and a life of crime.

But while it is easy for us to smile condescendingly at the constrained and even bigoted attitudes of the era, a sober look at the comic books of the times reveals that most professional pornography today, focused as it is on power, domination, and violence, in fact derives more from popular-culture forms like early comic books than from *Playboy* or the bondage shots of Bettie Page. It might seem strange that comic books could bear more responsibility than, say, stag films, for violent porn, but what matters in that assessment is not so much the appearance of bare breasts or genitalia as the way many comics reveled in scenes of arcane, brutal, and extremely sexualized torture of women.

By the time the hammer came down on the comics industry

(literally, in the hand of Kefauver as he opened the Senate hearings), comic books had become one of the most popular forms of entertainment in the country, read by every sort of American. Indeed, in 1947, 41 percent of adult men and 28 percent of women read comics regularly. By 1950 (before the industry peaked), 54 percent of all comic books were read by people over twenty. Adult readers of comics read on average eleven titles a month, and nearly half of all readers, adults and children, were females, driving the massive growth of so-called working-girl comics and romance comics. And while various adult groups read comics in roughly equal numbers, white-collar workers read more than any other adult market. It was an immense—and powerful—industry.

The Kefauver hearings, however, put an end to more than a decade of massive growth. At the beginning of 1943, Americans were buying between 12 million and 15 million comics a month, a number that would seem minuscule in 1954, when industry circulation peaked at 150 million issues a month, with 650 different titles. Even more important, the average comic book was read three or four times, meaning there were between 450 million and 600 million readings every thirty days. In a population of 150 million people, this is what corporations call saturation.[4]

Kefauver depended heavily on the work of Fredric Wertham, a psychiatrist whose 1954 book, *The Seduction of the Innocent,* supported the links between comics and deviancy upon which the senator would base his arguments. (Wertham's book also famously postulated the homosexuality of Batman and Robin.) Joining the cause were national institutions like the General Federation of Women's Clubs (GFWC), which organized community responses to comics across the country in church organizations, PTAs, and other groups.

In an attempt to appease the growing public outcry over comic book content and to avoid government interference, the industry instituted its own version of the Hays Code, ending what most historians call the golden age of comics. The Comics Code Authority, established in 1954, attempted to excise all sex, violence, gore, sadism, crime, and horror from the industry, and as a result, within one year, more than half of all comic book titles had disappeared. Superhero comics, which had been in decline since the end of the war, made a comeback, but the industry had lost the sophistication and wit that had earned the medium a large adult audience in its heyday.

THE GOLDEN AGE OF COMICS

Comics' golden age had begun with a superhero—*the* superhero. In 1938 the sons of Jewish immigrants, Jerry Siegel and Joe Shuster, first published Superman, who would be the most popular comics character ever and one of the most recognizable images in the world. He was, however, in the early years, a man apart from sex. While he certainly had an interest in Lois Lane, it was the most chaste of pursuits and always lower on his priority list than apprehending the merest of criminals.

Seldom given anything near equal credit for creating the industry is the second costumed hero, Sheena, Queen of the Jungle, who debuted in America only three months after Superman.

From the beginning, comics offered idealized versions of men and women. While Superman and his kind were presented as virile incarnations, the comics themselves remained sexless in any overt way until 1942, when the United States entered World War II in earnest. The comics industry, despite the burdens of paper rationing, can thank the war for the growth of its adult readership. Stories changed, grew more overtly patriotic, and hundreds of thousands of issues were shipped across the globe to servicemen, two-thirds of whom read comics and enjoyed the pop-culture connection to home. On military bases, comics sold ten times the combined sales of *Life* magazine, *Reader's Digest,* and *The Saturday Evening Post.*

In response to the new, adult readership, comics grew more overtly sexual. Female heroes that had appeared rail thin in revealing but relatively modest costumes now flaunted voluptuous curves, covered by the scantiest of attire. Comics were, in many cases, narrative pinups.

On the home front, women began reading comics as female characters assumed more powerful roles within them. Career-girl comics and women superheroes proliferated and gave women their own vicarious thrills. William Moulton Marston, the psychologist who created Wonder Woman with the explicit purpose of promoting a feminist philosophy, never allowed her to be presented as a sexual object. Most leading female characters, however, even in comics aimed at a female audience, grew more sexual as the war continued.

By the last years of the war, many comics—though seldom the marquee superhero titles—depended on what has come to be called "good girl" art, hypersexualized female characters who faced peril that usually emphasized their bodies and their vulnerability. Common "headlight" covers depicted women bound with their arms behind their backs, tied to posts, their backs arched to emphasize their breasts. Nazis, Japanese soldiers, generic natives, and even aliens bent over them, ready to despoil, mutilate, and murder. Leering villains threatened good girls with every imaginable death: dismemberment, burning, and beheading (the most popular).

After the end of the war, with paper rationing over, the comics industry began its meteoric rise. With every passing year, the superheroes appealing mostly to kids fell in importance while adult adventure, crime, and romance stories multiplied, often featuring good girl art with more psychologically complex threats posed to the women.

The 1946 cover of *Rangers Comics* no. 31, provides a perfect example of the uses to which women's bodies were put in the early

Rangers Comics, October 1946 (Fiction House).

Uncredited illustration. From the authors' private collection.

postwar years. The victim is a good girl with Bettie Page hair. Most obvious in the image is the anger and dark joy of the tormentors as they menace a voluptuous woman. The "woman in peril" theme is far older than American culture, but the threat on display here, and on thousands of other comic book covers, renders that theme in explicitly male terms, and makes graphic sexual violence the promise of the issue.

The cover image is a Freudian nightmare. The woman is tied to a post, her arms behind her back, and her breasts, with nipples erect, thrust forward. The natives clutch long sticks, and the American rescuer, small and pathetic, clutches his tiny gun in the background. The star of the drawing is, of course, the large, fire-spouting serpent, a *penis dentata* (symbolic "toothed penis") that threatens both to burn her alive and consume her.

The tiny, distant rescuer visually contradicts earlier versions of the powerful American male hero. Here he appears as an ineffectual sham version of the traditional hero, just as the serpent itself, if we follow its length around, is also a phony—merely an empty tube manipulated by natives pulling strings. Because the serpent is not the real thing but just a device manipulated by hand, the image plays as a representation, perhaps, of sexual frustration and masturbation, with an imperiled American woman as the object of arousal. The cover exemplifies the turn comics had taken from the war era to the postwar years.

For one thing, after the war, comic book covers shifted away from depicting enemy soldiers (Nazi and Japanese) being overwhelmed by larger, and more masculine, American heroes. Nazis remained popular villains, but were joined after the war by generic dark-skinned savages of undiscovered lands, who thrilled to white female flesh and dominated the American would-be rescuers (if they were even present). The visual language of the covers increasingly designated the villains, rather than the American heroes of the war years, as the vicarious thrill providers. The perspective of the implied viewer of *Rangers* no. 31, for instance, is that of one of the victim's tormentors, not a rescuer.

While male characters were also often threatened in arcane ways (Batman's sidekick, Robin, was a common victim), the threat was generally outlandish (giant fanged teddy bears controlled by the Joker, for instance), unlike the more distinctly imaginable, real damage the good girls faced.

Given the adult readership of comics and the social changes

overtaking America—scarred servicemen returning home and ex-Rosies returning to the workplace after their forced retirements—the growing anger and sexual violence of the comics suggests a response to women in which violent sexuality negotiates the new order.

Fiction House provides a fascinating example of the sexual politics of the era. Comic book publishers resembled nothing so much as assembly lines, with writers cranking out stories and sending them to rooms of artists who, nearly shoulder to shoulder, penciled, inked, and lettered the stories. At the beginning of the war, women found work in these factories just as they did in many industrial ones. In general, women worked as artists only, but at Fiction House women not only drew, but also wrote and even edited, comics titles.[5]

Moreover, alone among major publishers, Fiction House did not fire its women employees as servicemen returned home expecting to regain their jobs. More than at any other publishing house, women provided a strong creative voice throughout the remainder of the company's existence.

The cover of *Rangers* no. 31 provides an interesting example of how these gender politics worked themselves out. Specifically, we can see in that cover how Fiction House attempted both to respond to the growing public desire for sexually violent imagery and, at the same time, to promote an awareness of women's changing social status.

Like most comics, *Rangers* was an anthology of six continuing storylines. In issue no. 31, none of the stories includes any event resembling the action on the cover. The threat to burn and consume the bound woman is a bait and switch—a tease to attract interested eyes and open wallets.

Quite unlike the cover, the eight main characters within the comic include one female villain, one female victim, four heroic females, and two heroic males. None is harmed in any significant way. Top billing is given Firehair, Frontier Queen, a protector of Native Americans and the enemy of wealth-seeking white men. The issue utilizes a common paradigm: women in peril featured on the cover, and smart, heroic women inside. Similar cover images graced the titles of many publishers, and while the promised brutality was seldom delivered, only Fiction House straddled both sides of the divide, depicting eroticized threats against voluptuous women while at the same time acknowledging the evolving position women were assuming in the culture.

Looking back on this moment when comic books in their own way negotiated a turning point in the social order, their efforts might appear promising: the culture seemed, in the inside pages of the comics, to be slowly coming to grips with an empowered female population. The cover images might then represent merely a vestigial resentment over the loss of male supremacy. In all, the comics were perhaps about to mature into positively feminist conduits.

Sadly, such was not the case.

THE HORROR! THE HORROR!

A number of developing social changes took clearer shape as the nation passed the midcentury mark. Women began returning to work in more noticeable numbers, though generally not to jobs as well paying as the ones they had left. And public intellectuals like Schlesinger began to note that there was trouble brewing with American males. The comic book industry, serving an increasingly adult and dramatically expanding readership, responded to women in the workforce and the consequent "crisis of American masculinity" by publishing fare that did indeed deliver on the promise of sexual brutality—and in spades.

In 1950 William Gaines, the publisher of Entertaining Comics (EC), led a revolution that spiked the industry's circulation but that also ordained its demise. EC specialized in horror comics. Conservative groups had long complained about the sex and violence in comics, but public and governmental concern did not gain any traction until the horror comic asserted its grisly dominance in the public imagination. War, romance, and crime comics retained their popularity, and even outsold horror, but horror comics gave the industry a ghastly new face—which now became the target on which every foe of comics could draw a bead.

Invariably, groups protesting comics cited their harmful effect on the young. But several crime comics included the phrase *for adults only* on their covers, and in any case featured stories interesting only to adults.

EC's writers and editors certainly saw themselves as serving an adult audience, and dealt with adult social topics. Bigotry against minorities, non-Christians, and the disabled, among other marginalized groups, was excoriated as an all-too-common, knee-jerk American reaction to difference of any kind. In fact, EC comics stood firmly and openly on the side of progressivism in general— on every social issue except gender equality. EC's titles championed the weak and the vulnerable, and punished the guilty in ever more creative ways. Even animals came under EC's protective wing. Women, however, were another story. As far as Gaines was concerned, women were on their own.

Of necessity, horror comics like EC's took fear as their primary subject. Murderers, aliens, and cannibals inspire obvious brands of fear, but in EC's antibigotry stories, the fear was often of being surrounded by an American mob, itself afraid of threats to the traditional order of things.[6]

The most common source of fear in EC comics, however, and in a host of imitators, was not monsters or zombies but women. Specifically, women who challenged accepted notions of masculinity. The paradigmatic EC story introduces someone—or sometimes a group—who commits some sin (pride, selfishness, and cruelty are typical) and receives a harsh punishment as a result.

The tales always convey a moral, with endings that often include explicit discussions of the social issues in play. While men earn punishments for cruelty and bigotry, women, on the other hand, earn their grisly rewards for infidelity, for promiscuity, for bad mothering, and for placing their careers ahead of their husbands. All these prospective wrongs were, of course, commonly attached to women's position in the workforce.

In "Beauty and the Beach," for example, in EC's *Shock Suspen-Stories,* a dual story covering two women embarking on modeling careers, we see how their success turns the women into harpies who reject their husbands. When the husbands snap, pushed past their limits of tolerance, we are meant to sympathize with their righteous anger. One encases his wife in plastic while the other burns his wife to death under those emerging symbols of vanity—sunlamps. In three years (eighteen issues) of *Shock SuspenStories,* women were punished for gender-related sins by, among other means, being stabbed, strangled, chopped in half, decapitated, electrocuted, devoured by a shark, and suffocated.

In story after story, EC encourages its readers to take satisfaction—and to learn from—the consequences of female moral failure. Women should understand their role, these comics said, by accepting their subordinate marital status and their nature as mothers. We don't wish to argue here that EC comics encouraged actual violence toward women, but in the context of a perceived American masculinity crisis, the tales identify nontraditional women as the primary cause of trouble for both men and society. And their punishment for threatening the social dominance of men is violent and highly sexualized.

Beset manhood served as the regular subject of EC comics and others. In "Made of the Future" (1951), from EC's *Weird Science,* poor Alvin suffers when his fiancée abandons him for a wealthy man. When he happens across a guided tour from the future, he quietly follows it to 2150, where he obtains a kit for a Deluxe

Wife—just add water—and takes her back to his former life. The wife is perfect, beautiful and subservient, but Alvin loses her as well when she is accidentally returned to 2150. The story is a fable about the disappearance of traditional gender roles, and of the hopeless efforts of men to retain them. Alvin is presented as pathetic and, in the end, lonely. Another *Weird Science* story, "Lost in the Microcosm" (1950), about a scientist who grows ever smaller until he disappears, predates the more famous film *The Incredible Shrinking Man* (1957), but both explore the sense of manhood's shrinking as a result of a society that no longer valued it.

Men, however, were ready to fight back, hard.

"HITLER'S HIDEOUS HAREM OF AGONY": MEN'S ADVENTURE MAGAZINES

After the Comics Code Authority put an end, in 1954, to the work that made EC and Fiction House profitable, adult readers, and men in particular, largely abandoned comic books. They turned instead to men's adventure magazines (MAMs), where, over the next fifteen years, they could find pictorials of voluptuous women in bikinis and lingerie, as well as increasingly explicit illustrations of their torture fully dramatized in the stories. Popularly called "sweats" (for the obvious reason) MAMs had been around since 1949, with the creation of *Stag*. The bastard love child of pulp fiction magazines and men's literary magazines, such as *Esquire*, MAMs ascended during the same years that the comic book industry declined.

Martin Goodman, the publisher of *Stag*, knowingly pitched his magazine low. Betting that there was a large, underserved market of veterans who had not gone on to wear gray flannel suits but had, rather, returned home to boring lives and unchallenging work, Goodman believed these men wanted to remember the heroism and action—and even the gore—of war, to see themselves, vicariously now, as powerful and masculine. Circulation numbers proved him right. By the late 1950s, over fifty different MAMs crowded the local drugstore shelves, where, unlike *Playboy,* they were generally welcome. Even the lower-tier magazines enjoyed sales numbers of 100,000 to 250,000. While the total circulation of MAMs never equaled that of the comics, their total circulation roughly equaled that of *Life* and *The Saturday Evening Post* combined.[7]

MAMs depended on the faltering comic industry for more than its swelling readership. Goodman also published the Timely Comics line—what is now known as Marvel Comics—which had created figures like Captain America. In the next few years, some comic book publishers added MAMs to their lists, transforming titles like *Battle Cry* in MAMs. Others abandoned comics altogether and turned wholly to the popular new trend. After all, the restrictive comics code had left many editors, writers, and artists looking for work, and they now found a place for their skills on the pages of magazines like *Stag, True,* and *Man to Man.* And because MAMs clearly targeted an adult audience, conservative groups worried about children did not interfere with their publishing and distribution.

Publishers did, however, have to contend with groups like the GFWC (General Federation of Women's Clubs) and the Catholic National Organization for Decent Literature (NODL), which felt that they had battled the comics successfully and often included MAMs on their banned books list (along with the work of William Faulkner, Ernest Hemingway, and others). Local NODL groups, sometimes with the help of the police, would pressure drugstores and newsstands not to stock books and magazines they found unacceptable. Because such groups faced pressure in return not to appear to be banning everything, adventure magazine publishers could walk a tightrope, remaining as lurid as possible while still taking care not to become the first to appear on the conservative groups' hit lists.

During the first years of the growth of MAMs, which is to say those last years before the comics industry was compelled by growing public furor to create the code, *Stag* and its imitators relied on cover illustrations of heroic American men with good girls at their sides. These buxom women provided readers a visual transition from the comic book to the magazine. In addition to the illustrations and stories contained in the magazines, they offered American men the first mainstream portal to products they previously had a difficult time finding: ads sold lingerie by Lili St. Cyr, sex manuals, and yes, hard-core pornography.

The revolution *Playboy* started in 1953 contrasted starkly with the marketing appeal of the MAMs. Whereas MAMs sold fear and anger, *Playboy* sold pleasure and joy, whether in the form of centerfolds or in the reviews and ads for the best new products. Nearly every MAM featured at least one title such as "American Men Are Sex Saps," "The Homosexual Epidemic," or "Americans Are Lousy Lovers: Why Our Women Prefer Foreign Men." *Playboy*, on the other hand, was explicitly corporate, materialistic, and driven, promoting a vision of the good life.

Playboy's good life, however, seemed foreign to many working-class men. The resonant message of the MAMs was that American men, many of them former combat soldiers, triumphed through the power of guns and clenched fists. If "they" want to steal your masculinity, the MAMs implied, you'll have to keep it through violence and the sheer force of your will. Had the silk-pajama-clad, smoking-jacketed Hugh Hefner appeared in a men's action magazine, he would have seemed more an example of the "homosexual epidemic" than anything else.

The MAMs enjoyed a tremendous legal advantage over *Playboy* in many states and communities because they contained illustrations rather than photographs. The local drugstore usually wouldn't stock *Playboy*, with its images of topless, smiling girls-next-door, but magazines featuring illustrations of women in bondage, wearing only strips of clothing, and, let's say, about to be dipped in lye—those were fine.

Illustration enjoyed another advantage over photography. In 1954 *Man's Magazine* published its February issue with two covers, one a standard illustration of a heroic American fighting Australian Aborigines, the other featuring a pinup photograph of Eva Meyer (wife of the porn film director Russ Meyer). The illustration outsold the photograph.

Why might this be so? The way that illustration facilitates fantasy is different from the way photographs work. Illustration can emphasize detail difficult to capture on film and render the impossible believable. The early MAMs had experimented with staged photographs of scenes of violence and sexual threat, but the desired effect was minimized by their obvious dramatization. They were clearly fake photos. While it seems a contradiction, illustration, though obviously "not real," facilitates a closer identification with the fantastical experience—whether it be wrestling an octopus or caressing, or flaying, the skin of a beautiful woman. After *Man's Magazine*'s experiment, MAMs depended almost wholly on illustrations.

In the mid-1950s publishers would begin to test the limits of men's ability to identify with extreme images and stories. Till then, most covers and interior illustrations depicted men in combat, against men or animals, and the blood on display often belonged to the protagonist, whom we were meant to believe would fight his way to safety. In 1956, however, two new trends surfaced. A few magazines began including pictorials of lingerie-clad women not just as eye candy, but menaced by the same kinds of attackers that, until recently, only male heroes had to battle, thereby ramping up the level of violence involving scantily clad women. In 1958 the Supreme Court made the government's task of regulating obscenity much more difficult, by giving protection to "unorthodox ideas, controversial ideas, even ideas hateful to the prevailing climate of opinion," and the second new trend appeared: publishers of MAMs realized they were free to publish nearly any image or story they wished, no matter how outrageous the sexualized violence. If there was a dormant misogyny in the comic book industry before 1954, with the MAMs it had awakened, hungry and lustful.

Immediately, the visual and narrative treatment of women in MAMs became even more extreme than in the comics, a difficult feat. The lion that had previously been roaring at the terrified woman now had its claws in her flesh. Clothing became more tattered and the poses began to look suspiciously like those of a woman during sex, despite the arms of the octopus wrapped around her. Simultaneously, the American male figure began to shrink both visually and in the storyline.

By far the most obvious expression of this trend was the reappearance of Nazis—Nazis everywhere! And all of them tormenting and torturing beautiful, half-naked females. Earlier MAMs had made the heroic American male the center point of the illustrations and stories. Now, leering Nazi officers and their fat, shirtless henchmen subjected supple-limbed women to an endless variety of grisly deaths. After 1959, Nazis torturing women became the most common theme of the genre. By assigning to the Nazi officer the same power and authority previously given to the American hero, the MAMs began a decade-long trend in which the reader's vicarious thrill was no longer heroism and victory but torture and death.

The November 1965 cover of *New Man* shows a Nazi officer preparing to impale a bound woman from behind with a spear still red hot from the brazier. Nearby, a Nazi soldier binds another woman, the next in line for torture and death. Roughly half of the MAM titles featured images of women being branded, burned alive, thrown to voracious animals, beheaded, stretched, drilled, frozen, dipped in acid, dismembered, engulfed in molten metal, and, in cover after cover, whipped bloody. In all these images the female is tightly bound, as if otherwise wild, uncontainable, and dangerous.

Strikingly, the women in the MAMs from the 1960s seem to have all been busy preparing for a glamorous night out when they were kidnapped, bound, and readied for torture. Wearing lacy bras and deep red lipstick, they were apparently ready for sex when captured. The *New Man* cover from November 1965 is typical in this: block out all of it except the faces of the victims and their expres-

New Man, November 1965 (EmTee Publishing).

Uncredited illustration. From the authors' private collection.

sions could easily be interpreted as sexual arousal rather than pain and horror. And the sexuality is deliberate, of course. The images offer us the women's death as the ultimate climax.

These are, then, immensely angry images that act out the sexual and social frustrations working-class men felt as their world shifted underneath them. The countless scenes of torture offered men the vicarious thrill of reasserting the control and dominance they felt they deserved but were losing. Oddly enough, since many of these men were veterans, they reasserted themselves by turning to images derived from an act of incomprehensible nihilism, the Holocaust. The signature atrocity of the Nazis consisted of the attempted total destruction of the other, the non-Aryan, Jews, as a way to legitimize themselves and create their own identity. In the fantasized images on the covers of MAMs, as in the actual Holocaust, the powerful regarded themselves as superhuman and denied full humanity to their victims.

In the worldview of the MAM, women were the usurpers of a fully realized masculine identity, which could be regained only through sexual domination and violence. Being a Nazi, via the pages of a magazine, made such violently sexual domination possible. The Nazi figure may also have revealed the suppressed self-hatred and guilt MAM readers felt, stemming from their desire to subjugate a whole category of human beings and to torture as a means of pleasure.

Though not nearly as popular as the scenes of Nazis torturing women, the American soldier also regularly faced torture in the MAMs—by huge-breasted, Teutonic Nazi officers, shirts open to their waists, sneering at the degradation of the American hero. This was a far cry from the heroic images of a decade earlier, in which American GIs conquered all foes. And who, after all, brought him so low? Women! Powerful women whose self-possession and independence shows on their grinning faces.

Seldom would a 1960s MAM cover show an American man

and woman side by side, facing a common threat, as happened often in the 1950s. In the MAMs, men and women were citizens of different countries, permanently at war.

Readers of adventure magazines also believed that the war against comics and the less successful battle against men's magazines, by groups like the GFWC and NODL, was part of a larger social effort to force them into moral conformity—a movement led mainly by controlling women who would even decide what men could and could not read. The bondage and torture covers can be seen, then, as a pulp-paper revenge.

As the adventure magazines aged, the culture changed, and the Nazi became too distant a figure for its audience to depend on consistently for violent thrills. In the late 1960s the Nazi morphed into the hippy and the outlaw biker. Just as American men had, during the 1940s, defined themselves against their Japanese and German enemies, they now, as they entered middle age, defined themselves against new, barely fathomable groups. Yet the magazines continued to adopt these groups as the stand-ins for their audience's resentments, even providing some transition, as most of the bikers—and, strangely, even many hippies—wore swastikas or the Iron Cross.

In late 1967 the Supreme Court again widened the protections for obscenity, allowing full frontal nudity, and many adventure magazines again transformed (as they had done in the 1950s from comic books to adventure magazines), this time into "skin" magazines. But after 1968, the number of adventure magazines plummeted as competition winnowed the ranks of skin magazines down to a supportable number.

The new men's magazines were still not in any way silk pajama clad, and they did not try to compete with Hefner's *Playboy*. *True*, one of the more popular survivors of the transition, chose a flamboyantly crass approach that mixed the old with the new. One 1976 cover advertised "12 Pages of Hot Nudes!" along with a story about

"The Depraved Orgy-Master Who Makes Manson Look Like a Boy Scout." But the misogynistic violence of the adventure magazines of the 1960s had largely evaporated.

OF SHE-WOLVES AND HE-MEN

Physicists tell us that energy cannot be destroyed, merely changed into new forms. The cultural force behind the success of men's adventure magazines, especially the Nazi-focused issues of the 1960s, moved from page to screen in the 1970s. The Naziploitation film, as it has been called, is considered largely apart from the porn renaissance of the 1970s, but it's worth noting.

Porn historians call the 1970s the golden decade because of the big budgets available to the industry and porn's growing popular acceptance. Genre films like *Love Camp 7, SS Hell Camp,* and, the most popular, *Ilsa: She Wolf of the SS,* flew under the radar of many Americans who worried about the growth of mainstream porn. Imported from Italy or produced in the United States with comparatively low budgets (*Ilsa* was made on the leftover sets from the television show *Hogan's Heroes*), these Naziploitation films featured medical experiments, graphic torture sequences, and sexual debasement. Making the sexualized anger of the adventure magazines explicit, Ilsa, for instance, castrates her male prisoners and uses a giant electrified dildo to torture her female inmates.

The Naziploitation trend did not outlive the 1970s, but its underlying philosophy—of denying the humanity of the other through sexual violence—did indeed survive. Subgenres like the "women in prison" film, for example, maintained some of the more obvious violent aspects.

But in the 1980s the video porn industry began to grow into the massive enterprise it is today, and porn developed its own class system, much like the one that divided *Playboy* from the adventure magazines. Today, rape porn and snuff films (featuring deaths that are simulated, but increasingly realistic) are underprivileged in comparison with the near-Hollywood-quality porn films being produced. But the lion's share of video porn is rooted in anger and resentment directed against women, and so looks more like the men's adventure magazines of an earlier era than like *Playboy*.

4. Porn Exemplars
Advancing the Front Lines of Porn

The figures responsible for the porning of a culture are legion. We present here just a sampling, not a comprehensive catalog, of a half-dozen on America's A-list. Because we discussed *Playboy* and Hugh Hefner, arguably the premier exemplar of America's porning, in Chapter 1, we have left him out here. To hold the number to six, we had to make some either/or choices, such as Al Goldstein over Larry Flynt. The two are in some ways alike in what they bring to the porning of America, but Goldstein, never the subject of a major Hollywood movie, is less well known.[1]

Discussed here, then, are Russ Meyer, Al Goldstein, Madonna, Snoop Dogg, Jenna Jameson, and Paris Hilton. What links these individuals, in our view, is their role in what we referred to in Chapter 1 as the normalizing of the marginal. That is, each has been instrumental not only in bringing porn into mainstream American life, but doing so in such a way that it has been absorbed into the fabric of the culture. For example: Jenna Jameson. Whereas at one time many women in porn were impoverished, drug-addicted prostitutes, Jameson, in contrast, is an enormously successful career woman, in many ways a model of the strong woman Americans so admire. Her attractiveness, intelligence, independence, and wealth then become attached to porn, her chosen career, by association. Undoubtedly there are those who would question her career choice, but because her overall profile is positive, Jameson is considered "normal," one of us.

We do not, however, tell the same story six times over: each of our porn exemplars is unique, and all have normalized the marginal in strikingly different ways.

RUSS MEYER

We exaggerate only a little in saying that what was left of the modesty of 1950s America went up, at the end of the decade, in a mushroom cloud of Russ Meyer tittyboom. *Tittyboom* was the former World War II combat photographer's term for the still and moving pictures he took of gorgeous leggy women with stunningly large breasts. In the late 1950s Meyer unleashed an atomic dose of tittyboom in his first movie, *The Immoral Mr. Teas*. America, especially Hollywood, would never be the same.

It is a surprisingly funny term from a man seriously obsessed with breasts. But exploring the humorous possibilities of nudity and sex, at a time when nudity and sex could hardly be explored directly in any way at all, would become a trademark of Meyer's work.[2]

And it is a strange fact that some of the most important modern American porn is humorous, or at least has a comic side. Even before the goofy humor of the 1972 blockbuster porn movie *Deep Throat*, in 1959 Meyer's groundbreaking *The Immoral Mr. Teas* established a cartoon-like comic tone—not surprisingly, really, since Meyer often cited Al Capp's *Li'l Abner* comic strip as one of the most important influences on his work.

Presenting sex as funny may have been the perfect strategy, whether intentional or not, to break the prevailing ice of sexual suppression. Men's magazines of the 1950s (with titles such as *Peep Show, Frolic, For Men Only*, and *Adam*) very carefully remained on the safe side of the line separating allowable glimpses of bare skin from arrest on obscenity charges. Exploitation films of the period, with titles like *Is Your Daughter Safe?* and *This Is My Body*, often masqueraded as educational films about the dangers of drug addiction or back-alley abortion or some other social peril. Sexually, they promised everything in advertising pitches, but on-screen they delivered little.

The national libido was conflicted, even schizoid: it panted with barely containable excitement at the men's mag fringes—the *Frolic* cover photos, say, of babes in bikinis—while the center remained as crisply buttoned as the housedress over June Cleaver's bosom. And at just this cultural moment, along came Mr. Teas in his straw hat, pedaling a bicycle, a door-to-door false-teeth salesman so cartoonishly ridiculous that neighborhood urchins hooted, pelting him with rocks and clods. *Come on, loosen up, Mrs. Cleaver!* Teas seemed to be saying. *It's all in good fun.*

When Teas has an impossibly oversized molar extracted by a dentist, the shot of painkiller, proportionately oversized we must assume, produces an unexpected result: he hallucinates a kind of visual superpower and imagines seeing through the clothes of every woman he meets. The film is pure voyeurism as Teas, the embodiment of ineffectuality, can do no more than ogle the array of ample breasts for which Meyer's movies would become famous.

Or infamous. Twenty minutes into the premiere screening of *The Immoral Mr. Teas* in San Diego on May 27, 1959, the police raided the theater and stopped the show, seizing the reels and holding them for almost a year. If anything, however, the bust helped the movie, creating a buzz in the industry and on the street: here at last was a film that delivered gorgeous women in naked abundance. In January 1960 the movie reopened to a packed house in Los Angeles. The following summer it opened big in Seattle. Then on to Philadelphia and Washington, D.C., attracting large and even record-breaking audiences at every venue. On April 26, 1961, under the headline "28,810 for 'Mr. Teas,'" the *Hollywood Reporter* announced, for instance, that *The Immoral Mr. Teas* had set a house record in its seventh week at the Paris Theatre in Los Angeles.

Just as later, in 1972, the stunning profits of *Deep Throat* would spawn greedy imitators, so *The Immoral Mr. Teas* launched a new genre just on the basis of its bottom line. If a film about the mating rituals of the monarch butterfly had been shot for $24,000 and grossed a cool million—as was the case with *The Immoral Mr. Teas* —the numbers alone would surely have inspired a new genre of monarch butterfly films. Just so, a new genre was born in the nest of *Mr. Teas* greenbacks: the nudie-cutie. The old exploitation tease was dead, replaced by the sexploitation *Teas*. Meyer's sexploitation films would feature gorgeous heroines with immense and frequently uncovered breasts. And Meyer could crank out these films, sometimes two in one year: *The Immoral Mr. Teas* in 1959 was followed by *Eve and the Handyman* in 1960, *Erotica* and *Wild Gals of the Naked West* in 1961, *Europe in the Raw* and *Heavenly Bodies!* in 1963, and *Lorna* and *Fanny Hill* in 1964.

Meyer can be credited as the filmmaker who proved the truism *sex sells* beyond any doubt. But we must also credit him for figuring out how to pitch that sale to America in the late 1950s. As Jimmy McDonough says in *Big Bosoms and Square Jaws: The Biography of Russ Meyer, King of the Sex Film*, "Meyer dragged the hairy sex monster into the noon sun and turned it into a seemingly innocent cartoon. Where Americans had shuddered, they now laughed."[3]

For the next couple of decades Meyer found himself competing against the porn industry as well as Hollywood, as mainstream movies revved up the sex in their offerings and porn movies increasingly played in the same grind houses and drive-ins that featured Meyer's movies. He would do well in the race against Hollywood, always outpacing the studios in sheer quantity of nudity and in daring. The race against hard-core porn, however, was one he simply refused to run.

Even before *The Immoral Mr. Teas,* Hollywood studios had begun to push the envelope of nudity and sexuality in mainstream movies, and they pushed it harder after *Teas.* Posters for *Baby Doll* (1956), for instance, had showed a seductively pouting girl-woman in a tiny nightie (called a babydoll thereafter). *Psycho* (1960) featured a shower scene that revealed no significant nudity but was considered risqué simply for depicting a woman in the shower. *Walk on the Wild Side* (1962), set in a New Orleans bordello, came with a warning on posters and in previews: "This is an adult picture! Parents should exercise discretion in permitting the immature to view it." In 1963, *Promises! Promises!* featured the Monroe wannabe Jayne Mansfield, and included nude shots of her ample bosom. The late 1960s saw *Bob & Carol & Ted & Alice,* about swingers, and *Midnight Cowboy,* which flirted with homosexuality, showing (while not quite showing) fellatio in a movie theater.

In 1972, the second development, the growing popularity and accessibility of hard-core porn movies, manifested itself dramatically in *Deep Throat,* whose graphic, hard-core sex totally eclipsed the nudie-cutie. Even before *Deep Throat,* tamer porn movies, many from Europe (such as Sweden's *I Am Curious (Yellow)* in 1967) still far outstripped the sexuality of Meyer's sexploitation movies.

Although Meyer always referred to himself as a pornographer, he loathed hard-core porn. He was contemptuous of movies that showed the sex act itself, especially the close-up shots of the piston-like penis-in-and-out-of-vagina that would appear in the hit porn movies *Deep Throat* and *Behind the Green Door,* and that in fact remain as obligatory fare in most porn movies today. He vowed that he would never diminish the power of the mystery of female eroticism by such cinematic dissection.

What to do, then? How could Meyer continue to compete with Hollywood and hard-core porn, and yet resist crossing a line he was loath to cross? His single response to Hollywood's encroaching nudity and porn's unacceptable explicitness was a heavy admixture of graphic violence.

Meyer's movies, then, became as much about violence as sex, beginning with *Lorna* in 1964. Splattered blood began to mix in equal quantities with bare breasts in a new genre sometimes called the roughie. Some critics see Meyer's turn to violence as a weakening of his genius for voyeuristic sex, but with this new formula he was indeed able to continue to produce moneymaking movies.

Meyer made sixteen movies between *The Immoral Mr. Teas* (1959) and *Beyond the Valley of the Dolls* (1970), his two most well-known films, including *Faster, Pussycat! Kill! Kill!* in 1966 (which has something of a cult following) and the very successful *Vixen* (1968), which may well, as some claim, hold the record as the longest-running movie at a drive-in theater—fifty-four straight weeks in Aurora, Illinois.

Along with making movies one after another, Meyer also battled obscenity charges one after another, sometimes prevailing, sometimes not. *Vixen*, for instance, which broached the taboo of incest, was shut down or otherwise censored in Florida, Georgia, Illinois, Michigan, North Carolina, Ohio, Oklahoma, Utah, and Wisconsin.

Meyer was a fighter, and thanks to the financial success of *Vixen*, he was able to hire some of the best lawyers to represent him in these contests. In many instances charges against him were dropped or cases dismissed. The stiffest and most successful resistance came in Ohio, where a wealthy and influential businessman, Charles Keating, led an impassioned anti-pornography crusade to ban *Vixen*. Keating would later become nationally famous as a corrupt banker, convicted of fraud in 1993 in the Lincoln Savings and Loan (aka the Keating Five) scandal. The crusader against porn had perpetrated a different kind of obscenity, one that cost many company retirees their entire life's savings.

Meyer's legal battles with Keating in Ohio were an important part of the larger battle that raged throughout the 1960s regarding First Amendment protections of free speech, especially as applied to artists. In 1961, for instance, the ban on Henry Miller's *Tropic of Cancer* was lifted. But in that same year, the comedian Lenny Bruce was arrested for obscenity at the Jazz Workshop in San Francisco, the first of many such arrests (in Los Angeles, Chicago, and New York) until Bruce's death by morphine overdose in 1966. Ralph Ginzburg, publisher of *Eros* magazine, was convicted of obscenity in Philadelphia in 1963; the ruling was reversed by the U.S. Court of Appeals for the Third Circuit in 1964, and the case ultimately went before the Supreme Court, which upheld Ginzburg's conviction in 1966. On the very same day that the Court announced its unfavorable decision for Ginzburg and *Eros*, however, it lifted the long-standing ban on *Fanny Hill: Memoirs of a Woman of Pleasure*, a novel it found to have some "redeeming social value."

AL GOLDSTEIN

Al Goldstein not only stepped into the donnybrook of a legal tussle Meyer found himself in (Goldstein launched the porn magazine *Screw* on November 4, 1968, the day before Richard Nixon was elected president), he sucker punched, so to speak, none other than J. Edgar Hoover, calling him a "fag" in an early issue of the magazine.

Goldstein was subsequently charged with obscenity nineteen times in a two-year period, 1968–70, something he has stated he regards as Hoover's vendetta. According to Goldstein, the FBI director's last words were, "Get Goldstein!"

Before Al Goldstein, pornography was just plain dirty. After Goldstein, pornography was still dirty, maybe even dirtier, but it was no longer plain. Goldstein's *Screw*, and then later his cable television show *Midnight Blue* beginning in 1975, opened pornography out in new directions. In print and on television, Goldstein offered pure porn—explicit images of nudity and sex acts—but added political and social commentary, wicked satire, intellectuality, and a goofy *Mad* magazine kind of humor. *Screw*'s porn was still dirty, but now it was also edgy, funny, and socially relevant—in a word, *hip*.

Through this unique publication, then, which appeared at a critical time in the shifting sexual mores in America, a rebellious Al Goldstein became not merely another pornographer, but a leader of the sexual revolution of the late 1960s and the 1970s. Perhaps even more important, Goldstein became a public champion of free speech at a time when the limits of First Amendment protections and the related issue of defining obscenity were hotly argued in academic and legal circles. Ultimately, these matters were litigated in courts from the state level all the way up to the Supreme Court, with Goldstein and *Screw* often at the center of it all.

For all these reasons, *Screw* attained a certain antiestablishment kind of respectability entirely new to pornography, especially among the intelligentsia and celebrities. At the same time, it turned a good profit by appealing to large numbers of readers who bought it simply for the dirt. *Screw* regularly offered reviews of pornographic books (which had never before been treated with the seriousness that a book review automatically confers), and the reviewer of these "fuckbooks," Michael Perkins, was an English professor with a Ph.D. Along with hard-core porn stars such as Seka and John Holmes, celebrities such as Jack Nicholson (November 1972) and John Lennon (June 1969) were interviewed in *Screw*.

In Al Goldstein, then, porn had, for the first time in America, a well-known and interesting representative to help nudge it into mainstream American culture—a sort of ambassador of smut. Goldstein would, in print and on his cable show, make references to Aristotle and Spinoza while talking about oral sex techniques with Seka. He would pal around with celebrated writers like Philip

Roth, Gay Talese, and Jerzy Kosinski, who once accompanied Goldstein on an excursion to the swingers haven Plato's Retreat in New York City.

Goldstein's trademark became the middle-finger salute, which he memorialized in an enormous poolside sculpture that faced the ocean at his Florida mansion. His was an in-your-face style of pornography for which, however, he would pay a hefty price.

For all his arrests on obscenity charges, Goldstein was generally successful from a legal standpoint, thanks to dropped charges, hung juries, and not guilty verdicts—until December 1974. He and his partner, Jim Buckley, were then charged by federal authorities with mailing obscene material (*Screw* magazine) into Kansas. And for the first time they were convicted.

The conviction, however, was reversed. The judge ruled that the prosecutor had made inflammatory and prejudicial remarks in his closing arguments, and declared a mistrial. A retrial began in October 1977, and this one ended the following month with a deadlocked jury. So again there was ultimately no conviction. But the stress of three years of an intense legal battle took a toll on Goldstein's health, and cost him about three-quarters of a million dollars in fines and legal fees.

In an unpublished article, Goldstein offers an interesting take on his federal indictment.[4] In May 1974 Goldstein was the featured interview in *Playboy*. Always outrageous in his efforts to shock the bourgeoisie, he outdid himself before an audience of millions. In his words, "My interview in *Playboy* was volatile, fiery, rambunctious, provocative, and contained an insane verbal assault on Richard Nixon, his attorney general and coterie of attack dogs." And that puts it mildly. In fact, he commented that Nixon had his daughters perform oral sex on each other in front of the Secret Service. He also said that Nixon and his best friend, Charles (Bebe) Rebozo, regularly sodomized each other. Then Goldstein took off the gloves and got nasty. As Goldstein puts it, "My attack on Nixon was like a Ginzu-wielding sushi chef, overdosed on crystal meth, trying to slice and dice the universe."

The exposure he gained from the *Playboy* interview led to his appearance in further high-profile venues. And more foaming-at-the-mouth rants. On CNN's *Crossfire*, Goldstein asked the conservative commentator Pat Buchanan what images he used for masturbation. In a debate with Jerry Falwell, Goldstein wanted to know what color panties God wore. Meanwhile, the publicity rocketed *Screw* sales to 175,000 a week. "My newspaper was filled with hooker ads and in this new millennium God smiled on the world of fucking and sucking." And so, Goldstein concludes, "This is the world Nixon wanted to punish me for helping to create."

Through high-profile trials like those in Wichita, Goldstein's public identity had gradually assumed its most important form: he became a kind of sexual outlaw, in his words, "taking on the world." The posture linked him to two of his personal heroes, the brilliant and controversial comedian Lenny Bruce, who was also frequently arrested for obscenity, and the expatriate writer Henry Miller, whose "obscene" books *Tropic of Cancer* and *Tropic of Capricorn* were banned from importation into America for decades.

Bruce, like Goldstein himself a bit later, was often arrested for his defiant—sometimes tauntingly defiant—flaunting of social and legal strictures. Perhaps Bruce's most famous arrest was after his 1961 performance at the Jazz Workshop, where he performed a now famous comedic riff on the term *to come*.

Though he saw Bruce perform live, Goldstein never met him personally. In 1970 he did, however, undertake a cross-country trip to the Los Angeles home of Henry Miller, a journey—more a pilgrimage—that he made, as he later put it, "awash in hero worship." Goldstein's adulation of Miller sheds much light on Goldstein himself, and on the roles he played as America's crusading pornographer.

Miller's authorial voice is Goldstein's as well, and can be described as angry working class—the voice of a common man, a working stiff who is disgusted by the deadening conditions of menial employment, and by a conventional, hypocrisy-ridden morality. In the early 1920s Miller worked for the Western Union Telegraph Company, which he renamed in his writing the Cosmodemonic Telegraph Company. Goldstein, too, despised his work for newspapers, which he began while still a student at Pace University, moonlighting as a photographer, gofer, and driver of the radio car for the New York newspaper the *Daily Mirror*.

Like Miller, whose father was a tailor, Goldstein resented not only his own deadening employment, but also that of his father, who worked as a photographer "eighty hours a week, running with the news hacks chasing down headlines." He was a man who, as Goldstein says in his 2006 autobiography *I, Goldstein: My Screwed Life,* "never had a close friend, never went to a movie, never read a book, never had an original thought."[5] For both men, the example of the father became something to resist, to rebel against.

One manifestation of this struggle was that Goldstein, like Miller, developed an insatiable appetite. *Tropic of Cancer* and *Tropic of Capricorn,* Miller's most famous books, are almost as much about eating and drinking as about sex. Goldstein, five foot eight, at one point in his life, before undergoing gastric bypass surgery, ballooned up to 350 pounds.

For both men, though, literal hunger also became abstract, metaphorical: Goldstein hungered for the perfect pastrami sandwich, certainly, but, more generally and more importantly, he hungered for fully alive, vital experience. Like Miller, he hungered for pleasurable sensation, for the joys of sensuality, for the excitement of shocking the bourgeoisie—for a life that refused to gnaw on the dry bones of meaningless work and hypocritical convention. In short, Goldstein, like Miller, hungered for a life unlike the wasted life of his own father, unlike the wasted lives of the masses of "walking corpses," in Miller's term, one sees everywhere. It was an insatiable hunger for a life worth living.

That hunger might have led Goldstein in many possible directions. And in later years, dead broke, homeless, shunned by his only child, maybe Goldstein himself wondered about alternative paths. As he observed in 2007, now seventy-one years old: "All the battles I had, all my arrests, all my struggles to legalize pornography have produced a product I am ashamed of. The pornography of today is horrendously ugly, desensitizing—I would call it almost a . . . fleshy catastrophe."[6]

But in fact hunger led both men into lives of unbridled, uninhibited sexuality. And that untethered sexuality, in turn, further led them to their vocations: one as a controversial chronicler of his own sexual exploits, the other as a rebellious, free-speech-crusading pornographer.[7]

One wonders how many Americans, like Goldstein himself, find in porn (and in strip clubs, porn chat rooms, swingers clubs) a release from hated jobs and a resented conventionality. One subtheme of *Deep Throat,* after all, is that bourgeois life is boring—and is relieved only by the edgy, promiscuous sex of hard-core porn.

MADONNA

In Madonna we have the single most evocative—and provocative—figure in the porning of America. From the beginning of her career, a time when the entertainment industry busily promoted images of masculinity such as Rocky, the Terminator, and Gordon Gecko, she spoke openly about her close friendships with homosexuals. Even more bravely, Madonna was one of the earliest—and certainly the most famous—of stars to speak publicly against the sexually repressive attitudes that slowed the nation's response to the AIDS crisis in the 1980s. On the other hand, Madonna also made it her explicit purpose to bring the images and themes of pornography into the mainstream. And in these efforts, as in all others she has undertaken, she was stunningly successful.

Born Madonna Ciccone, she began her almost unbroken string of successes early. Earning straight As in school and a dance scholarship to the University of Michigan, she headed after graduation for the mecca of aspiring performers, New York City. Whereas most such aspirants do little more than wait tables, Madonna soon earned a coveted place with the Alvin Ailey American Dance Theater troupe. She also began recording dance singles, and her first successes gained particular popularity with gay audiences, signaling the creation of a career-long fan base that would lead to her being hailed as the biggest gay icon of all time.

As is true of most successful vocalists, Madonna was talented, hardworking, and lucky. Her greatest talent, however, has never been her singing voice. Instead, as would become clear in the gathering momentum of her career, her greatest gift is her ability to construct the persona of Madonna as a multimedia phenomenon. By the time of her second album, *Like a Virgin*, Madonna's cultural presence reached far beyond the limits of her voice. There was also the sexy, outrageous Madonna of MTV videos, wearing, for instance, nothing but strategically placed leather straps, grabbing her crotch, and even simulating masturbation. And Madonna the actress, starring in major (if generally unsuccessful) Hollywood films. And, most especially, in the endless interviews an insatiable media demanded of her, the Madonna of the powerful public voice, guaranteed to raise eyebrows and cause a stir.

Indeed, the single theme running through all of these manifestations of Madonna is power. Appearing in 1984 on *American Bandstand*, Madonna said, in response to Dick Clark's question about her plans, "I want to rule the world." It was an odd comment from a woman who had just sung "Holiday"—the bubblegum pop encomium to the idea of fun. To Madonna the comment was, however, more prediction than joke, and she would soon prove to be nothing less than the most famous woman in the world.

Like a Virgin foreshadowed what would become her career formula: begin by tapping in to a previously ignored audience, add sexual provocation, and find colossal success. Wearing lacy lingerie in the title song's video and in performances, with a large belt buckle proclaiming BOY TOY, she made herself the scourge of parents and the idol to millions of adolescent girls, many of whom became "Madonna wannabes." Her live performance of "Like a Virgin" at the 1984 MTV Video Music Awards startled even that worldly audience as she sang prostrate on the stage, writhing in orgasmic pleasure. Madonna was a savvy manipulator of image, her fans would soon come to realize, and such components as the label *boy toy* needed to be understood ironically. Boy toy was what she wanted, not what she was.

The Madonna story, as she herself often tells it, attributes her Herculean work habits and mania for control to her mother's death when she was five, and the eventual remarriage of her father, a conservative Catholic. These disappointments gave her a fascination with and a desire for power—to control in adulthood what she could not as a child.

Madonna's captaining of her own career and her pro-sex stance has made her an important figure in what is commonly called the postfeminist movement. In 1990 the scholar and public intellectual Camille Paglia wrote, "Madonna is the true feminist. She exposes the puritanism and suffocating ideology of American feminism, which is stuck in an adolescent whining mode. Madonna has taught young women to be fully female and sexual while exercising control over their lives."[8]

Indeed, the two characterizing traits of Madonna are sex and control. What may be limiting, and troubling, about Madonna's larger vision of the world—of culture, politics, and personal relationships—is that her career has always conflated sex and control, as if neither were conceivable without the other. From her earliest videos, sex was the field upon which the battle for power was played out.

Sparking one of her early controversies, Madonna played a peep-show performer in the video for "Open Your Heart." Wearing lingerie that can best be described as dominatrix lite, Madonna re-creates within a strip club the watcher/watched relationship she was developing with American culture itself. Yes, she seemed to be saying, you can view my performance, you can even thrill to my body, but in doing so you give me control over you.

The sexual gaze is explicit throughout the video, the gaze of the peep-show audience and her own in return, but she takes com-plete control of it. The audience, after all (the peep-show audience within the video and, by extension, the actual audience viewing the video) must *pay* to keep open the panels through which they gaze. She may, then, in a sense give them sex, but without surrendering one iota of control. The power in this exhibitionist/voyeur relation-ship of exchanged sexual gazes, in other words, is completely un-shared. It is Madonna's alone.

The peep-show audience in the video includes two gay sailors and a woman dressed in a man's suit. From this point on, Ma-donna's productions would regularly promote a cross-gendered sexuality, a "political" message that she continues to see as her fight against a repressive culture. "I'm constantly trying to chal-lenge the accepted ways of behaving sexually," she has said. She is waging, in other words, another battle of control on the field of sex.

Is there, we want to ask, any sexuality at all that doesn't require someone to dominate? Madonna has always been very open about her own desire to dominate. Her interviews are regularly peppered with declarations about the size of her balls, especially in relation to the men around her. She regularly calls men (Warren Beatty and Kevin Costner, for instance) "pussies." She has said she finds effeminate gay men intriguing because she sees them as alter egos to her own mannish or butch identity. She regularly characterizes her dancers and performers as children: "They're naughty children. They're needy children. They're gifted children. I love them all to death," she said on her 2006 *Confessions Tour* DVD. She herself, then, is their firm but doting mother—though she often better resembles the stern father she frequently includes in her productions as an avatar of control and repression.

In her controversial and successful—if critically hooted—1992 coffee-table book *SEX*, she wrote, "I wouldn't want a penis. . . . I think I have a dick in my brain. I don't need to have one between my legs."[9] For all her gender unorthodoxy, she accepts the traditional view that all relationships inherently have a dominant partner and a submissive one, and that the dominant power remains distinctly masculine, a "dick in the brain" if not between the legs. This dick in the brain of a gorgeous female body may explain her fascination with cross-gendered identities.

In the early 1990s Madonna would focus almost solely on the issues of power and sex, in multiple ways: the Blond Ambition tour, the documentary *Truth or Dare*, the release of *SEX*, the video for "Justify My Love," and her sixth original album, *Erotica. SEX* is at the center of this flurry of activity.

SEX functions as a primer on nontraditional sex acts, including bestiality, sadism and masochism, bondage, and a host of others. While some of the images are almost quaint, such as longing looks from same-sex partners, many are startling, such as a topless woman threatening a bound Madonna with a switchblade held to her crotch. All the images, however, have such a theatrical feel, like a girl playing X-rated dress up, that no real threat is conveyed, even in the mild and almost playful S&M pictures. The book is interesting mainly for the way, as in almost all of Madonna's work, it portrays sex in terms of dominance and power.

Critical backlash was one principal response to her book and her other productions of the early 1990s, and it triggered a heated reaction from Madonna. In her next album, *Bedtime Stories,* she expresses apparent surprise that her work, so clearly calculated to provoke, had actually done so. One track, "Human Nature," opens with the demand that we express ourselves, and not repress ourselves, and goes on to argue that because sex is human nature she has no apology for anyone she might have offended.[10]

But in this put-down of sexual repression and suppression of free speech, and in other ways as well, Madonna represents much that is positive in the porning of America. She is emphatically and unapologetically pro-sex. She has spoken and acted against injustice, beginning in the 1980s with her criticism of the nation's slow response to the AIDS epidemic. She has been a powerful force in America's hesitant but steady welcoming of gays and lesbians into mainstream culture. And she has been arguably the most influential figure of the last three decades urging women to take control of their own sexual and professional lives.

Yet she has also been a part of the general sexualization of American culture, and of young women in particular. In a 2007 *New York Times* article about the proliferation of campus-based porn magazines, Alecia Oleyourryk, the founding editor of Boston University's *Boink,* cited a girlhood influenced by Madonna: "All she was was naked all the time." It's the porning of America in miniature, a generation of young women who, like Madonna, take charge of their own lives, but increasingly view themselves through a prism of sex. Worse, Madonna has created a template too easily adopted and poorly executed by her pop music progeny. When Britney Spears dressed up like a porn movie schoolgirl and sang "Hit me baby one more time," she reversed Madonna's power relationships and established herself permanently—and, later, disturbingly—as the object of power rather than the holder.

As American culture has grown increasingly porned, and increasingly drawn to domination as a way to think about sex,

Madonna has literally and figuratively moved away, relocating to the English countryside with her husband, Guy Ritchie, a movie director. When she began a new international tour in 2006, the Confessions Tour, the accompanying, almost obligatory "Madonna controversy" had nothing to do with sex at all, but rather dealt with her placing herself on a cross to relay a message about violence overseas.

Going completely unremarked upon, however, was the opening of the show. Madonna, drawing on her growing interest in all things equestrian, appears as the master of the hunt, with several of her dancers in the roles of horses, wearing the horse-derived fetish gear of leathers and bits. (The porn industry calls the fetish "pony play.") Much reining, riding, spurring, and whipping follow. A production number so heavily laden with bondage and domination imagery, relying for its thrills on the suggestion of sado-masochism, would certainly have made headlines during the *Erotica* era. But in 2006, nary a raised eyebrow.

Of her intention in *SEX*, Madonna told *Vanity Fair* in October 1992, "I'm out to open their minds and get them to see sexuality in another way. Their own and others." The simple fact that Madonna no longer shocks us sexually is proof of how thoroughly she has succeeded.

SNOOP DOGG

The rapper Snoop Dogg (born Calvin Broadus) asserts that he *is* America. This sweeping claim does two things at once: it positions him as the new normal and suggests that his values are America's as well. Once we understand that, we'll be all right, he assures us. If that assurance sounds as much threat as stoner humor, the assertion may well be correct either way.

Snoop Dogg often speaks of himself in the third person—as a creation, an act, or a brand. As his career as a rapper has waned—his records still do quite well, but more as party music than as the "voice of the streets"—his cultural presence has actually increased, moving him away from his original fan base of mostly young black men to an ever wider and whiter audience, an expansion that has earned him the unofficial title of King of All Media. Starting in 2001, his media kingdom began to include porn.

Much has been made of Snoop's background. His impoverished youth in Long Beach, California, his slide into gang life with the notorious Crips, his time as a drug dealer (for which he was jailed), and his arrest and trial for murder—all of these are still leveraged in the maintenance of his gangsta image. In his 1999 autobiography, *Tha Doggfather,* Snoop is quick to explain that his time as a gang member was less about violence than it was about money. "We liked money and we liked what we could get with money and we weren't too especially particular where we got the money to get what we wanted. We were straight up capitalists."[11] He credits his drug dealing with training him for his career in rap, as well as for his entry into every highly competitive market from cell phones to barbecue grills to pornography.

His entry into pornography (as a producer and narrator, not as a performer) brought together his two loves, money and the pimp lifestyle. When Snoop discusses *pimpin',* he uses the term in several overlapping ways. One is to refer to the clothing and style made famous by the character Huggy Bear on the 1970s television show *Starsky and Hutch,* a role Snoop filled in the comedic 2004 Hollywood film reprisal. Another meaning of *pimpin'* is the achievement of absolute authority over a group of women who are eager to fulfill the pimp's every whim and wish, especially in a public display. Snoop established himself as the most famous pimp in the world when, at the 2003 MTV Video Music Awards, he arrived leading two scantily clad women in dog collars. In 2006, Snoop told *Rolling Stone* that some years earlier, at a high school Halloween costume party, he and a friend had won first place by dressing as pimps. The next year, a girl volunteered to portray their prostitute. "So we put the bitch on a leash and walks the stage. We pimpin,' she's the ho, and we won back to back."

Around the time of his stunt at the MTV awards, Snoop took up actual pimping as a hobby, fulfilling what he called a childhood dream. Snoop Dogg managed prostitutes for two years, until, in late 2004, he realized it was a barrier to reconciling with his wife, against whom he had started divorce proceedings.

Another barrier to reconciliation was Snoop's short but immensely influential career as a porn impresario. Working with Hustler Video, Snoop wrote, narrated, and composed the music for *Snoop Dogg's Doggystyle,* widely hailed as something new in porn: the hard-core hip-hop music video. *Doggystyle* was immensely popular, winning two Adult Video News awards, for best music and best-selling release of the year. Shot in Snoop's California home, it was the first hard-core video to appear on Billboard's Music Video chart.

The movie fulfills the promise many music videos make but never deliver on. A clever mixture of the conventions of hip-hop videos and hard-core pornography, the video established hard-core hip-hop as a new genre recognizable to both worlds.

The hypersexuality of hip-hop videos has long been controversial, within the African American community and beyond. While most music videos would hardly be described as sexually cautious, hip-hop videos have generally moved sexuality to the foreground in more literal and less stylized ways, often by filling the screen with women shot from behind, thonged and bent over, their rears bouncing to the rhythm. Further, in keeping with his valorization of the pimp image, Snoop's videos regularly portray servile women, "hos," as proof of masculine power and virility.

Yet Snoop Dogg's videos marked a milestone of sorts in black equality. While the pornography industry has long produced videos targeted for black audiences, these have seldom been major productions or enjoyed big sales, as was the case with *Doggystyle.*

Because of its financial and cultural success, *Doggystyle* created a small renaissance in hip-hop pornography, with figures like Mystikal, Ice-T, Digital Underground, and others getting involved in the industry—though, so far, none as performers. (R. Kelly's sex tape is an infamous and inadvertent exception.)

In 2002 Snoop Dogg himself followed up on the success of *Doggystyle* by producing *Snoop Dogg's Hustlaz: Diary of a Pimp*, and appearing in *Girls Gone Wild: Doggy Style*. Snoop's Girls Gone Wild (GGW) entry became the center of controversy when the two young women pictured raising their shirts on the cover of the DVD sued Snoop and the company. The women, one of whom was seventeen at the time the video was produced, alleged that Snoop offered them the drugs ecstasy and marijuana in return for showing their breasts. After settling his part of the lawsuit, Snoop ended his relationship with GGW, complaining about the lack of black women in the videos.

Indeed, the role of blacks in pornography can be seen as a microcosm of American race relations. The depiction of blacks as animals has traditionally been a familiar theme in porn. When a white female porn star has sex with a black male star, her presumed degradation in the act is often one source of the "pleasure" derived from the scene. Historically, one way to differentiate major porn stars from the lesser lights is whether or not they have had to perform in interracial scenes in order to maintain their place in the industry. (Jenna Jameson, famously, has never performed with a black actor.)[12]

Doggystyle and *Snoop Dogg's Hustlaz*, on the other hand, are brazenly positive about blackness in general and about black male sexuality as a distinct and powerful cultural trait. For this reason, coupled with their high production values and enormous sales, they mark a breakthrough in pornography. It must be noted though that they do not similarly empower women. In Snoop Dogg's videos women are if anything even more objectified, treated simply as bodies that serve men's pleasure, than in the typical hip-hop video.

In the years after his porn heyday, Snoop's corporate popularity has soared. He even starred in a GM commercial with Lee Iacocca, as sure a stamp of cultural approval as any rapper is likely to receive. Richie Abbott, his publicist, has said, "Nowadays, Snoop is for the kids." This, of course, is precisely the worry, since Snoop's fascination with porn remains a significant part of his persona. During a 2005 performance in Sweden, for instance, Snoop projected on a screen explicit girl-on-girl pornography during his rap set.

Rolling Stone captured the contradictions within the fascination with Snoop in a December 2006 cover story titled "America's Most Lovable Pimp." The cover showed him smoking a large peppermint stick—bringing to mind his drug of choice—and wearing a Santa hat. In that same year, however, the lovable pimp, the kiddie Santa, was arrested three times on drug and weapons charges. Music critics have speculated that these arrests were actually managed, created to maintain his street credibility, which remains a crucial part of his popular appeal. He's a gangsta and a sexist, yes, but *our* sexist gangsta.

If our fascination with Snoop is filled with contradiction, he himself is a walking contradiction. Snoop lived a life of sex, drugs, and violence as a youth. He has periodically revisited that life as an adult, and also renounced it. He is a peacemaker, having created a program to keep kids out of gangs. At the same time, however, he maintains his membership in the Crips. He was an important part of the tenuous 2005 ceasefire between the Crips and the Bloods, yet he continues to release songs that glorify criminal activity and murder.

The contradictions continue in regard to his treatment of women. He credits strong women with saving his life, yet his songs and his actions are misogynistic by any measure. In "Can You Control Yo Hoe," he sings that you have to put a bitch in her place, even if you need to slap her face. He uses the traditional explanation for the violence of his lyrics: Snoop told the *Courier-Mail* in 2006, "When I call a woman a bitch, it's an act. I'm acting out my scene. I'm expressing my true art. If you don't respect it for what it is, then please don't listen to it, don't criticize it." It is an effective defense, reminding his critics of the fallacy of equating art with reality. (Nobody believes that Johnny Cash ever shot a man in Reno, let alone simply for the enjoyment of watching him die.) But Snoop admits to having actually "strong-armed hos" during his career as a pimp. If the Snoop Dogg persona is a creation, it seems to have taken over its host.

Nevertheless, Snoop's star continues to rise. He has taken on porn as a lifestyle, and, with the help of corporate America, he has made it *cute*. The violence, misogyny, and homophobia of Snoop and other rap stars may at one time have been an understandable—though not defensible—reaction designed to reclaim black manhood in a culture that has systematically undercut it. This image of the rapper, however, has been co-opted and commodified, packaged for an increasingly white audience taking a vicarious pleasure in aggressive black manhood, a process that harkens back to blackface minstrelsy.

With Snoop, however, the meeting of gangsta rap and commerce have a special significance. In commodifying Snoop's vision of the fully porned lifestyle, corporate America has taken on the role that pimp Snoop has abandoned (as a career if not as an image). While Snoop bragged that he once had hos "on every exit from the 10 freeway to the 101 freeway," as the King of All Media he can bring the porn lifestyle to everyone.

JENNA JAMESON

Earning the title World's Most Famous Porn Star is a bit like being named a McDonald's employee of the month fifteen times in a row: a lot of work to get there, but a dubious honor nonetheless.

   The title, which adorns the covers of several of her self-produced videos, may actually be far too humble a description for Jenna Jameson, who, according to *New York* magazine, has reached the status of a cultural icon. Only trauma has brought iconic status to porn performers in the past, such as Linda Boreman (aka Linda Lovelace) and John Holmes, who participated in the short-lived porn chic era of the 1970s, only to have their lives publicly spiral into despair and violence. In contrast, career management and steadily increasing success may well be the central themes of the Jameson biography. Jameson videos often sell twenty times the average porn video, her ClubJenna website profits about $15 million a year, and she has achieved an unparalleled mainstream presence. It's hard to argue with the claim that Jenna Jameson is in fact the most famous and successful porn star ever.

   With the 2004 release of her postmodern memoir, *How to Make Love Like a Porn Star: A Cautionary Tale,* Jameson publicized a life story that seems to take direct aim at a host of conceptions about her and her industry. Yes, she suffered a tough childhood, early sexual abuse, and an underage entry into sex work. No, she doesn't believe it led to her making a career of pornography. Yes, porn can be humiliating and degrading. But it can also be empowering. Yes, she's proud of the title Porn Star. No, she doesn't want her children to have a mom who is one. She has also said that she would lock her daughter in a closet if she wanted to go into pornography. These tensions characterize not only her memoir but much of her career as well.

   Jameson made her first film appearance in the eleventh edition of the Up and Cummers series, dedicated to new industry talent, but she graduated quickly to starring roles and just as quickly began to turn her burgeoning popularity into greater control of her career and image, a rare thing in the industry. A perfect example of the cult-of-personality marketplace that characterizes American culture of the past few decades, Jameson has turned herself into a

highly diversified corporation within the sex industry. She has appeared in video games (including one in which winning means
bringing "Jenna" to orgasm), in cameos in mainstream movies like
Private Parts, in a recurring role on a 2003 NBC series, *Mr. Sterling,*
and as an interviewer for the E! cable channel and for the ECW
professional wrestling series. In 2000 Jameson created Club-
Jenna, profitable in its third week, that at first produced only her
own videos. It has, however, expanded and now hires its own contract girls, a few of whom earned their contracts by winning Jameson's reality show on Playboy TV, *Jenna's American Sex Star.* In the
tradition of big Internet successes, in 2006 Jameson sold Club-
Jenna to Playboy Enterprises for an undisclosed (but undoubtedly
very large) sum. She continues, however, to run the company for
Playboy.

If it weren't for the fact that Jameson's empire is built on
pornography, she would be universally embraced as a great American success story, a powerful woman living a twenty-first-century
American dream.

It's another example of the push-me-pull-you tensions within
pornography, and also between porn and mainstream American
culture. In this as well, Jameson provides a complex and revealing
illustration. After entering porn, her fast-rising popularity gave her
a power over her career that she put to firm and uncommon use.
Most female porn performers find themselves inexorably drawn
along the traditional career arc for a porn star—which moves
roughly from girl/girl scenes, to girl/boy, to anal sex, to "double
penetration," to interracial, and, finally, to the dark zones. Jameson, however, stopped her progress in the arc at girl/boy interac-
tions, and while online forums are full of complaints about her
lack of adventurousness, Jameson's popularity has grown without
falter.

Indeed, at the same time that Jameson has reveled in her
Queen of Porn status, she has performed not in more films, like

most porn successes, but rather in fewer and fewer. Her rise to porn superstardom developed at about the same time that she met and married Jay Grdina, and she responded to marriage by eliminating girl/boy scenes until she could convince her husband, a successful porn film director, to perform with her. In 2006, after the breakup of her marriage with Grdina and the sale of Club-Jenna, Jameson began dating Tito Ortiz, a mixed martial artist who competes in the Ultimate Fighting Championship series, and with this union she committed to ending her career as a performer altogether.

While still a performer, the evidence of Jenna's "empowerment," of her special status at the top of the porn star hierarchy, could be seen in her refusal to participate in the acts for which porn is known. Jameson avoided anal sex, double penetration (vaginal and anal), and interracial scenes. In most porn these are standard fare, and the women simply must comply, upping their hard-core ante, in order to maintain their place in the porn hierarchy. Pornography's audience eagerly await "Her First Anal!" for their favorite stars, and accepting the inexorable movement to harder-core performances is generally requisite for industry success. Jameson's refusal—confident that she would star nevertheless—constituted an assertion of superiority over what second-tier stars have to do. It is also, counterintuitively, an assertion of independence from her audience's expectations and desires. Porn, yes, but on her terms.

That interracial scenes are near the bottom of the list of undesirable porn acts for performers but are immensely popular with consumers of mainstream (white) heterosexual porn suggests an implicit desire in the viewers to see porn stars lower themselves—regarding sex with a black man as degradation, and thereby combining racism with misogyny. It is possible that Jameson's decision to avoid interracial scenes has more to do with staying at the upper end of the porn marketplace than with racism per se, but it is, nevertheless, a reiteration of gender and racial hierarchies.

In 2006 Jameson moved behind the camera with her directorial debut, *The Provocateur*. Produced on film, a mark of quality in the porn world, it is a high-production-value fantasy featuring wall-to-wall sex. In a special DVD segment describing the making of *The Provocateur*, Jameson described the film as "couture porn," and, of her visual style, she explained, "I don't want it to be porn. I want it to be something you would see on a Marc Jacobs runway." It's a telling comment that demonstrates her desire to differentiate herself from the vast majority of what sits on the racks in the video stores next to her own productions. This desire to, in a sense, de-porn pornography, to make it more broadly acceptable, is apparent in most high-end porn films.

Porn's actors and directors regularly discuss how closely their productions meet Hollywood standards. For example, a huge adult film success in 2005, *Pirates* (unconnected to Jameson), had over a $1 million budget and was also released in an edited, R-rated version, made available in rental stores like Blockbuster—a move openly intended to widen porn's audience, especially among women. High-end pornography operates almost as a separate industry within the larger industry, and Jenna Jameson is its avatar.

As well, in *The Provocateur* and in most of the products in Jameson's niche in the porn world, the films are committed to the idea that the women characters are enjoying themselves in a fully consensual and mutual way. Facial expressions of pain are nearly nonexistent, and pleasure is tied to mutual cooperation with a partner. While *The Provocateur* remains pornography—decidedly hardcore—intended primarily for men, most of it is clearly intended as well to be tolerable to and even enjoyable for women. In general, Jameson's films tend to be sex positive, and they generally explicitly support women's personal and sexual agency. In the plots of such films (the large majority), women usually play either powerful characters or characters who gain power over both their professional and sexual lives. Seldom does the act of sex leave a female character in the thrall of her male partner; indeed, the reverse is much more often true.

These films are not merely pro-sex. The most common theme is of female self-empowerment—an odd by-product of the necessary focus on women in porn for straight men. Yet the narrative conjoins all modes of empowerment with sex. The main character begins as unsure, unsuccessful, and unsexed, and each vector is reversed by the film's end. This seems to assert a positive message about women's innate strengths, but the implication is that for a woman to be fully empowered she must also become not just sexually active but sexually voracious, participating in sex constantly, intensely, and, often, with multiple partners. In this sense, it replaces one confining standard for women—of the "good little wife"—with another, the multiple-orgasming *uber*woman.

Jameson's films figure importantly in the crucial argument over whether pornography is inherently misogynistic. In her film roles and in her personal and professional lives as well, Jenna Jameson presents herself as the very model of the self-possessed successful woman. If she and those following in her footsteps are able to make this point convincingly, the American culture may well resolve the question of porn as misogyny in the negative. But maybe even more importantly, the line between adult and mainstream films will also become even thinner than it is now, perhaps to the point of vanishing altogether.

PARIS HILTON

The oft-heard characterization of Paris Hilton is that she is famous for being famous. But that is not completely right. In fact, she became famous as the beautiful young heiress everyone got to see down on all fours having sex on an Internet video. Before that event, Paris Hilton was only a moderately successful occasional model, and a bit actress in forgettable films. But in a culture mimicking porn in innumerable ways—decked out in slutwear, speaking what Tom Wolfe has called "fuck patois," hooking up—Paris gained fame for going whole hog in her own porn imitation. In May 2001, on computer screens everywhere, she appeared naked with her boyfriend Rick Salomon in four minutes of heaving flesh and pumping buttocks. Just like a porn star.

And yet, she was not a porn star! She became famous, then, as the un-porn porn star, the outsider who was not part of the industry per se, but rather was usually part of porn's audience—a member of that audience in effect speaking back to the world of porn and saying, "Here, look at me! I'm every bit as good at making porn as you!" Her video got millions of Internet hits, and a longer, twenty-seven-minute version, marketed by an adult film distributor, sold very well. She was not the only member of the porn audience, then, who thought she had succeeded.

But not only was she in fact not a porn star, she was about as far from the typical kind of female found in porn as could be imagined. The back-alley elements of personal misery and deprivation are lacking. It's clear that she likes to party, but she is not perceived as an alcoholic or drug addict. Her childhood, according to some accounts, may have been short on parental attention and affection, but it's by no means a story of abandonment and abuse. Far from poor, she is indeed the heiress to an enormous and well-known fortune.

Who is Paris Hilton, then? And why does she act like a porn star, both on and off camera? (In the fall of 2006, for instance, she was "caught," along with pal Britney Spears, partying in clubs pantyless. Even in our seen-it-all, jaded society, the resultant barecrotch photos shocked many.) The critiques of Paris Hilton's personality are well known, and we needn't belabor the issue. Even her self-portrait in the 2004 book *Confessions of an Heiress: A*

Tongue-in-Chic Peek Behind the Pose presents little more than a superficial, self-absorbed, vapid young woman. In a *South Park* send-
up of Hilton, her lap dogs finally can no longer bear her ennui,
arrogance, and utter emptiness. The poor pooches commit suicide, shooting themselves with her driver's revolver.

We are interested, however, not in the strictly personal, but
rather in what Paris Hilton represents in our porned culture, and
with who she is in that iconic sense. Along those lines, it well may
be the case that Paris Hilton has all the vices of the contemporary
porn star she imitates—superficiality, narcissism, materialism—
and none of the virtues. For instance, Jenna Jameson is, like some
others in the contemporary porn industry, clearly a working girl.
Whatever we may think of her career choice, she nevertheless
brings to it intelligence, independence, and hard work. Although
Hilton has earned millions via soft-core commercial ads and paid
appearances at all sorts of public and private events (where she is often required only to wave at the photographers), our heiress is not
in it for the money.

She is in it, apparently, for the attention. Culturally speaking, it
is a perfect match: exhibitionist meets voyeur. And this match can
be said to play itself out in a little porn drama that is so familiar as
to be in fact a cliché. We'll call it, "The Gardener's Affair with the
Rich Man's Daughter."

In this overused plot, the voyeuristic gardener becomes a
stand-in for the viewer. At first, we see the daughter only from
a distance: beautiful, provocatively dressed. The gardener gets his
first close look at the daughter when he happens upon her having
sex with her boyfriend. He can't leave without alerting the pair to his
presence, so he must, like the porn audience itself, quietly watch—
a trapped situation that confers a kind of innocence upon voyeurism, his own and that of the audience. Near the end of the sex
scene with her boyfriend, the daughter notices the gardener, but in

a combination of kinky thrill and utter condescension, she finishes with her boyfriend anyway.

Of course, even if you haven't seen this plot in action, you know where the narrative must inevitably lead. The daughter watches the strapping gardener at his chores and eventually goes to him in his shed, where he sleeps.

From this point the storyline may take one of a few possible directions. The daughter and the gardener may run away together. Or, in another common version, the daughter may, after a short and intense affair, abandon the gardener and go back to her rich boyfriend (and snobbery). Or the gardener may turn the tables on the rich daughter (who always sneered at him anyway, even when they were locked in carnal embrace), by reversing the condescension, scorning her decadent luxury, and haughtily abandoning her—which is indeed what happens in our version of the porn drama involving Paris as the rich man's daughter and the gardener as, essentially, the American public.

Though Hilton, the daughter of real estate tycoon Richard Hilton, was known by readers of fashion magazines for a few years before she became famous, most Americans saw her for the first time on the Internet, in the "doggie position" with her boyfriend. Like the lower-class gardener, we were all at that moment given almost unwilling access to the sexual lifestyles of the rich and famous. And from that moment on, we have been engaged in a highly sexualized and volatile "affair" with her.

What makes our fascination with Hilton so odd is that, except for a small number of readers of men's magazines, like *Maxim*, the American public doesn't like her at all. This is unusual. Generally, we like our sex symbols, even the ones we ghoulishly watch self-destruct, like Marilyn Monroe, or, recently, Anna Nicole Smith.

Indeed, our fascination with Paris Hilton is almost completely negative, and she has become a cultural touchstone signifying ignorance, vacuity, and fame without merit. We take pleasure in her troubles and public humiliations, even the smallest of which feeds our schadenfreude (such as her being pelted with cigarettes and lipstick tubes by members of a crowd in a mall in Austria in February 2007). She sneers at us with her glossy, plastic, celebrity face, and we sneer back with our blank, John Q. Public faces.

And yet, despite the mutual animus, she continues to perform for us, begging for our attention. And we continue to offer it up, raptly. This porn movie we are engaged in with Paris Hilton, then, is a degrading one in which our pleasure and hers are based on disliking and dehumanizing each other.

Contrast this perversity with the—at least relative—sanity and spirit of the 2005 remake, *The New Devil in Miss Jones,* starring Jenna Jameson. The setting in the remake is the business world, and the movie suggests that the damnation of Justine, the main character, is a result of her unwillingness to take charge of her life personally, professionally, and sexually. The message is a bit of a stunner for a porn movie. The implicit linkage of the three areas, after all, makes for a reasonable thumbnail description of feminism.

This porned vision for women's complete self-possession is, however, the single most common theme in high-end pornography. That the movie dominated the film category of the 2006 Adult Video News Awards makes for a compelling argument that at least one part of the industry is engaged in a purposeful effort to move porn toward a contemporary, woman-friendly ideology, which would enhance its full acceptance into the mainstream film industry.

This comparison is not intended to convey an endorsement of the Jenna Jameson brand of pornography, or of any brand of pornography, for that matter. Rather, we are arguing that if the culture had to choose between the two narratives of American sexuality for which Jenna Jameson and Paris Hilton are the exemplars, it would do well, in our view, to go with Jameson's version.

The Paris Hilton brand of porn, based on mutual contempt and dehumanization, is consistent with the degradation porn represented in the images issuing from the Abu Ghraib prisoner-abuse scandal, discussed in Chapter 6. And humiliation and debasement form the basis as well of a metaphorical porn evident in many areas of our culture—for instance, in the field of political commentary.

METAPHORICAL PORN AND ITS EXEMPLARS

Reviewing the exemplars of porn, we observe a distinctive characteristic of the entertainment culture that is also driven by porn: from one exemplar to the next, the shock bar, so to speak, must always be raised. For Russ Meyer, the nudie-cutie raised that bar enough to garner widespread attention. By the time we come to Snoop Dogg, however, the bar is all the way up to hard-core porn.

Entertainment must keep exceeding itself to remain captivating; it must constantly outdo its previous performances. The grinding relentlessness of this ethic can be seen dramatically in cases where it almost literally takes over as the shaping force in someone's career. The late daredevil Evel Knievel, for example, jumped his motorcycle over increasingly longer lines of cars, then moved from cars to trucks and buses, then, many bone fractures and near-fatal crashes later, attempted to jump the Snake River Canyon in Idaho in a rocket-powered Skycycle.

Some fifty years ago, Marilyn Monroe attracted enormous attention for photos showing her standing on a subway grate in Manhattan, her pleated white dress blown up around her hips to reveal her thighs and just a tiny peek at her panties. Today, no female sex star would attract much attention with such a limited display of skin. In fact, from Marilyn to later sex symbols, we can sketch an exponentially upward-curving line of "shock value." The line passes through Jayne Mansfield, who exceeded Marilyn in daring some well-publicized fully nude shots; through Bridget Bardot, who dared a few more than Mansfield; through Ursula Andress, the first Bond girl, who appeared in *Playboy* in 1965 and appeared nude in countless photos; through Brooke Shields, who elevated the shock bar by appearing nude at the age of twelve in the 1978 movie *Pretty Baby*; through Madonna, who further raised the bar by incorporating bondage and S&M images in her music videos of the 1980s and in her book *SEX*; and finally, to the likes of Paris Hilton, Britney Spears, and Lindsey Lohan, who in the fall of 2006 were all photographed in clubs and elsewhere flashing their shaved crotches. If at this point we revisit the photos of Marilyn on the subway grate, they seem by contrast almost innocent in their self-consciously naughty transgression.

Porn, too (which can be defined imperfectly but not altogether incorrectly as "sex as entertainment"), is subject to this imperative to exceed itself. It has arguably responded to this imperative by becoming increasingly dark: that is, more and more marked by humiliation and real violence. But in this postscript we'll briefly look at the way in which "porning" can be understood as a cultural metaphor that applies to areas apparently disconnected from actual porn, such as, for instance, political punditry. In recent years, in this understanding, we have witnessed the porning of politics, so that we now have not only literal porn exemplars but also metaphorical porn exemplars, chief among them Rush Limbaugh, Al Franken, Bill Maher, and Ann Coulter.

In the late 1980s (his very first syndicated radio show aired on July 4, 1988), Rush Limbaugh made a discovery that would transform politics in America: political commentary was lucrative popular entertainment! Political commentary could be so entertaining that if one did it right, a huge audience of radio listeners would be the reward. But just as we can trace an upwardly curving line from Marilyn Monroe to Paris Hilton in the raising of the shock bar, so we can trace a similar line from, for instance, Limbaugh to Franken to Maher to Coulter. Once political commentary had become entertainment, the bar had to be continually raised. And, as with porn, the method of raising the bar became increasingly dark: politics as entertainment began to rely, like porn, on heightening levels of degradation, evidenced in commentary as increasing levels of personal insults and attacks.

In 1996, when Al Franken wrote a book to attack, or counterattack, Rush Limbaugh, that work of ideological disagreement was titled *Rush Limbaugh Is a Big Fat Idiot*. Rather than analytical political argument, the book consisted, as the title suggests, mostly of ridicule, insult, and invective.

Coulter, for her part, attracts enormous attention by in a sense outdoing the shock level of deliberately outrageous regular features on Limbaugh radio shows, such as the "Animals' Rights Update." The lead-in to this bit from early Limbaugh programs consisted of the sounds of automatic gunfire tracked over the howls and yelps of the slaughtered animals. How do you top that?

Coulter, in 2006, on national television called former vice president Al Gore "a total fag." She also accused some 9/11 victims' wives of "enjoying their husbands' deaths."[13]

What we have in all this, then, is not political analysis in any intellectual sense, but rather a highly lucrative entertainment spectacle driven by the willingness to reach down into lower and darker depths of ridicule, humiliation, and debasement. In other words, using the term not literally but metaphorically now, we have the porning of American politics.[14]

And just as it is disturbing to contemplate what will follow the violent porn that is growing in popularity on the Internet, so it is unsettling to contemplate the metaphorical-porn exemplar now waiting in the wings, whose outrageous insults and calculated humiliations will upstage even Limbaugh, Franken, Maher, and Coulter.

5. Would You Like Porn with That Burger?

In 2006 Clinique, a popular line of skin care and beauty products, released an ad for a moisturizer that even a decade earlier would have been not so much unacceptable to potential customers for its objectionable sexuality as just plain incomprehensible to most female viewers. Unless one was familiar with hard-core porn, the close-up of a young woman's face splashed with a milky substance extending from her lips, across her cheek, and over the lid of her eye would be simply baffling: *What's she doing?* you can imagine the viewer thinking. *That can't possibly be the suggested application...*

But the ad execs, a culturally savvy group, who designed this promotion knew that their target audience of young women would instantly read this image as a playful take on the most common, obligatory sex finale in hard-core porn, the cumshot or facial. For the last decade or so, most sexual sequences in heterosexual porn, whether on Internet sites or in movies, culminate with the male ejaculating on the face of the female. The Clinique ad is both a visual pun ("facial") and an allusive verbal joke ("dramatically different moisturizing lotion") intended to appeal to a sexually sophisticated, hip (as in *Sex and the City*) female sense of humor.

The female face in the ad has a mannequin-like perfection of smooth features and skin as well as the almost complete absence of hair. In this regard, like a mannequin she represents not an individual but a kind of everywoman. And like a mannequin, she is

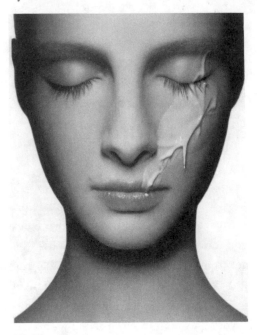

Clinique ad.

all about surfaces, completely devoid of emotion, as her expressionless face makes clear. The eyes are closed, suggesting privacy, or, even more, a transcendent peacefulness. The only familiar suggestion of sexuality is in the mouth: the wide, full, sensuous lips contrast in their red tint with the blandness of the other colors and the starkness of the lighting. The lips alone are textured, the only part of the total image that looks like it might contain nerve endings and feeling (and thus, pleasure).

Putting everything together, then, we have a portrait of emotionless superficiality—so deliberately cultivated as to mimic the mannequin's perfect surfaces and complete absence of feeling. Inasmuch as the image is about sex at all, it is about oral sex, which is suggested in the sensuous mouth, and is explicit in the streak of semen-like fluid across the face. What we have, in other words, in the Clinique ad is an iconic representation of sex in twenty-first-century America: the emotionless, impersonal hookup.

There is, however, no sell in just representing the hookup. And so the image is not so much about sex, after all, as it is about how Clinique can help young women in making their way through this new world of the hookup. The message is that the mannequin-like perfection of one's exterior (and that's where Clinique comes in) can serve as a kind of armor against emotional vulnerability in these days of impersonal and highly porned (cumshot) sexuality. Clinique is selling, then, a personal ideal for young women, as well as the means to achieve it, and we could call that ideal *mannequin sublime.*

As a cultural artifact of our hypersexual times, the Clinique ad finds much company in the world of porn-derived advertising, dating back at least to the 1980s and the image of the fifteen-year-old, presumably pantyless, Brooke Shields in her Calvin Klein jeans. Of course, sex has always been used in American advertising. But in the past few decades the sex in such advertising increasingly derives from hard-core porn. Consider, for another example, a 2007 ad by Old Spice, which markets Red Zone, a bath product for men.

Whereas the Clinique ad is pitched to young women, the Old Spice ad is pitched to young men, and the intended demographic accounts for some important differences in how the ad is to be read. For one thing, unlike the more oblique and subtle Clinique ad, which offers an image without comment, the text of the Old Spice ad comments directly on the image, and does so in a locker-room, jesting way: "This is simply a picture of a woman eating a vanilla ice cream cone" is the verbal equivalent of an elbow dig, inviting a "Yeah, sure it is!" from the male viewer. (Indeed, the next word in the text is *Sure.*)

Still, the ad is carefully crafted and highly porned. In the short text, the word *eat* and *eating* appear, and the word *it* occurs four

Old Spice ad.

times, including in the phrase *eating it*. Instead of the semen-like splash of lotion in the Clinique ad, we have semen-like melted ice cream on the young woman's tongue, from an ice-cream cone that resembles an erect penis right down to the pastry cone shaft.

The sell in this case is a personal hygiene that is commensurate with the angelically backlit, all-American blonde, whose sultriness (which the text alleges) is actually nowhere apparent in the image except in the dark eyebrows and eyelashes that contrast with her hair, which itself has only hints of the darkness of sexual appetite.

Having repeated the word *it* three times in the text, the fourth appearance, in which the word is underlined, is in the phrase *keep it clean*. The ad makes it explicitly clear that the woman is "only eating it because it tastes good," which is to say that if you, the young male viewer, do not "keep it clean," she will not eat it. The heavy-handedness of the text is deliberate, reinforcing the guy-to-guy humor that is essential to the ad's message.

The hookup, subtly implicit in the Clinique ad, is in the Old Spice ad suggested by the odd phrase *it is hot where she happens to be*. The word *happens* implies something unarranged, unpredictable, which is characteristic of the contemporary hookup: a meeting leading to sex could happen at the mall, or it could happen at a party, or it could happen in the apartment elevator. You never know. Unlike the traditional date, in preparation for which you could get it clean, in the era of the hookup you have to *keep it clean* because you just never know.

A recent ad for Orbit gum can be seen as a female companion piece to the Old Spice ad, and connects with the Clinique ad as well. This ad shows a young woman with a manhole cover in her hyperextended open mouth, with the text beneath the photo reading, "Dirty mouth? Nothing cleans it up like Orbit."

Orbit ad.

Like the Clinique ad, which makes no apparent sense at all except in a porned culture, this ad is unreadable to anyone not familiar with the conventions of porn. Why, after all, would bad breath be
described as a dirty mouth? The loaded term *dirty mouth* is applied
to someone who talks dirty—or, perhaps, does dirty things with
her mouth.

As with the Clinique ad, however, the culturally attuned advertising executives who went forward with this promotion knew that
they could count on their young clientele's familiarity with the conventions of porn. The photo of this attractive young woman with
her mouth entirely filled by a circular object recalls the images
rampant on Internet porn sites of women performing oral sex on
men. The message of this ad to its young audience is simple and
clear: her mouth is dirty because it's an orifice for male sex, a
"manhole."

Just as the males in the Old Spice ad are told that they need to
keep their genitals clean and ready for a woman who might, at any
time in the unpredictable world of the hookup, fellate him, so here
young women are told that oral sex leaves their mouths dirty. This
might of course refer to an unpleasant aftertaste as much as to
moral regret. But in either case, Orbit gum will take care of it. (The
promise in the ad implies a mess, something that must be cleaned
up rather than just cleaned.)

Like the Clinique ad, the Orbit gum ad addresses conflicted
young women in a porned, hookup culture. They are expected to
provide oral sex (the new second base, according to Tom Wolfe in
Hooking Up), just as the young woman in the Clinique ad has to be
emotionally prepared in her own sex life to deal with the potential
insult of the facial.

Rape victims are often said to shower compulsively after the
assault; Orbit gum promises to deal with the defilement of oral sex
by similarly "clean[ing] it up." Why this young woman might be

conflicted about having a dirty mouth is evident in her angelic, girlish face (if we mentally remove the manhole cover and see her as she would normally appear). The aura around her head, as well as her white blouse, further suggest that "dirtiness" is contrary to her nature. Indeed, this ad, like the Clinique ad (and we could cite many more such examples), speaks to the emotional discomfort many girls and young women in America experience as a result of their sexualization.

TWO-DIMENSIONAL PREENING

We are interested here not in chronicling the phenomenon of porned advertising (which, just from Brooke Shields to Paris Hilton, would require a book in itself), but rather in examining the repercussions of such advertising on the culture. We begin with a self-evident proposition: advertising works. Profit-driven businesses and corporations would not spend billions of dollars a year on advertising (in many enterprises advertising dollars comprise the biggest piece of the budget pie) unless it was known demonstrably to be effective.

Advertising works, but in unintended as well as intended ways: every ad that uses porn to sell a product is also, at the same time, an ad for porn. When Paris Hilton, for instance, looking every inch the porn star, performs something resembling oral sex on a hamburger, everything about the ad—that it comes into our homes on our familiar television screens, that Hilton is a rich, beautiful celebrity, that the choreography and cinematography are slick—everything, in short, about the ad that makes it work to sell us Carl's Jr. hamburgers also makes it work in a real sense to sell us porn. If Hilton's beauty, wealth, and celebrity, for instance, make the Carl's Jr. hamburger in her hands more desirable by association, so do they make the porn star look more desirable by the same association. In this way, porn is marketed through its presence in glamorous and effective advertisements for all sorts of products. Ms. Hilton, via the Carl's Jr. ads, sells us a side of porn with every burger.

Further, this combo of burger and porn subtly imparts to porn the familiarity and acceptability of that most all-American of food staples. (And, to complete the symbiotic relationship, the porn element in the ad lends new excitement to what might otherwise become a too familiar and even tired staple, the same old hamburger.)

Advertising works in more general ways as well to promote porn. The use of porn—which is to say the sexual use of female and male bodies—to sell us everything from clothing to food items to music CDs to automobiles, implies that our own bodies, our own sexuality, are in themselves commodities in a vast marketplace. This process of seeing oneself as a commodity assists the normalization of porn because we live in a culture driven by consumerism. We feel familiar with, comfortable around, things for sale, even when we ourselves become, to use the current word, commodified and marketed. Let's look at some very clear examples of this phenomenon.

As we've seen, in the late 1990s clothing manufacturers introduced what they themselves called slutwear, and the fashion quickly became popular with high school and college-age girls and young women. Slutwear can be defined as clothing that presents the female body as a sexual commodity on display.

Some staples of slutwear are, for instance, the thong bikini, which, like thong underwear, entered popular usage via strip clubs and porn movies of the 1980s. (These sources also, by the way, introduced women to the current fashion of shaving their pubic hair.) Thong underwear can also be considered slutwear when worn (in a fad that has for the most part lapsed) so as to be partially visible from behind. In that case, the elastic waistband and the top of the V that gradually disappears into the cleavage of the derriere is called a "whale tail." (At least a half-dozen websites are dedicated to publishing "seen on the street" or "voyeur" photos of whale tails.)

Push-up bras lift and shape the breasts for maximum cleavage. Belly shirts button low from the top to reveal cleavage, extending just below the breasts, leaving the midriff exposed. Extremely low-slung jeans sit just above the pubic bone. Along with belly rings and other piercings, tattoos, heavy eye mascara, and glitter (applied to breasts and legs as well as to the face), the effect is to imitate the porn star.

In the 1950s, if a teenage girl wore a tight sweater and skirt and an angry parent said, "You look like a little tramp!" the teenager would probably protest that the parent simply didn't understand what kids were wearing these days. In 2008, if a teenage girl is attired as described above and an angry parent says, "You look like a little slut!" the girl might well respond, "Hey, thanks!"

If the popularity of the slut look surprises you, consider the advertising climate in which young women have grown up. Twenty-year-olds in 2008 were born in 1988. If we lump MTV music videos into the category of ads, which they certainly are in part as they promote the sale of music albums, today's twenty-year-olds were just four when Madonna simulated masturbation in some of her Blond Ambition tour numbers. They were six years old when Calvin Klein began running ads featuring the model Kate Moss, who was in fact eighteen but looked prepubescent. One of the most famous of these ads showed her nude, lying on her belly on a sofa, the visual focal points being her childlike face and bare bottom. Today's twenty-year-olds were fifteen when Abercrombie & Fitch began running increasingly sexual ads in its *A&F Quarterly* catalog. In the space of a few years these ads progressed from partial to complete nudity, and from complete nudity to suggestions of group sex.

Again, this list is simply a quick gleaning, merely representative and not at all exhaustive. Suffice it to say that teens and twen-tysomethings have grown up in a culture saturated with porned advertisements, relentlessly promoting the notion that their bod-ies and their sexuality are marketable commodities.

Such commodification is everywhere evident in our culture, ranging from the relatively benign to the highly porned. The web-site Facebook is among the benign, an online yearbook of sorts, with photos (mainly headshots, as the site name suggests) and profiles of high school and college-age males and females. The profiles cite interests, turn-ons and turn-offs, favorite quotes, and so on.

Appearance in Facebook is virtually *required* of everyone in their teens to early twenties. In a *New York Times Magazine* (March 4, 2007) article about college sex magazines, "Campus Exposure," a student at Harvard says of the holdouts who refuse to participate in Facebook, MySpace, and other such online networks, "They're treated like pariahs, people will just harass them until they join." If you pose the question in a college classroom as to how many of the students assembled are in Facebook, typically everyone in the room will raise their hands. It is hard to think of any other ques-tion likely to elicit such unanimity. Alexandra Jacobs, author of the *Times* article, explains the near-universal willingness to join such networks this way: "To attend college now means to participate in a culture of constant two-dimensional preening, for males and fe-males alike."

MySpace, which recently surpassed Google as the most popu-lar website, and which claims about 125 million member profiles worldwide, is a more complex phenomenon than Facebook, and the two-dimensional preening is more consistently porned. My-Space clearly demonstrates the culture's comfort with the com-modification and marketing of the individual.

Such marketing occurs on many websites, including in innu-merable personals in classified ads all over the Internet. Craigslist, for instance, publishes personal ads for women seeking men, men seeking women, men seeking men, and so on, as well as separate categories for "strictly platonic" or, at the other extreme, "casual en- counters." Some matchmaking sites, such as AdultFriendFinder, are so specialized as to cater only to those looking for no-strings- attached sexual encounters, whether hetero, same sex, or bi, part- nered or group. Reliable membership numbers for such sites are hard to determine, since the operators have a vested interest in in- flating them. But if one considers MySpace and its countless spin- offs, along with all the dating and matchmaking sites in existence —some of which, like Craigslist, are huge in themselves—the number of Americans marketing themselves via online advertise- ments is unquestionably immense.

Compared to Facebook, the demographics of MySpace are far more wide-ranging, including the elderly as well as the very young, high school dropouts as well as college grads, and even profession- als with postgrad degrees. And members can market themselves in sophisticated multimedia formats using text, photos, graphics, and music.

Those who post on MySpace are in a tough market, with mil- lions of competitors. Often many thousands compete for attention within a twenty-mile radius of their own zip codes, which shop- pers use in narrowing their searches and perusing profiles.

Profiles are formatted like advertisements, so the typical My- Space page is an easy read. Essential information is presented suc- cinctly, in headed columns. An "About Me" column, for instance, lists such details as marital status (one can simply identify oneself as being "in a relationship"), sexual orientation, favorite music, tel- evision shows, and books, along with schools attended, current job, and even annual salary.

The "I am here for" section typically lists one or more of the following purposes: dating; networking; long-term relationship; or friends. "Who I'd like to meet" is also standard fare, though the chosen individuals can be surprising. One Pennsylvania woman, who identified herself as "born again," indicated that she'd like to meet: (1) Dolly Parton and (2) Jesus.

Along the right side of the page is a mandatory column of friends consisting of other MySpace members who log on to a profile page with photos of themselves, along with greetings and a brief personal message to the host. The creators of MySpace regard this particular feature as so vital—perhaps to uphold the sense of community, of an online meeting space as welcoming as an actual neighborhood gathering spot—that lest some page be sadly without a single friend, the site automatically provides everyone with "Tom," an agreeable-looking twentysomething buddy in a T-shirt.

In the case of older members, lists of friends often include their own children, as well as nieces and nephews, stopping by to offer a palsy, affectionate greeting, addressing the parent or relative as "my best friend" or "my good bud." Similarly, on the pages of young members, moms and dads, aunts and uncles, pop in with a chummy word or two. In the virtual MySpace world, the social leveling described by Robert Bly as "the sibling society" very much prevails.

To assist even the computer-naive in creating a suitable page, boilerplate layouts are available free of charge from many providers, as well as such standard features as glitters (images and words that literally sparkle), flash toys (graphics, often photos, that suddenly appear on the page), and colorful backgrounds, often with a design motif of, typically, unicorns or Harleys. Surfing the pages of MySpace, however, one is struck by how many of the pages include material that is pornographic, both soft core and hard core.

MySpace has clear guidelines prohibiting, for instance, nude photos of the members. Offers of prostitution are also forbidden and violators are booted off the site. Many profiles, however, especially those created by self-described swingers, push the envelope of the acceptable, including photos in which members are shown wearing thongs or similarly revealing lingerie. One expects the risqué on swinger pages.

But even on the most ordinary of pages, one often finds pornographic cartoons, photos, and GIF images of sex acts, glitters with porn messages, and so on, much of which is easily available as free downloads from a number of providers, such as the website Sexpeeppages ("What you need, when you need it"). The seamlessness with which material such as glitters with the words *nice tits* and *blow me* coexist on a page along with, for instance, photos of children's birthday parties and Colorado ski vacations, is visual testimony to the porning of America—that is, of porn so thoroughly absorbed into the culture that we hardly notice it anymore. It does not stand out as taboo, or even in poor taste. Rather, it is part of who we are, in carefully constructed public presentations. In the sophisticated advertisements for the individual known as MySpace profiles, porn is used in much the same attention-getting way that Calvin Klein and Carl's Jr. use it in their advertisements.

The phenomenal success of MySpace has, as mentioned, spawned countless spinoffs, many of which attract members by lessening the sexual restrictions that apply on their site. Stickam, for example, an Internet newbie, consists of MySpace-type member pages, or "rooms," but is heavily populated with webcam users. In 2007, about four hundred Stickam-member live webcams were online at any given moment, increasing to seven hundred or more at night.

Webcam broadcasters have the option of restricting viewing access to selected visitors by, at any time they choose, designating their room as private. The designation *private* often indicates that the webcam broadcaster will strip (known as "showing" or, if done very briefly, "flashing") or engage in solitary or partnered sexual activity. Further, those who enter a room can display their own nude webcam images, in a small format, on the host's page.

Craigslist, another mammoth Internet presence, exemplifies a somewhat different form of porned advertisement. Craigslist consists of a vast bulletin board of advertisements of all sorts, the overwhelming majority of which are not in any way sexual. Among its offerings, however, are personals ("women for men," "men for men," and so on) and "services," which includes a category labeled "erotic."

The personals category typically contains, among postings from real people seeking face-to-face sexual encounters, "cloaked" ads the intention of which is to shunt respondents to phone-sex lines or subscription cam websites. The erotic services category, however, is another matter.

For most big cities (one logs on to Craigslist by city designations), clicking the "erotic" link instantly summons a lengthy list of sex workers of all sorts, from those offering massages "with happy endings," to fetishists peddling, for instance, the worship of their feet, to mistresses specializing in domination and/or bondage (with varying degrees of sadomasochism, from light spanking to whipping), to full-service providers (who sometimes refer to themselves as GFE, for "girlfriend experience," if they are willing to kiss mouth-to-mouth). Full-service providers, whether GFE or not, offer vaginal intercourse as well as sexual specialties (coded as "languages spoken," such as "French," for oral sex, and "Greek," for anal).

As we saw in Chapter 4, between 1968 and 1970 Al Goldstein, of *Screw* magazine fame, was arrested nineteen times, partly for publishing in his magazine ads for escort services and independent prostitutes in New York City. In the porned America of the twenty-first century, on the other hand, the erotic services section of

Craigslist publishes such ads with impunity, including ads featuring pornographic pictures.

Many sex-specific sites on the Internet publish ads by prostitutes, including e-mail addresses and phone numbers. On Craigslist, however, one can shop for jobs and apartments in, say, Boston, and at the same time locate the specific erotic services one might hope to find there. Lumping together sex shopping with other kinds of shopping removes the stigma from the sex trade, making Craigslist a prime example of the porning of America. The site reinforces the commodification of the body and sexuality by including them as items for sale in the vast marketplace we all browse.

The Craigslist online community adds to the normalization of the sex trade by, for instance, referring to the women and men that advertise their services there not as prostitutes, but as *providers*, substituting a neutral, or even positive, term (providers are, after all, simply answering a call) for a stigmatized one. And the men who hire providers are not johns, another stigmatized term, but rather hobbyists, innocuous as, say, stamp collectors. Further, listings on the site regularly include reviews, in which a hobbyist who has done business with a particular provider offers other hobbyists an assessment of the provider's services—a sort of informal consumer reports of the local sex trade.

FROM MYPLACE TO EVERYPLACE

As we've suggested, if the porning of America describes a process, the final stage of that process would be the disappearance of porn altogether, not through its absence but rather through its ubiquity. When porn is totally absorbed into a culture, when its styles, vocabulary, and behaviors are completely normalized, it is no longer visible as porn. We are not yet at that stage. And we might not ever get there, since cultural developments do not always extend into the future in a linear way. But we are not far from that stage, either.

In the 1980s, when professional porn was typically shot in 35-mm-film format and featured stars, on sets, with a director and sometimes even a script, a pornographer named Mark Krinsky, under the pseudonym Ed Powers, used handheld video cameras to produce a series he called Bus Stop Tales and, later, Dirty Debutantes. (The "debutantes" were making their sexual debut on camera.) In these films, Powers interviewed women he picked up on the street, and then videotaped himself having sex with them. Powers is often credited with having invented amateur porn.

Ed Powers was not, in any real sense, an amateur, but rather an innovator within the porn industry. He marketed his videotapes widely and so successfully that many imitators began using the videocamera and nonprofessional women to produce a high-profit product. Innumerable Internet websites still feature the Powers style of "amateur" porn, including the impromptu interview followed by videotaped sex.

In the past few years, however, a true amateur porn has not only emerged, it is rapidly becoming the most popular form of porn, as evidenced by burgeoning websites, magazines, and DVDs. In the opening chapters of this book, we described a cultural convergence: porn stars had become more like us (as was epitomized in Timothy Greenfield-Sanders's XXX exhibit), and we, in turn, had become increasingly like porn stars, imitating their physiques (both via the gym and plastic surgery), their fashion styles, their language (a fuck patois, to again use Tom Wolfe's term), and their anonymous, no-strings style of sex.

At a certain, inevitable point in this convergence, porn stars and ordinary people so closely resemble one another that the former become superfluous, obsolete, the dinosaurs of a porned culture. Simply put, who needs them anymore? To this question, true amateur porn emerges as the answer: "We don't need them. We *are* them."

College porn magazines, while not the purest manifestations

of amateur porn, are perhaps the most surprising. The *New York Times Magazine* feature "Campus Exposure," referred to earlier in this chapter, examined these publications. If one considers the stereotype of the women and men in early American porn—marginalized, drug addicted, disadvantaged—one can hardly imagine a more complete opposite than, say, the students of Boston University. But in fact *Boink*, an outright porn magazine (that is, unlike some other college sex magazines it describes itself as "user-friendly porn"), was founded in 2005 by Alecia Oleyourryk, then a senior at BU. *Boink* is completely staffed by college students, and features only actual students from BU and other nearby colleges and universities. Its sales, however, are not confined to the campus: it retails for $7.95 in its hardcopy form (single copies or subscriptions are also available in online versions), with a press run of ten thousand copies.

Other similar college magazines operate on a smaller scale, and many disdain the porn label. The oldest of these, *Squirm* ("a magazine of smut and sensibility") has been published at Vassar since 2000. In 2004 students at Harvard began publishing *H Bomb*, followed by *Vita Excolatur* at the University of Chicago, and *Outlet* at Columbia University.

College students, then, in significant numbers are comfortable in highly sexualized situations: posing nude, masturbating, and having partnered sex (in the case of *Boink*) on camera, writing erotic fantasies as well as reviews of vibrators and other sex toys, giving explicit advice on sexual techniques, and so on. The long-running series Girls Gone Wild features college girls on spring break (currently comprising about sixty DVDs), with titles such as *Extreme Orgy* (in three volumes), *Extreme Sex, First Timers* (also in three volumes), and, as discussed earlier, *Doggy Style* (hosted by Snoop Dogg). In a 2006 book, *Female Chauvinist Pigs,* author Ariel Levy chronicles the ease with which camera operators for Mantra Films, the production company, find young women who—for no more compensation than a T-shirt or a hat with the GGW logo—are willing to flash their breasts, their bottoms, deep kiss one another, and engage in other sexual activities (with girl-on-girl action a specialty).

Shane Enterprises, a porn film company founded in Van Nuys, California, in 1996, shoots "reality based" movies around the country (*Small Town Sluts*, for example), including some on college campuses using porn stars (in one movie—almost inevitably— Ron Jeremy appears) along with students. The series is called Shane's World College Invasion. The company's website currently offers nine such DVDs, packaged in three three-volume sets.

Porn featuring college students received frenzied media attention in 2002 when Shane shot a porn movie in a freshman dormitory, Teter Quad, at Indiana University in Bloomington. Shane Enterprises reportedly sent out a casting call for their porn movie on the campus radio station and hundreds of students, male and female, responded. The Fox News Network's show *The Factor,* hosted by Bill O'Reilly, aired footage of crowds of would-be porn stars carrying on lasciviously for the news cameras as they lined up to interview for possible inclusion in the porn movie.[1]

Even allowing for media hype, the student response was lively, at least, and sufficient to result in a movie that featured credited cast members such as Drunky the Bear, Belladonna, and other students "playing themselves." In that same year, another College Invasion by Shane (called *Frat Row Scavenger Hunt 3*), filmed at Arizona State University in Tucson, somehow drew little media attention, even though, according to the *New Mexico Daily Lobo*, the student newspaper of the University of New Mexico, two teams of ASU students composed of fraternity members and females searched for sex toys hidden around campus and then earned points for finding and performing sex acts with them. The *Daily Lobo* reported that the student body president and vice president did not see the production of the video as "a big deal."

Further, many websites, such as CollegeFuckFest, purport to show porn featuring only college males and females, usually in off-campus party settings. The complete picture of college porn, then, from student-run magazines to professional production companies and Internet websites specializing in college students is a very big picture indeed.

Most of what we have mentioned regarding college students appearing in porn is more or less on the Powers model of amateur porn. The phenomenon is significant in the porning of America, however, simply for its scope: clearly, many college men and women regard themselves as de facto porn material, as porn stars, and are willing, for very little or no financial compensation, to present themselves publicly that way. The sophisticated production facilities and distribution of many of the endeavors we have cited here, and their high profitability, especially GGW, make them, however, decidedly nonamateur.

The most genuinely amateur porn consists of ordinary people of all adult ages, from the very young to the elderly, posting online video clips of themselves having all manner of sexual activity. In almost all cases, the product is technologically very basic: a webcam or digital video recorder is set up and pointed at the participants, who simply turn it on and then perform for the camera.

They then select a clip, from a minute or two up to twenty minutes or so, and send it electronically to the host site, such as YouPorn, PrivatePornMovies, or YourAmateurPorn, where it is available for viewing as a link. The phenomenon is nothing less than an Internet wildfire, with such sites multiplying exponentially with every passing month.[2]

Those who create the websites do so for profit. Many are free to viewers and make their money selling banners and links to advertisers. Others sell subscriptions. But those who create the porn itself on these truly amateur sites are not paid at all.

Who, then, are these people? They are truly a cross-section of the American population, and as such they have democratized the notion of the porn star. Older performers are referred to as "matures," ranging in age from forties to seventies, and, though this is rare, even older. Hardbodies occasionally appear, including silicon-breasted females and eight-pack-abs males, but most do not resemble the porn star template at all, with sagging breasts and thick middles more the norm than the exception. Sometimes the camera angle deliberately leaves the faces of the performers unseen, but such was more often the case even just a couple of years ago than now. As the stigma of porn recedes more and more completely into the past, the amateurs are bolder in facing the viewing public, facing the camera, as they perform.

Amateur porn clips in many ways resemble the home videos we all know, sometimes out of focus, the picture shaking, the action occasionally interrupted so the camera can be repositioned. Indeed, we half-expect the performers to lean in close and smile and wave for the camera. Like the individuals featured in our own home movies, we know these people. They're our moms and dads, cousins, nieces and nephews. They're *us*.

6. The Nexus of Porn and Violence

Abu Ghraib and Beyond

If the Clinton/Lewinsky scandal was a trench-coated national visit to a blue movie house, the Abu Ghraib prisoner-abuse scandal was a furtive venture down to the room under the room, for pornography too disturbing to be made light of on late-night television.

In late April 2004 the CBS television program *60 Minutes II*, followed in May by articles by the journalist Seymour M. Hersh, online and in print for the *New Yorker,* revealed several of the now infamous Abu Ghraib photos. The story of the highly sexualized, brutal treatment of detainees by American soldiers would continue to develop after those first weeks following the unveiling of the photos. Our sudden realization that the flower of American youth were purveyors of violent pornography and snuff films was another in a long line of losses of American innocence.

By that time, we'd sat through lengthy televised discussions of a president's semen. Heard the news reports of female teachers having sex with their schoolchildren. Videos of celebrities in flagrante delicto had become ho-hum. We were unshockable.

The first batch of photos from Abu Ghraib ranged from the explainable all the way to the horrifying. Some photos were of naked Iraqi detainees bound at the wrists and ankles and lying on the ground. Others included a hooded Iraqi forced to simulate oral sex with another prisoner, and the now totemic image of a hooded man hooked up to electric wires while balancing precariously on a box.

In the days following the graphic revelations, some discussions of Abu Ghraib became de facto conversations about porn in general and Internet porn in particular. Dozens of print, television, and online news reports and commentaries covering the scandal described the photographs in terms of pornography. Indeed, pornography and America's porn-infused culture became the most common targets of a feverish effort to find someone, or something, to blame.[1]

Writers as ideologically different as the liberal intellectual Susan Sontag and Rebecca Hagelin, vice president of the conservative Heritage Foundation, agreed that pornography and a violent and lascivious culture were at the root of the sexual abuse and torture at Abu Ghraib. Sontag, in one of her last pieces of writing before her death in 2004, sounded notes dear to the hearts of conservatives when she cited violent video games as an important factor in preparing young Americans to commit these kinds of atrocities. One wonders what she would have made of the revelation, in the summer of 2005, that one of the most popular and most realistically violent video games ever, Grand Theft Auto, included an animated porn "Easter egg," a secret component of the game. Players in the know, or those with enough Internet skills to find out how, could unlock and run the program, which allows the player to have simulated sex with a digital prostitute.

The events at Abu Ghraib became the subject of a national discussion in which Americans tried to come to grips with how our soldiers, the good guys, we like to think, could commit acts that ranged from abuse to torture—and even to murder. (The death of Manadel al-Jamadi, whose corpse Private Charles Graner and Specialist Sabrina Harman happily pose over, thumbs up, in separate photographs, was ruled a homicide by the military.)

Most porn, as immoral and destructive as many Americans believe it to be, is still less frightening than what we saw in those photos. Describing the photos as porn condemned them at the same time that it placed the acts they document in the realm of the merely distasteful rather than of war crimes. Rush Limbaugh, for instance, all but pooh-poohed the controversy, describing the events as "fraternity hazing" and calling the photos "standard good old American pornography," as if there was a place reserved for "American porn" right beside Mom and apple pie.

Limbaugh's intention was to minimize the growing damage to public support for a war begun by a Republican president, but in actuality his assessment was valid. Good old American pornography, of a particularly violent and degrading sort, provided the source and structure of the photographs that continued for months to trickle out through a variety of magazines and websites.

Porn was a crucial factor in the scandal, and over the next few months the national conversation about Abu Ghraib became a conversation about porn; real porn, fake porn, amateur porn, and, if we believe the pundits, all manner of rhetorical porn. The story of Abu Ghraib became a porn story, in the events themselves, in the immediate aftermath, and in the cultural response.

PORN AS THE LANGUAGE OF CONTROL

In the hubbub of commentaries about the scandal at Abu Ghraib, and in several well-publicized announcements by conservative figures like the Christian broadcaster Charles Colson and organizations such as Concerned Women for America and the Family Research Council, porn was identified as indeed a cause, if not *the* cause, of the events at the prison. The porn industry was already reeling when the Abu Ghraib photos surfaced—a highly publicized rash of AIDS diagnoses among performers had led some companies to shut down temporarily. Now accusing fingers pointed at it from every direction.

As details continued to emerge, it became clear that the guards at Abu Ghraib were intensely involved, on a daily basis, in porn. The military police at Abu Ghraib apparently organized much of their professional and personal lives around porn while serving in the prison.[2]

Originally brought to Iraq to serve in more routine jobs like directing traffic, the reservists of the 372nd Military Police Company (of the 320th MP Battalion) found themselves involved in dramatically more intense and complicated duties as prison guards. According to the investigative report of Major General Antonio M. Taguba, the soldiers were undertrained (having in fact received no training for work in a military prison) and subject to too little oversight. Further, the prison was understaffed, and these were all factors in the abuse and torture. Despite the nationwide search for root causes, actual factors turned out to be relatively banal.

Taguba's report, and subsequent investigative journalism, has shown that military intelligence (MI) personnel encouraged the guards to "soften up" detainees for interrogation (a directive prohibited by Army Regulation 190–8). Further, Hersh's *New Yorker* article "The Gray Zone" argued that the type of abuse and torture that detainees were subjected to was part of a program of intelligence gathering code-named Copper Green, which was based on the idea, confirmed by Arab scholars, that because of cultural factors making masculinity and honor the highest priorities of Arab men, they are particularly vulnerable to sexual humiliation. Such a program, then, turns sex into threat. And porn into policy.

The military and the CIA have denied the existence of Copper Green or any such program. Multiple credible reports in sources such as the *New York Times* and the *Washington Post*, however, have documented the pressure put on military intelligence to get information out of the prisoners, often through interrogations conducted by the CIA. The practice of "ghosting" security detainees to keep them out of the eye of human rights groups seems also to have been common. According to Hersh's article and other sources, military intelligence, planning an interrogation the next day, would instruct guards to, for example, "Make sure this guy has a bad night" or "Loosen this guy up for us."

Also well documented is the use of civilian contractors as interrogators. MI officers appear in some of the abuse photographs, which were put up as screen savers in areas used by guards and MI officers.

Finally, the confession and conviction of MI Specialist Armin Cruz, the testimony of Graner that MI officers directed him to use sexual humiliation, and the release of internal government documents (through the Freedom of Information Act) show the involvement of Department of Defense operatives in these kinds of interrogation tactics. These reports and others provide credibility to Hersh's core thesis that the military police did not think up this type of abuse and torture independently. The reason that soldiers of the 372nd participated in the torture at Abu Ghraib is fairly clear: they did what they were told. Then they expanded on the orders.[3]

But how to explain the sexual humiliation the photographs show? Why was the visual language of violent and degrading pornography brought to the goal of extracting information from prisoners? And why did the sexual humiliation of prisoners extend beyond those detainees suspected as insurgents? Subsequent reports have shown that most of the victims at Abu Ghraib depicted in the circulated photographs were ordinary criminals, not security detainees likely to have information about the insurgency. This fact makes much of the inflicted abuse and torture recreational, or "for entertainment," as Cruz is reported to have said. Army captain Chris Graveline, who prosecuted Graner, made the assessment that "it was for sport, for laughs."

So while the MPs were officially directed to loosen up detainees for interrogation, the abuse caught on as entertainment and developed a momentum of its own. Much of what the public has seen in these photographs, then, was sexual degradation for the fun of it.

What did this degradation include? The following list of "sadistic, blatant, and wanton abuses" is from General Taguba's report:

- Punching, slapping, and kicking detainees; jumping on their naked feet
- Videotaping and photographing naked male and female detainees
- Forcibly arranging detainees in various sexually explicit positions for photographing
- Forcing detainees to remove their clothing and keeping them naked for several days at a time
- Forcing naked male detainees to wear women's underwear
- Forcing groups of male detainees to masturbate themselves while being photographed or videotaped
- Arranging naked male detainees in a pile and then jumping on them
- Positioning a naked male detainee on a MRE Box with a sandbag on his head, and attaching wires to his fingers, toes, and penis to simulate electric torture
- Writing "I am a Rapest" (sic) on the leg of a detainee alleged to have raped a fifteen-year-old detainee, and then photographing him naked
- Placing a dog chain or strap around a naked detainee's neck and having a female soldier pose for a picture
- A male MP guard having sex with a female detainee
- Using military working dogs (without muzzles) to intimidate and frighten detainees, and in at least one case biting and severely injuring a detainee
- Taking photographs of dead Iraqi detainees

Taguba also reported as credible accusations that MPs had broken chemical lights and poured phosphoric liquid on detainees, threatened detainees with rape, and sodomized a detainee with a chemical light and "perhaps a broom stick."

Since the scandal broke, further reports, some deriving from testimony at military hearings and others coming from eyewitness accounts of the seventeen hundred additional photographs and videos shown to Congress behind closed doors, have surfaced, adding to the list and increasing the detail.

- Detainees forced to masturbate into the mouths or onto the bodies of other detainees
- Detainees handcuffed together in poses of homosexual sex
- Female detainees forced to bare their breasts
- Male detainees forced into homosexual acts
- A detainee forced to use a banana to simulate anal sex
- MPs videotaping the rape of a fifteen-year-old detainee by a private contractor

Some reports cite multiple instances of young Iraqis being raped. In a 2007 interview with Hersh, Taguba added that he saw images of "a naked detainee, lying on the wet floor, handcuffed, with an interrogator shoving things up his rectum," and "a video of a male American soldier in uniform sodomizing a female detainee."

Some of these acts clearly borrow from the kind of porn many Americans can imagine, such as that depicting bare breasts and masturbation. But many derive directly from that growing segment of the porn world catering to the desire, overt and unashamed, to degrade and humiliate a victim. Often the means is violent.

Was pornography responsible for what happened at Abu Ghraib? Surely this is not the whole story. Rather, lousy training, poor leadership, bad orders, and a variety of other systemic flaws created a situation in which soldiers—several of whom astonished their family, friends, and previous commanders with their actions—could indulge the kind of dark impulses that find full expression in violent pornography. Porn was not the cause of abuse but rather the language of abuse at Abu Ghraib—a language in which these young soldiers were fluent.

TURNING CRIME INTO PORN

The reasons that degradation porn became the language of detainee abuse at Abu Ghraib are perhaps too complex to examine here in their entirety. As discussed in Chapter 3, pornographic use of the military figure has a long history, though it evidently now needs to be expanded to include both genders. And the military has long suffered from sex scandals, with the 1991 Navy Tailhook convention being the most famous of recent ones.

In its very conception, a military is based on the premise that, when necessary, one nation asserts its will—and its identity—over another. That philosophy necessarily and understandably trickles down to the individual soldier. But it becomes especially problematic when such domination involves sex. The history of warfare is rife, for example, with accounts of the victorious soldiers' rape of the women of the conquered people.

The theme of asserting one's will over another is also found in most porn, fascinated as it is with narratives of the exploitation of power differential. Doctors and dentists seduce patients, teachers and tutors seduce pupils, city slickers, sometimes traveling salesmen, seduce farmers' daughters, and innumerable other such scenarios. The prison guard/prisoner fantasy has been popular in porn for decades, in print and film.

Also, soldiers at work in their primary purpose, waging war, have to engage in a psychological distancing from the objectified enemy, "us versus them," that is similar to what happens in most porn narratives—someone is on top, in control, of a more passive "other" (the patient, the student, the farmer's daughter, the prisoner). The viewer is generally discouraged from identifying with the weaker, more passive, player in the drama.[4]

Built into the military mindset, then, is a more general process that scholars call "othering." This refers to the social and psychological processes by which a group in power defines, usually in opposition to itself, a less powerful group. In the specific case of the military, the less powerful group would typically consist of the defeated enemy, the vanquished. Othering serves simultaneous purposes: first, it justifies whatever actions the dominant group feels it needs to use to control "them," the weaker group, and second, it reaffirms the superiority of the dominant group. Othering is on full display in the Abu Ghraib photos, as it is in all violent pornography. To their tormentors, the detainees at Abu Ghraib prison are clearly nonentities.

But the abuses at Abu Ghraib prison did not simply reflect brutality. The photos and videos did not just record the torment and torture, separate from it all. Rather, these materials were in fact an integral, defining part of it: sexual sadism turned into violent pornography. The visual images, carefully posed and even staged with some complexity, turned a crime into porn—and that got everyone's attention. Reports of abuse, after all, had been leaked to the public well before the storm of scandal broke in the spring of 2004. Until the photos surfaced, and the story took on the patina of porn, few Americans knew or cared about how prisoners were being treated in a prison whose name even most reporters couldn't pronounce.

As indeed became clear, a culture of porn existed among the soldiers involved in the abuses at Abu Ghraib. An Army Criminal Investigation Command investigation report, written in 2004 by Special Agent James E. Seigmund, compiled all of the images collected from the prison—more than 2,800 photographs and videos.

As it turned out, 660 of these were images not actually from Abu Ghraib, but were, rather, professional pornography likely collected from websites by the MPs and passed around, on the same discs, with the violent pornography they created themselves.[5]

These soldiers created for themselves a world that integrated porn into their lives and jobs, and that took pornography as the organizing principal of othering the detainees in their charge. The soldiers themselves have described the environment in the prison as "chaos," a "hodgepodge," and the "Wild, Wild West." Indeed, the stories that have surfaced suggest a mix of teen sex comedy, porn movie plot, and horror movie. "Almost everyone was naked all the time," one congressman reported after seeing seventeen hundred of the classified photos and videos, a report confirmed both by soldiers and detainees. According to Taguba's report, beer was smuggled in to the prison and soldiers regularly got drunk, which also contributed to the sexual free-for-all that developed. An officer sexually propositioned a female subordinate, prostitutes allegedly had regular bunks in the prison, soldiers sneaked into off-limits areas of the prison to have sex with one another, and, in a scene straight out of *Porkies,* an Army captain photographed female subordinates without their knowledge while they were showering in outside stalls.

While beer-soaked orgies, clumsy passes, and peeping toms might sound more like *Animal House* than like serious crime, they were part and parcel of the same broken military command—poor leadership, insufficient supervision, vague orders—that produced the worst of the abuses. Colonel Ralph Sabatino, who visited Abu Ghraib at the time the events took place, reported in a deposition that he saw the name of the porn star Ron Jeremy written outside the cell door of a prisoner who had evidently been given the nickname by guards. "It didn't strike me at the moment, but after hearing the allegations, I understand very clearly why they perhaps used that nomenclature to describe that particular prisoner."

Sabatino's testimony shows that the guards themselves saw what they were doing as pornography, and not only in this case but in the preponderance of cases of abuse described their actions in the language of porn. Jeremy is a heterosexual porn star, but we know that some of the guards involved in the abuse, to more effectively sexually degrade male Iraqi detainees, forced them to dress like women and treated them sexually like women. In a May 3, 2004, Associated Press story, one detainee, Dhia al-Shweiri, was quoted as saying that he would rather be beaten and tortured than sexually humiliated. "We are men. It's OK if they beat me. Beatings don't hurt us, it's just a blow. But no one would want their manhood to be shattered. They wanted us to feel as though we were women, the way women feel and this is the worst insult, to feel like a woman."

The deep irony in al-Shweiri's complaint lies in its dependence on the cultural beliefs, common among Arab men, and especially so with the kind of men attracted to reactionary Islam, that women are fundamentally less than men and should naturally be in a position of submission. The further logical implication of these views is that to be a woman is to be, by definition, degraded.

The guards structured their behavior around these assumptions. In their actions, the male and female American guards created an ongoing violent porn movie, or a series of such movies, with themselves in the role of the dominant male performers, and the Iraqi detainees, male and female, in the role of the female performers—which is to say, the degraded, passive victims.

When Armin Cruz, along with others, handcuffed male detainees together in a sexual position and put his boot on their buttocks to simulate anal sex, he "feminized" the detainees. In the ideology of al-Shweiri and in the view of the guards as well, shaped by violent porn, women are inferior, weak, passive. Only women, then, can be raped. To degrade a male, you must first turn him into a female by raping him.

Twenty of the photographs show a guard with a swastika drawn between his eyes, recalling the misogynistic Nazi imagery of the men's adventure magazines discussed in Chapter 3. The swastika represented, in those images, absolute authority maintained through sexual violence. The guards at Abu Ghraib, like the adventure magazines of old, and like the violent porn movies of today, recognized only two possibilities with no middle ground: one was either the torturer or the victim. The torturer enjoyed a firm sense of identity and value. The victim had neither. In Abu Ghraib, the guards made their choice.

Intermixed in the hundreds of photographs shown to Congress were dozens of shots of the soldiers themselves. The justification several of the soldiers gave when the scandal broke—that they were just following orders, or doing what they assumed their superiors wanted—evaporated once this fact emerged. One female soldier, reported in many newspapers to be Lynndie England, had sex with several different partners in front of both still and video digital cameras, sometimes in front of Iraqi detainees. This "amateur porn" demonstrated the kind of violence characterizing the abuse of prisoners. England and Graner, reportedly her boyfriend at the time, recorded their own mock violent, sadomasochistic sex. It is hardly surprising, given that these were public acts, that the soldiers made use of the digital technology of the Internet to distribute such pictures and videos among themselves, like trading cards.

By enacting pornographic scenes with their peers in front of the detainees, the soldiers communicated clearly to the Iraqis, who may have been unfamiliar with porn, a sexual template of the position the prisoners were in vis-à-vis the guards: they were the women—or, rather, the "bitches" and "sluts" that populate most pornography—and they were going to get fucked. No news sources have reported whether the sadomasochistic sex between England and Graner was performed in front of detainees, but whether it was or not, it reinforced the guards' own sense of their absolute authority and power over their charges. In that sense, the guards performed, documented, and later viewed the violent sex photos and videos as a reproducible rehearsal of sorts for their treatment of the detainees.

When they copied and distributed these pornographic images to one another, they completed a circle, integrating porn that they had created "on the job" into their everyday lives, but now in the guise of "entertainment." Once their mundane lives, which included the torment and torture of detainees, was in this way transformed into material for entertainment, they could further exploit it for its potential to produce even more porn. The fun of it all, the sheer joy evident on the faces of the guards in so many of the photographs, may have been the most startling, to many Americans, aspect of the images.

Imagine for a moment a guard's night of pornographic entertainment at Abu Ghraib. The soldier sits down at his computer, onto which is loaded a variety of the photographs and videos that became familiar to us once the scandal was exposed. The first button he (or she) touches on the computer will automatically remove from the screen abuse photos used as screensavers. (The heap of naked Iraqis was apparently a favorite.) Now, if he wants to be titillated, he can view some pornography. He could go to the Internet, the source of the vast majority of violent pornography today, or he might simply call up the amateur porn files created by the guards themselves, featuring one another as "actors." These would have been transferred to him by compact disc. (Graner evidently enjoyed spreading the photographs around on disc, sending some to Sergeant Joseph Darby, who eventually turned the abusers in.) In either case, the porn files exist side by side with abuse files, setting up an easy-to-imagine evening of entertainment: a little porn, a little abuse, a little more porn, a little torture, and then some more porn.

Given the pleasure taken by the guards in both their homemade porn images and those of detainee abuse, such evenings, depressing as it is to contemplate, almost certainly were routine.

PORN AS REALITY, REALITY AS PORN

At Abu Ghraib, the interspersion of traditional heterosexual porn, often featuring the guards themselves, with sexual degradation and violence against Iraqi detainees can be said to reflect that segment of the professional porn world that mixes sex with (usually) simulated violence. And just as the guards at Abu Ghraib imitated the world of porn in their treatment of detainees at the prison, the world of porn soon began imitating the guards. However unwittingly, the mainstream media participated in this faux Abu Ghraib porn by publishing samples in newspapers and on television news programs.

On May 1, 2004, the *Daily Mirror* of London published several purported prisoner abuse photos, including one showing a man in a British military uniform urinating on a bound captive—a common fetish in hard-core porn. The photos were quickly exposed as fakes created by Stuart MacKenzie, a private in the Territorial Army. For days, however, the hoax photos were a constant presence in the British and American media, and even now they maintain a presence on the Internet.

Even more important, the *Boston Globe,* on May 12, 2004, published photographs of men, presumably American servicemen, raping and abusing Iraqi women. The images were extremely graphic, showing genitalia. The women wept and grimaced in pain. These images, too, however, were fake. Or, rather, they were genuine porn.

The photos, as it turned out, had been under discussion on Internet news and blog sites for days. On May 4, the online news site World Net Daily exposed the fact that violent pornography from two porn websites, Sex in War and Iraq Babes, was being presented as documentary on Arab websites and used as anti-American propaganda. Demonstrating the momentum that online articles can gather, the anti-American story and images spread across the Internet like kudzu.

On May 11, the day before the *Globe* ran with the story, Boston city councilman Chuck Turner held a press conference and presented the photographs as legitimate. The next day, the *Globe's* page B2 story about the press conference, written by Donovan Slack, was accompanied by a large photo of Turner holding up several of the photos for display. The "abuse" photos within his photo were clearly visible: women screaming, crying, and writhing. That these women were later found to be performers was understandably disturbing to Bostonians. (Later editions of the newspaper minimized the photograph, but left it on the page.)

World Net Daily contacted Slack and informed her of the source of the bogus photos. Embarrassed for herself and the *Boston Globe,* she said, "It's insane. Can you imagine getting this with your cup of coffee in the morning? Somehow it got through all our checks. Our publisher's not having a very good day today." Actually, in her story, Slack expressed some doubt about the authenticity of the photos. Her verbal skepticism was, of course, overwhelmed by the powerful visual images.

The intersection of porn and reality became evident to Slack when she was directed to the Sex in War website. "This is ridiculous," she said. "I'll be working at *Penthouse* soon."

FINDING ABU GHRAIB IN THE U.S.A.

The *Boston Globe* scandal was sorted out within a few days, and the Iraq Babes website shut itself down because of the anti-American use of their images. Sex in War was eventually bought by tamer porn producers. The photographs of fake Iraqi rapes, however, are still available on a number of free Internet sites. In fact, photos from the defunct Iraq Babes site appear now mostly on jihadi websites or in leftist American blogs—some of which repeat the accusation of GIs raping Iraqi women and use the images as proof.

Given the fact that Taguba's investigation documented various brutal acts, including the rape and sodomizing of prisoners, belief in the fake photographs is understandable. Indeed, in the summer of 2006 five soldiers stationed in Mahmoudiya were charged in the rape and murder of a fourteen-year-old Iraqi girl and the murder of her family, including a five-year-old girl.

In researching the intersection of the Abu Ghraib story and pornography, we found that Google searches on the prison scandal regularly returned porn sites alongside news venues like the *New York Times,* the *Washington Post,* and Fox News. As it turned out, when the media began reporting the additional hundreds of photographs and videos kept classified by the government, the lawmakers who viewed them described them with many of the same terms that violent porn sites use to promote their product. The most popular adjective such sites use to describe their product is *brutal.*

On Google, a search using the keywords *Iraq, brutal,* and *rape,* yielded 333,000 possibilities, and about half of those (of the first several Google list pages we took time to read) were for violent porn sites, with the rest fairly evenly divided between news sites and blogs. Some of the listed sites were examples of an Internet marketing strategy in which a site consists solely of a list of terms likely to be searched attached to another list of links to commercial sites. On the first such portal site we visited, *Iraq* was nestled between *girls raped* and *gay young teen boys getting raped.* The links, drifting down the long page, were a Dantesque descent past "violent sex movie" and "teen rape movies" to "illegal pedo rape." The linkage of Iraq to these sites suggests a belief on the part of the site producers, at least, that their target customers are likely to connect it with a catalog of sexual violence. Given the events at Abu Ghraib, such ideas cannot be dismissed.

According to Bill Asher, president of Vivid Entertainment, one of the largest producers and distributors of hard-core pornography, fetish porn (which he sees as including violent porn) is the fastest-growing segment of the porn industry. It is worth repeating that our goal in this book is to investigate the growing dominance of porn in our culture without, as much as possible, passing judgment on the morality of its production or consumption. It is difficult, however, to delve into the subindustry of violent porn without coming away disturbed. Given the presence of porn in their lives, it seems likely that the guards perpetrating the abuse at Abu Ghraib deliberately imitated the violent porn that now thrives on the Internet.

The other possibility is that such images of domination and cruelty—of standing on and urinating on prostrate victims, of bondage and torture, violent rape, and strangulation—are sunk in a Jungian collective unconscious, just waiting an opportunity to emerge, like creatures from a black lagoon. If this is the case, both the anarchic freedom of the Internet and the near-chaos of an Iraqi prison would offer such fertile opportunities for emergence. This seems to us the darker possibility.

After all, the imagery of Abu Ghraib is readily available online, with actual women instead of male prisoners playing the role of "woman, the object of abuse." In two popular subgenres of violent porn, prison porn and military porn, the porned images of Abu Ghraib have filtered back into pornography in fairly direct ways, adding realism to the violent imagery.

One of the most popular violent porn sites on the Internet is Scream&Cream, dedicated to all forms of "violent extreme forced sex fantasies." Despite the fact that sites such as Scream&Cream—and there are many others—use words like *fantasy,* every effort is made visually and through accompanying text to heighten the "reality" of the rape narratives to which the site offers access. Much like an Abu Ghraib video that Seymour Hersh and others allege shows the rape of a teenage Iraqi boy, Scream&Cream promises that their online videos include all the sounds of rape, in the highest audio quality.

Indeed, the uncountable sites that provide violent porn have entered into a realism race. The premise of the website Violent-Russians, a popular site, is that women are first stalked and then raped. Despite enlarged "fantasy" disclaimers added in the summer of 2005, the videos make use of the gritty film techniques that Hollywood directors have chosen to convey "realism" (ambient lighting, film stock, and camera movement, for example). The site imparts to the viewer a sense of the lived reality of the onscreen stalking and rape.

Sites like Scream&Cream depend on free online tours to convince viewers to pay the subscription fees (usually around $30 per month), tours that show explicit stills and excerpts from videos. The "fantasies" these sites offer highlight pain and fear even more than they do hard-core sex. Camera angles focus on faces, goggle-eyed and streaked with streaming mascara. Mouths are open in screams sometimes silenced by large ball gags. The rapid intercutting between shots of penetration and terrified faces makes the locus of "pleasure" clear.[6]

Sites like Rotten and Goregasm (its tagline: "Where bones meets boners") present a mix of photos and videos of actual violence and gore with hard-core pornography. Within a number of such sites one can easily go back and forth from violence to porn, navigating from rape pornography to videos of American hostages being beheaded in Iraq, from the homemade porn of "my wife's hot pussy," to hundreds of photos and videos of the bodies of American soldiers and Iraqi men, women, and children mangled and killed by gunfire and bombs.

It should surprise no one that the murder of Nicholas Berg, an American civilian taken hostage in Iraq, is widely available online, and that some watch it for entertainment. But the fact that violent porn sites became the most common purveyors of the video suggests that those site producers understand that a linkage does exist between staged rapes and actual beheadings, that simulated violent sex and actual violence are not only appealing separately, but for certain viewers gain in appeal when brought together, side by side, so that one can easily go from one to the other and back again.

What these gore sites do, then, is provide the Internet consumer with the opportunity to relive the activities of the Abu Ghraib prison guards, who similarly moved back and forth in their daily activities between porn, including violent porn, and the violence of beatings and abuse. Sites like Scream&Cream, Goregasm, and Rotten make commercial use of the same dehumanization that was literally on display at Abu Ghraib.

WHAT IS PORN WHEN IT CEASES TO BE FANTASY?

The exploitation of dehumanization is abundantly evident in the violent pornography of Extreme Associates, a company that attracted a good bit of public attention after its production of the porn film *Forced Entry* was featured on the February 2002 episode of PBS's investigative news program *Frontline*. Extreme Associates is owned by Robert Zicari and Janet Romano, whose "porn names" are Rob Black and Lizzie Borden. The two were charged by the Justice Department in the first major obscenity prosecution in ten years, in August 2003.

Romano's description, on *Frontline,* of the plot of *Forced Entry* makes clear what sort of enjoyment is to be found there. "A girl [is] being kidnapped, being forced to have sex against her will, being butchered at the end and spit on. She's being degraded." The butchering that Romano mentions is the cutting of the character's throat, after which she dies in a pool of blood. (After a series of appeals and setbacks, the Justice Department's prosecution was ongoing at the time this book went to press in late 2007.)

On the *Frontline* segment, Zicari openly challenges the government to "come after us for obscenity!" Even more notable was the admission by Romano, who directed the video, that the film's star, Veronica Caine—Romano's real-life best friend—was unaware of the punishment she would take during the filming of the video. The kicking and punching inflicted on Caine were not fake, but real. The fleshy sounds of smacking and pounding are real, the cries of pain real. The entire beating was filmed by the *Frontline* crew until, overwhelmed and distraught due to the graphic nature of the scene, they made the decision to leave.

The Extreme filmmakers are perfectly aware of the expectations customers bring to their videos. Zicari claims that porn consumers are simply bored with typical industry fare, an argument that resonates ironically with the Christian conservative view that porn becomes an addiction requiring ever greater, darker thrills.

Romano's understanding of her personal motivation in producing violent pornography is surprisingly insightful, and can be applied to the situation at Abu Ghraib. "When I was a child, my stepfather was an alcoholic, so I think I have, like, deep issues, and this is kind of therapeutic for me, and takes my aggression out on other people. So, in a way, I'm exploiting people. I'm taking all my inner demons and aggressions [out] on them, but...it's good for me. So I guess that's all that matters."

What Romano describes here as therapy is an assertion of the self through the negation of the other, a feat accomplished through physical abuse, sexual degradation, and, simulated in *Forced Entry*, murder. In making this argument for herself, she makes it, by extension, for the guards at Abu Ghraib as well.

Unlike *Forced Entry*'s female victim, in Abu Ghraib the positions of "male" and "female" became performed roles rather than biologically gendered ones. The guards found their own identities thoroughly under assault at Abu Ghraib, by cultural displacement, an unclear mission, insurgent attacks on the building, inexcusable laxity in oversight, and contradictory instructions from superiors.

Their response to this deep confusion about who they were and what they were doing was to reassert themselves through the physical and sexual abuse and torture of the detainees at the prison. The Iraqis, male and female, collectively became "female," and the guards, male and female, collectively the dominant "male." The guards not only used pornography as the visual language of physical abuse. More important, they adopted the ideology of violent pornography: the brutal "male" using sex to degrade the weak "female."

The degradation of detainees at Abu Ghraib was of course real, not pretended. Violent porn increasingly crosses over the line from pretense into reality as well. Just as Veronica Caine faced actual violence in *Forced Entry,* more and more porn depends on real degradation. Though the Justice Department's prosecution of Extreme Associates centered on *Forced Entry,* four other movies were also cited that included, for instance, scenes in which a woman was made to drink bile, vomit, and the results of her own colonic (from *Cocktails 2*).

Actual degradation is certainly not new to porn. Midlevel porn producers have long depended on "First Anal!" editions that highlight a performer's introduction to the sexual practice. The pain she experiences in her first experience with anal sex, depicted in a still photograph on the cover of the video, is the real money shot of this genre. (Rarer and even more prized in the industry is the "loss of virginity" video, with the same purpose.) Similarly, videos ranging from the "rough sex" genre to the likes of Scream&Cream and Extreme Associates have long depended on images of women having their heads pushed so far down while performing fellatio that they repeatedly gag and even vomit.

In the past several years, however, hard-core pornography, especially on the Internet, has gravitated toward humiliation and degradation that cannot be defined as acting or "performance" in any sense. Take, for example (and only if you have a strong stomach), pinkeye and ATM. (We forgive the readers who might want to skim this section.)

On the website Pinkeye the male not only ejaculates on the woman's face, long a popular porn practice, but holds her eyelid open so his ejaculate will irritate and inflame her eyeball. Deliberately ejaculating into a woman's eye is certainly not a sensual act, but one having to do with violence and humiliation. The attraction for the male is simply the psychological kick of causing the woman discomfort. Whatever pleasure the viewer takes from the scene derives from the pain and humiliation inflicted on an actual woman.

Similarly, ATM, which stands for *ass to mouth,* locates the center of pleasure in degradation. In ATM, a man engages in anal sex with a woman, pulls out, and is immediately fellated by the woman. At least by suggestion, she "eats shit." Feces is, in general, increasingly present in humiliation porn. It also was one of the favorite mechanisms for degradation at Abu Ghraib, where detainees were handcuffed, smeared with shit, and made to stand for hours and pose for photographs. Porn videos that involve pinkeye or ATM or "colonic cocktails" do not even attempt to suggest that the women enjoy these acts. Indeed, the opposite is emphasized. The viewer is openly encouraged—through the liberal use of terms like *bitch, slut,* and *cunt*—to find satisfacton in their displeasure, their humiliation. Like the prisoners at Abu Ghraib, these women are being reduced, here to their bodily excretions.

In the 1982 book *Powers of Horror: An Essay on Abjection,* the psychoanalyst and philosopher Julia Kristeva describes the process of abjection as defining one's identity through "casting off" that which was once, in reality or symbolically, a part of oneself. Feces, urine, blood, hair, saliva, and semen are all physically part of us, but are rendered repulsive when separated from our bodies. Similarly, violent and degrading pornography, by smearing or filling women with these substances, renders the female body repulsive and entirely separate from the male body. The "female" is cast off and only the identity of the powerful and dominant male remains. The sexual abuse and defilement of Iraqi detainees similarly rendered them as utterly "other" to the American soldiers perpetrating the abuse at Abu Ghraib.

Anti-pornography activists have for decades described porn as angry and hateful toward women, a claim we don't think is true of all porn. Over the past decade or so, however, violent porn has advertised and sold anger and hate in increasingly actual—that is, not pretended or scripted—ways. It is as if the resentful anger underlying the men's adventure magazines discussed in Chapter 3, with misogynistic Nazis bayoneting bound and bleeding women, has returned to the surface of American popular culture in a new form. The male audience for violent pornography seeks literally to injure, through physical violence and humiliation, the flesh and spirit of American women.

In this sense, violent porn is perhaps no longer even porn at all, but something else, quite sinister, that exists not in an imagined world, but in the real world. For what it sells is not vicarious but actual: not the fantasized experience of sex with an attractive woman, long the hallmark of masturbatory porn, but the viewer's involvement in and responsibility for, through the sustaining financial support of his subscription to such sites, her bodily injury. The viewer's pleasure, then, is for the most part psychological, not sensual—a sadistic gloating over the female's actual blood and tears.

But Janet Romano—"Lizzie Borden"—is herself a woman, the object of victimhood in violent porn, isn't she? In an important sense, no. As Romano memorably put it, her exploitation of women is therapeutic. This is achieved through a kind of transgendering: through violent porn she becomes male. In fact, as the director of violent porn movies—controlling all the action—she becomes the dominant male, with the victims of degradation, as always, the females. Using male actors as her proxies, Romano becomes a version of the Nazi torturer well known from the covers of men's adventure magazines.

Violent porn implicitly accepts power as the male trait. Further, it views male power in only one way: dominating others through sexual violence. This is precisely the dynamic on display at Abu Ghraib.

But if the story of violent porn were confined to Abu Ghraib and the movies of Janet Romano, it would be a fringe phenomenon, isolated, certainly disturbing in itself, but not relevant to this book. Unfortunately, the story goes well beyond Abu Ghraib and Romano and is quite relevant to this book, because via movies and the Internet, violent porn has begun to seep into the mainstream, much as happened in the 1970s with traditional porn through films like *Deep Throat* and *Behind the Green Door.*

As we made clear in Chapter 1, the porning of America happened, first, because porn became mainstream by imitating ordinary people and ordinary life, and second, because the mainstream in turn began to imitate porn—in styles of dress, language, and behavior. We maintain that when porn becomes mainstream, the mainstream becomes porned.

To what degree will violent porn enter the mainstream? In what ways will fans imitate what they see in violent porn in their ordinary lives, in reality? Short of torture and murder, there remain many possible ways to inflict pain and humiliation on others, and to take sadistic pleasure in it. To put it another way, we have seen the porning of America. Will we now see the violent porning of America?

THE COOL THEATER TURNED CHILL...

In the summer of 2007, we visited the movie theater to watch *Hostel: Part II* on its opening day. *Hostel: Part II* extends the premise of the first *Hostel* (2005), in which members of an exclusive Slovakian club purchase kidnapped travelers (Americans are particularly prized) in order to torture and kill them in grisly and bizarre ways.

Viewers of films like *Hostel: Part II* are a savvy audience in that they know the conventions of the genre well, and can not only immediately spot the eventual victims, including the likely "final girl" (the requisite sole survivor of most horror films), but also predict the order in which they will be dispatched. In the first five minutes of the movie it is obvious to everyone that the homely girl will die first.

Lorna has been kidnapped and clubbed. She awakes, gagged and whimpering. Slowly the camera begins to rotate and zoom out, and we realize that she is naked and upside down, suspended by her ankles from the ceiling, hands bound behind her. We are treated to long looks at her body, her breasts taking on an odd appearance in her upended state. Unlike in most pornography, the acting is superb, and Lorna's abject terror and despair are convincing.

Director Eli Roth clearly wants us to feel doubly excited by the fearfulness of the threat Lorna faces as well as its sexual component. A Mrs. Bathory enters, disrobes, and lies down in a large tiled sunken bathtub. She picks up a scythe, first just to terrorize Lorna, but soon begins cutting her, causing blood to flow down Lorna's body and onto her. She then cuts Lorna's gag, so that she— and we, presumably—can savor all the sounds of Lorna's terror, every gasp, whimper, and shriek. Finally done with foreplay, Mrs. Bathory slits Lorna's throat, and the blood gushes down on her in a torrent. Drenched, massaging blood over her breasts, she writhes in orgasmic ecstasy.

The scene is disturbing enough in itself, combining riveting images of violent pornography with the torture depicted in men's adventure magazines. For us, however, sitting in the theater, by far the most frightening part of it all occurred not onscreen but in the audience. As the torture scene progressed, increasingly bloodier with every laceration of the scythe, a steady, throaty laughter from young men in the audience rolled through the theater. This wasn't buoyant laughter rising up from an audience, that almost luminous enveloping mirth, but instead a heavy staccato of laughs coughed out, filling the dark rows like smog. In the Abu Ghraib photos in which guards are pictured laughing—if we could hear them, this would surely be their laughter.

Then, at the moment Mrs. Bathory slits Lorna's throat in a shower of blood, in the theater a sudden, cooing chorus—*Ooooooh!* For us, the cool theater turned chill.

The orgasmic response of many of the men in the theater that afternoon renders irrelevant the countless defenses of "torture porn" or "gorno" (*gore* plus *gonzo*) movies offered by the genre's directors. Eli Roth has acknowledged that he was in fact inspired by the images of Abu Ghraib. But he has argued in many interviews that his films should be seen as social commentary, as critiques of American arrogance and ignorance about the rest of the world.

On the surface, his claims work. In *Hostel,* which earned ten times its $4.8 million budget, we watch two Americans and an Icelandic friend explore the seamier areas of Amsterdam. Outside a brothel, Paxton, one of the Americans, sees a prostitute through a window and says, "God, I hope bestiality is legal in Amsterdam because that girl is a fuckin' hog."

The young men, of course, enter, "paying to go into a room to do whatever you want to someone," as the reluctant Josh, the other American, puts it. His description ironically foreshadows their own fate.

All well and good. We see the arrogance and ignorance. But we see something else as well, and it is more in the foreground. For the men in the theater with us watching *Hostel: Part II,* the film was not a horror film at all. Their orgasmic responses expressed a very different emotion. It was erotic joy.

Interestingly, though these movies are known for gore and torture, there is often much less of it than one might expect. In *Hostel*, there are two scenes, both only a few minutes long, in which we see blood and exposed flesh. In one, Paxton escapes danger by hiding on a cart with severed body parts, and in the other, he and a young woman, Kana, evade recapture after she has had her face burned with a blowtorch. The scenes in which we watch actual torture—damage done to flesh—total only about ten seconds in the entire film.

Rather, the "pleasure" the audience derives from films like *Hostel* is in the close-ups of the victims' terrified faces—as it is in pinkeye and AIM. The murder of Josh, for example, is *Hostel*'s set piece. He is bound to a chair and gagged with a ball gag common in violent porn and in BDSM. The only damage we actually see, though, is a close-up of a drill bit piercing flesh, a shot that lasts less than two seconds. He is drilled at least three more times, has his Achilles tendons cut and his throat slit, all of which occurs offscreen. What makes his murder the center of the film is the terror the actor conveys, and the focus on bodily fluids, especially pain- and fear-induced vomit.

The film is in fact obsessed with sexualized excretions of every variety. When Paxton's turn for torture arrives, he spews bile, vomit, and blood, but his rescue of Kana epitomizes the sexualization of pain and bodily fluids. We do not see the blowtorch on her face, but after Paxton shoots the torturer, we see her ruined, dripping face and an eyeball hanging out of its socket. When Paxton uses scissors to cut it off, a white, pus-like fluid oozes out of the socket, a scene that Roth has called an "eyegasm."

Captivity, also released in the summer of 2007 and directed by Roland Joffé, created heated controversy well before its run with an ad campaign that rendered the genre's pleasures explicit. The ad is divided into four panels, labeled "abduction," "confinement," "torture," and "termination." The images emphasize the sexiness of the victim, especially the termination panel, which centers on one of her breasts.

The premise of the film is simple: a crazed fan kidnaps and tortures a fashion model, at one point forcing her to drink pureed body parts. The connection of such images from *Hostel, Captivity,* and *Cocktails 2* with the shit-smeared detainees at Abu Ghraib is obvious.

The sexuality of the scenes of brutalization and murder earns these movies membership in the torture porn genre. In *Hostel,* the man who will eventually torture Kana tells Paxton—who is pretending to be a customer of the club—that torture and killing is the natural next step in his search for a fulfilling sexual experience. But the fulfilling sex that characters in these films seek goes far beyond sensual, physical pleasure and crosses over into violence and killing. Violent, sexual murder becomes the language of dominance and power, an assertion of self that requires the utter denial of the humanity of the other.

Turistas (2006) develops this theme in a scene in which a young woman, dressed in a bikini through much of the movie, has her organs harvested by an angry doctor who sees her as the symbol of—you guessed it—American arrogance. Intercut with shots of her naked body are long, loving shots of her opened abdomen and of the organs as they are removed. In the final shot, the camera pulls back to show her extracted kidney wrapped in gauze lying next to a still-beautiful breast.

This is vivisection porn. If violent porn in general is filled with anger and hatred directed against women, in vivisection porn that negativity is used like a scalpel on female erotic power. As we see repeatedly on the beaches of Brazil in *Turistas,* a beautiful woman in a bikini holds ogling, horny men in the palm of her hand—the male characters in the film as well as the males in the audience. The vivisection then constitutes the literal deconstruction of female allure: The beautiful abdomen? Watch as it is slit opened to reveal a tangle of intestines and bloody, unlovely internal organs. A breast may still be beautiful with a kidney beside it, but the juxtaposition reveals the truth behind the illusion: a beautiful woman's body, after all, is blood, bile, excretions of all sorts, and wormy, pulsing, slimy organs. On the Internet, many sites (such as Allinternal) accomplish virtual vivisection not with scalpels but rather with tiny cameras mounted on dildos and inserted deep into vaginas and anuses.

Violent porn, then, is very much about stealing away power, and gaining it. The idea that torture offers the ultimate masculine power is most clear in *Hostel: Part II*. Except for Mrs. Bathory and her scythe, the main dealers of pain are two American men who discuss how killing young women will reclaim for them their power over women. Beginning with their bidding on young female victims, we follow them throughout their murderous reclamation of power. Todd has his victim dress up in lingerie before he uses a circular saw on her face, and Stuart selects his because she reminds him of his emasculating wife.

The movie exists in "Abu Ghraib world." Todd crosses the guards, and they sic attack dogs on him, reminding us of several frightening images of the prison. When Stuart attempts to rape Beth as part of her torture, she turns the tables on him and ties him to the torture chair. Throughout the movie, Beth has been depicted as rich and smart, but lacking confidence. When the guards of the torture club arrive to investigate the commotion, however, she has large scissors around Stuart's penis and uses the obvious threat to negotiate her release.

Informed that no one can leave without killing someone, she immediately cuts off Stuart's penis ("Let him bleed to death") and hands it to a guard, who throws it to ravenous dogs. Having committed sexual murder, Beth becomes confident and strong, striding away full of purpose and power. For her, sexual violence works.

The message is not, however, as Eli Roth has widely claimed, feminist. Instead, the clear message is that sexual murder makes the murderer not only a "man," but, indeed, *"the* man," the alpha male. Castrated Stuart—like vomit-spewing Josh and Paxton from the first film—becomes the "woman," or, using today's popular, porned lexicon, *the bitch.*

Many reviewers of torture porn movies see in the genre the coming fall of Western civilization. We can't say that we agree. But neither can we call these critics Chicken Littles. It is true, and un-settling, that the last time a Western society depended so much in its media and entertainment on sexual violence and murder was during Germany's Weimar Republic (1919–1933).

Unlike Weimar Germany, the United States has not recently lost a world war (though the 9/11 attacks, the failure of the Iraq war, and awareness of a world turned against us have created a sense of victimization for many Americans). We haven't suffered through periods of civil unrest and violence that threaten another civil war. Nor have we experienced the hyperinflation that de-stroyed the German economy and rendered much of the country destitute.

We do share with the Weimar period, however, a growing fac-tionalism and extremity in our politics. So intense is the personal-ized fighting between the forces of the right and left that rational political argument is nearly impossible. As we discussed at the end of Chapter 4, political commentary has become a porned enter-tainment, in which the desire is to humiliate and degrade political opponents, making them completely other. Both sides insult, ridicule, and taunt. A liberal commentator wishes for the death by assassination of the sitting conservative vice president. A conser-vative commentator calls the liberal former vice president a faggot. And so it goes. Much of the country seems to have joined in this ugly fun.

German culture during the Weimar period responded to the

contention and uncertainty of the era by developing a fascination with *lustmord,* or sexual murder. In its fiction, film, art, and journalism, Germany worked out its anger and insecurity through images of mutilated women. In this we share an eerie similarity to the nation that would become Nazi Germany. Over the last twenty years or so, sexual violence and murder have proven highly profitable in fiction, film, and television, with torture porn movies merely being the most recent and extreme examples. Our willingness to see men too as appropriate victims of lustmord might seem to represent a perverse brand of equal opportunity, but the position of the victim remains "the woman," and the purpose of the murder remains the "masculinization" of the perpetrator.

Again, we are not suggesting that our own fascination with lustmord will turn us into the next Nazi Germany. Rather, it seems likely to us that a culture that takes so much pleasure in images of sexual violence and murder, whether in its military prisons or its movie houses, is a culture that has lost its sense of strength and is searching desperately to recover its former authority.

7. Women and Porn

"A single book or a single picture," wrote Anthony Comstock well over a century ago, "may taint forever the soul of the person who reads it." And there we have it in a nutshell, the key issue in the argument against porn.

But is it true? Does pornography taint us? Does a dirty picture, once seen, skulk about deep in our consciousness and lay back trails connecting our polluted libidos to our feelings toward people in general? Or toward our lovers, or even our spouses?

Comstock certainly thought so. A former postal inspector, he was appointed by the New York City YMCA to chair its New York Society for the Suppression of Vice. No zealot before or after Comstock has been nearly so successful a suppressor. In 1873 he lobbied the U.S. Congress to pass the Comstock Act, which bars, to this day, the use of the mail to deliver obscene material. Though the definition of *obscene* has clearly evolved, in modern times the ban on sending obscene material through the mail was used by anti-pornography crusaders to pursue the likes of Ralph Ginzburg, Al Goldstein, and Russ Meyer, and many writers, including Henry Miller, whose *Tropic of Cancer* and *Tropic of Capricorn* could not for a time be distributed to booksellers through the mail.

Even in his own day, however, many critics hooted at the prudery of Comstock and his allies. They coined the term *Comstockery* to describe his overreaching antiobscenity movement, the targets of which came to include condoms and contraceptives, aphrodisiacs, "marital aids" (sex toys), and even anatomy textbooks.

Yet Comstock's belief that porn taints the soul remains relevant today. In fact, the arguments over pornography all have, at their core, one position or another on this supposed defilement. For Comstock, the taint was fundamentally moral. Over the last several decades, however, not only moral crusaders but groups with social and political allegiances have lobbied against pornography.

Of all these groups, women, the putative victims of pornography, have overwhelmingly dominated the public discourse on the subject since the 1950s. And since the growth of women's liberation as a powerful social movement in the 1970s, feminism has set the terms of the debate.

ARGUING THE TAINT: A SHORT HISTORY

During the postwar years, the debate over pornography paralleled the opposition to comic books. Many of the same groups organized national and local efforts against both porn and comics, such as the GFWC and NODL, discussed in Chapter 3. In fact, the 1954–1955 Kefauver Senate hearings lumped comics and pornography together as contributors to juvenile delinquency. As fervently as Comstock himself, the Kefauver panel believed in the taint of porn.

In identifying juveniles as the victims of this taint, the Kefauver panel foresaw a future in which damaged children would become the damaged adults running society. Not only the Senate panel, but also a growing antidelinquency movement led by women similarly saw pornography as potentially destructive to society.

These campaigns touted themselves as the guardians of the future of American masculinity. Focusing on boys as the most vulnerable victims of pornography, the female campaigners feared that pornography would turn their sons into sadists or sissies.

Porn in all its forms would, the argument went, lead young men into homosexuality and sadomasochism, which were seen as linked.

As previously noted, Cold War American propaganda issued both a clarion call for male power and a fervent warning about male violence. America wanted men ready to fight against communism, but it also worried that such men might grow too violent to fill their domestic role in the home.

The first modern anti-pornography campaigns, then, spearheaded by the Kefauver panel along with antidelinquency groups, sprang from deeply conservative roots, promoting the father-led nuclear family and strong patriotic values. Again, boys and men were identified as profoundly vulnerable to the taint of pornography. As such, they were likely to cause social turmoil, a libido-driven anarchy, with women bearing the brunt of their sexually damaged psyches.

These premises would underlie the dominant argument about pornography for the next forty years. In the mid-1970s, as the Kefauver panel and the antidelinquency groups of the 1950s faded into history, the feminist movement took over the fight against pornography. Working from the same premises of male vulnerability and the consequent danger men posed to society, the feminists of the 1970s saw porn's frightening potential to dehumanize and subjugate women.

Despite more than a century of earlier efforts by women to create an equitable society, pop history usually bestows upon Betty Freidan the credit for beginning the modern feminist movement. Freidan first shocked the culture with *The Feminine Mystique* in 1963. When, three years later, she founded, with others, the National Organization for Women (NOW), which she also led as its first president, Freidan set many of the terms in the social debate about women's liberation.

The Feminine Mystique challenged the dominant ideology of its era that the home provided women with their surest path to happiness and fulfillment. The "mystique," as Freidan identified it, was a complex set of cultural, social, and personal forces that conspired to convince women to participate in their own subjugation. NOW brought the matter of female subjugation to the public arena, assuming that many elements of the "feminine mystique" could be addressed by the group's social and political activism. NOW spent much of the 1970s, for instance, promoting ratification of the equal rights amendment (ERA).

At the same time that NOW began lobbying for the ERA, the pornography industry enjoyed what is still referred to as its golden age. Legal and cultural changes opened the door for a string of porn films and actors to gain a level of popular fame previously attainable only by Hollywood movies and stars.

Critics of porn thought they had a major victory when the Supreme Court, in *Miller v. California* (1973), made it more difficult for obscene material to gain First Amendment protection. Such material would need to be acceptable according to "contemporary community standards." But standards were changing fast in the 1970s, and relatively few communities took firm stands against porn. Prosecutors and police often felt unsure of their mandate. The overall result: porn proliferated.

For a while, feminists remained otherwise concerned. The Supreme Court legalized abortion with its *Roe v. Wade* decision in 1973, and, in general, American feminism focused on such specific causes. Until the mid-1970s, men, for the most part, led the anti-porn campaigns, from the point of view of decency and morality. Indeed, in 1975 a major anthology on the topic of pornography, *The Pornography Controversy*, edited by Ray C. Rist, a senior policy analyst at the Department of Health, Education, and Welfare, included figures such as Earl Warren Jr. but not a single woman contributor.

"PORN IS THE THEORY, RAPE IS THE PRACTICE"

All that changed in 1975. In that year, Susan Brownmiller published *Against Our Will: Men, Women, and Rape*. Rape, she argued, functioned as a social mechanism of control by which men maintained sexual supremacy over women. As a result, all men, even nonrapists, enjoyed the benefit of rape.

Brownmiller further contended that pornography was essentially rape on paper. "There can be no 'equality' in porn . . . [which,] like rape, is a male invention, designed to dehumanize women, to reduce the female to the object of sexual access, not to free sensuality from moralistic or parental inhibition."[1] Pornography, like actual rape, benefited all men, whether or not they were participants. Its very existence, then, constituted a de facto harm against women. Identified in this way as a crucial part of male oppression, porn became an urgent and compelling feminist issue.

The self-described radical feminist Robin Morgan famously stated, "Pornography is the theory, rape is the practice." That simple formulation became a slogan of the feminist anti-pornography movement, and appeared regularly on placards in the hands of women protesting in front of peep shows and porn shops. Further, an assumption that pornography depended upon violence against its female performers, which in turn led to violence against women in general, became the core belief of the movement.

The heat and scope of the protests startled the liberal establishment, traditionally committed to free speech and its First Amendment protections. Brownmiller articulated what for years to come would be a pivotal contention between feminists and many liberals: the unwillingness to consider the possibility that some speech could, in itself, constitute an act of violence against women. As such, porn should be subject to censorship.

Brownmiller's book, and its tumultuous reception, electrified the women's movement. As if on cue, in early 1976 the pornographic film *Snuff* was released in New York City; with it, Brownmiller's argument seemed to have been handed all the compelling evidence it could ever need. Arriving on the heels of citywide rumors that the NYPD had confiscated South American pornographic movies in which women were killed during sex, *Snuff* caused a powerful stir.

Originally produced in 1971 as a C-grade slasher film, then called *Slaughter*, it was loosely based on the Charles Manson killings. The title of the film was changed to *Snuff* when its distributor (the sometime pornographer Alan Shackleton) tacked on a startling finale. As the film ends, the camera pulls back to reveal the final scene as it is being shot on a movie set. A "script girl" and the director talk about the film and then have sex—during which he kills her, and then proceeds to dismember and eviscerate her. As the screen goes black, we hear broken bits of talk, including "Shit, we ran out of film" and "Let's get out of here," lending it the air of documentary. The marketing for the film suggested the shocking possibility that the murders of the women, including the script girl, were real. (The film's tagline: "A film that could only be made in South America—where Life is *CHEAP!*")

Shackleton had, as part of his marketing of the film, actually hired protestors to picket theaters where it was being shown. Soon, though, women's groups took up the action in earnest. Laura Lederer, the editor of the influential anthology *Take Back the Night: Women on Pornography* (1980), describes the film as "the powder keg that moved women seriously to confront the issue of pornography." In response to *Snuff*, women across the country formed protest groups, took legal action, and shut the film down in several venues. Over the next few years, groups like Women against Violence against Women (WAVAW), Women against Pornography (WAP), and Women against Violence in Pornography and Media (WAVPM) took on many other films and magazines, broadening their target to include soft-core advertisements and even events like the Miss America pageant.

WAP set up its headquarters on Forty-second Street in New York, then a hotbed of porn and prostitution, from which members staged protests and led tours of the area for everyone from housewives to nuns. In 1978 WAVPM organized a national conference, "Feminist Perspectives on Pornography," and, in conjunction with the conference, the first Take Back the Night March in San Francisco's pornography district. Even today such marches continue throughout the United States.

The first march through a pornography district, however, had occurred a year earlier in New York, as the result of a call by Andrea Dworkin. Dworkin and legal scholar Catharine MacKinnon would become the voices of the feminist anti-porn movement. Over the next fifteen years or so, Dworkin and MacKinnon, whose work together permanently linked their names, gave the anti-pornography movement a coherence and public prominence unequaled before or since.

Dworkin and MacKinnon took over the leadership of the anti-pornography movement at an oddly propitious moment. The golden age of porn was in part brought to an end by the election of Ronald Reagan and the political ascendance of the religious right. In 1985 Reagan appointed his attorney general, Edwin Meese, to head a commission to study the effects of pornography. Stocked with anti-pornography activists, the commission released a massive, vague report acknowledging that clear evidence of harm caused by pornography was unavailable—but assigning such harm anyway. The odd bedfellows—anti-porn feminists and the Reagan administration, along with much of the religious right—eventually created more long-term trouble for the feminists than short-term benefit.

Meanwhile, though, support for the dictum "pornography is the theory, rape is the practice" kept coming. In 1980 Linda Boreman, who had appeared under the stage name Linda Lovelace in the 1972 film *Deep Throat*, published *Ordeal*, in which she claimed that her then husband, Chuck Traynor, had used violence and threats to force her into prostitution and pornography. She would tell the *Toronto Sun,* "When you see the movie 'Deep Throat,' you are watching me being raped. It is a crime that movie is still showing; there was a gun to my head the entire time." Steinem, Dworkin, and MacKinnon (who would represent Boreman until her death in 2002) worked with Boreman during the promotion of her book, and together they developed the strategy of using civil rights laws to sue Traynor. When they discovered that the statute of limitations on such violations had elapsed on *Deep Throat,* Dworkin and MacKinnon continued to develop the "violation of civil rights" approach to combating other pornography.[2]

Bringing in the matter of civil rights focused the zealous but scattered anti-pornography movement. Feminists had grasped immediately that their campaign against pornography could not depend on the old arguments, morality and decency, because traditional concepts of morality and decency belonged to the same conservative ideologies that had led Freidan to write *The Feminine Mystique* in the first place. As a result, most of the successes of the anti-pornography movement up to this point avoided morality arguments altogether, relying instead on the simple force of protesting the sexual violence done to female victims. The feminists, in other words, lacked an overarching conceptual cause, some idea or principle around which feminists could rally as conservatives had rallied around morality and decency.

Dworkin and MacKinnon provided exactly that conceptual cause in civil rights. In regarding porn as a violation of the civil rights of women, they were proposing nothing less than a systemic legal change in the way society handled pornography and other images of violence against women.

Between 1983 and 1992, they worked with local officials in Minneapolis, Indianapolis, Los Angeles, and Boston trying to pass anti-pornography civil rights ordinances. Their model ordinance defined pornography as "the graphic sexually explicit subordination of women through pictures and/or words."

At the center of their approach lay the idea that pornography is improperly—incompletely—regarded merely as speech. Therefore, free speech protections should not be brought to bear. Just as Comstock, more than a hundred years earlier, considered pornography a happening, an event, that forever changes for the worse—*taints*—those who view it, so Dworkin and MacKinnon proposed that porn is in itself an *act* that harms women in measurable ways. Notice in their definition above that porn does not, say, "advocate" or "lead to" the subordination of women, it *is* the subordination of women through pictures and/or words.

Free speech, sacred to liberalism, does come into play, but in an unexpected way. Dworkin and MacKinnon argued that porn, by participating in a social system that perpetuates the inferiority of women, dehumanizes them and thus robs them of their own right to free speech.

Dworkin and MacKinnon testified at various hearings in support of the civil rights ordinances, along with a host of other experts of various sorts. Boreman, for instance, who had appeared anonymously and under many pseudonyms in countless porn films and loops, testified that coercion and rape were standard practice in the pornography industry. Prominent sociologists such as Edward Donnerstein and Diana E. H. Russell testified to a link between pornography and violence against women.

The hearings, despite their local settings, were national events. The testimony, often riveting, captured the public's attention. Dworkin was a brilliant polemicist, and MacKinnon a noted legal scholar whose first book, on sexual harassment, remains the most influential text on the subject.

But the ordinances all failed, one after another. Some went down by executive veto, others by court decision, and the rest were voted down by the citizens of the locale.

In other important ways, though, Dworkin and MacKinnon were dramatically successful. They had raised public awareness of the dark side of pornography, especially through Boreman's testimony. As Linda Lovelace, she was, after all, the most famous porn star of the most famous porn movie, and her celebrity was widespread. Johnny Carson, a gatekeeper of the cultural mainstream, admitted to seeing *Deep Throat*, and other celebrity giants praised it. She had appeared in interviews in the media and on the covers of popular magazines, including *Esquire*. Her fame was now brought to bear against pornography. If anybody knew the world of pornography from the inside, she did.

Dworkin and MacKinnon succeeded in mounting a compelling case against porn not on moral grounds, but rather as a crucial part of the oppression of women and a violation of their civil rights. Feminists and others would continue this approach in the fight against porn. And, most of all, the two anti-porn feminists had succeeded glowingly in bringing porn to the forefront of feminism's principal struggle for social advancement in the face of male oppression.

But all was not well. MacKinnon and Dworkin came to be seen by many, both in and out of the feminist movement, as rigid and doctrinaire. Critics even took to calling them MacDworkin, an effective epithet that dismisses even as it comments on the pair's monolithic take on pornography. In 1987 Dworkin published *Intercourse*, an angry, abstruse book that engages in such lengthy discussions as the warlike symbolism of sexual penetration, and led to a popular understanding of her thesis as "all sex is rape."

Dworkin's actual, more nuanced point was at least arguable: that in our unequal society, sex is impossible to think about, or to have, apart from gendered notions of submission and domination. But apart from the question of whether or not Dworkin was claiming that sex is rape, she and her allies promoted a leery view of sex that left very little room for any "approved" sexual activity at all.

Moreover, both in practice and in the public consciousness, Dworkin and MacKinnon had taken over the feminist argument about porn, and the public increasingly saw them as angry and accusatory. Many of their readers, including most of the next generation of feminists, came to reject what they saw as MacDworkin extremism.

Right from the beginning, some feminists worried about Dworkin and MacKinnon's type of activism. Even Gloria Steinem, who participated in the anti-pornography civil rights approach, had identified a "clear and present" difference between pornography and erotica as early as 1978. Steinem wanted to keep feminists from being labeled as neo-Puritans and prudes. Anti-porn too often bordered on anti-sex, and seemed to quash any possibility of an active and healthy sexual life for women.

Within the women's movement, resistance to the anti-pornography cause grew during the 1980s. Some, including Freidan, saw in the civil rights approach a misguided assault on free speech that could easily be turned against the feminist project itself. Others, assuming that the courts would continue to overturn any bans that might be legislated, preferred a return to the simpler and more direct street protests against pornography. Further, many feminists were dismayed, especially during the Indianapolis hearings, that self-described "militant feminists" were standing shoulder to shoulder with conservative religious figures who were foursquare against pornography—but also foursquare against abortion and the ERA.

Resistance to MacKinnon and Dworkin also resulted rather inevitably from the shifting demographics of feminism. A growing number of young women joining the women's movement simply disagreed with the way earlier feminists had framed the issue of sexuality and pornography. These "pro-sex feminists," generally less academic and less theoretical than the anti-pornography group, argued that sexual self-determination should be a foundational part of feminism. And such self-determination meant that a woman might choose to view pornography, or even perform in it.[3]

With Dworkin and MacKinnon as figureheads, feminism had earned a reputation as anti-male. Pro-sex feminists wanted to reverse that. A few, such as journalist and author Wendy McElroy, attacked the core idea of the anti-pornography movement—the notion of harm (or we might say, after Comstock, the damage caused by "tainted" men). The real harm, they argued, would come from censoring pornography, and such censorship itself would stifle the growth of women's equality. The debate, often called the sex wars or the porn wars, grew bigger and more heated throughout the 1980s. By the decade's end, the porn wars had seriously damaged feminism as a coherent national and international movement.

In the 1990s the conflict between feminism and pornography took an entirely new shape. Staggered by charges that second-wave feminism (identified mainly with Freidan and, later, Dworkin and MacKinnon) had been exclusively concerned with the lives of upper-middle-class white women, the movement now welcomed the voices of poor women and minorities. This openness to new causes removed pornography from feminism's crosshairs.

But it was gay and lesbian activists and scholars, increasingly in the public eye throughout the 1980s, who radically changed the dynamics of feminism and porn. Gays and lesbians had adopted much of their rhetoric and ideology from feminism—but not on the matter of porn. Homosexuals had long been aware that sex was for them a political act, in that gay and lesbian intercourse was still illegal in many places and considered immoral in many more. Sex, then, including pornography, became a crucial part of their activism and writing. And the porn industry responded by producing more target-marketed gay porn.

A shrinking number of anti-pornography feminists continue to fight on. Scholars such as Gail Dines and Robert Jensen have expanded the anti-pornography arguments, pointing out, for instance, the racism common in the products and rampant in the industry itself. In their view, pornography shares in the oppression and imperialism that underlie Western thought. Further, it's a toxic expression of a much larger problem: our capitalist, media-saturated society.

But even to educated audiences, the language of anti-pornography feminism has grown impossibly academic, abstruse, and foreign. And, as was true under Dworkin and MacKinnon's leadership, the movement remains dogmatic and intolerant of difference or dissent. For example, a 2007 national conference on pornography at Wheelock College invited only work clearly identifiable as anti-porn and excluded porn performers, sex therapists, and any consideration of recent developments like feminist porn.

For most feminists, however, the conversation has moved on to a new stage. Scholars like Laura Kipnis, Lynn S. Chancer, and Linda Williams have approached pornography not as a one-dimensional destructive force, but rather as a collection of the many ways a variety of groups have presented their own sexuality. For some of these groups, such as gays, porn can be a subversive act against the same straight male supremacy Dworkin and MacKinnon decried.

Most third-wave feminists, which is to say those at the forefront now, classify themselves as pro-sex, and have turned the conversation about pornography in new directions. For example, in one of the most influential feminist books of the 1990s, *The Beauty Myth* (1991), Naomi Wolf investigated the ways in which images of beauty dominate women's perceptions of themselves. In slavishly trying to measure up to male-derived ideals of beauty, Wolf argues, women perpetuate male supremacy even as it is in retreat.

Anti-pornography scholars and activists resent the third-wave feminists' description of themselves as pro-sex, implying, as it does, their own status as anti-sex. To many surviving second-wavers, the third-wavers offer "fuck-me feminism," a retrogression in which women confirm old gender stereotypes either by claiming to "choose" traditional roles, or by finding female power through adopting male behaviors, such as casual sex. Feminist defenses of pornography fall into this second category, they argue.

Some third-wavers, such as Naomi Wolf, also find pornography troubling, but not because of the supposed harm inflicted by tainted males. Rather, pornography connects good sex exclusively with the Barbie-like bodies of porn stars, and so interferes with ordinary women's enjoyment of sex—something that is very important to the third-wavers.

In *Promiscuities* (1997), which is in part a sexual memoir, Wolf examines the difficulties girls and women face in developing a healthy sexuality. And she finds a place in such development—if not quite for pornography—for erotica.

Most recently, the feminists garnering the most widespread attention have been young, nonacademic women trying to repair the divide within feminism created by the porn wars. For instance, Ariel Levy, an editor at *New York* magazine, argues in *Female Chauvinist Pigs* that young women, many of whom identify themselves as feminists, dress, talk, and behave in ways derived from "raunch culture"—of which the Girls Gone Wild videos are a good example. Levy neither praises nor condemns pornography, though it's clear she doesn't like most male-centered porn. Mainly, though, she is upset that so many young women have failed to find a way *not created by men* to enact their self-possessed sexuality.

Jessica Valenti, executive editor of the website Feministing, has a different project. With *Full Frontal Feminism: A Young Woman's Guide to Why Feminism Matters* (2007), Valenti wants to welcome everyone into a kind of big-tent feminism. Indeed, most young women are feminists, she argues, whether they know it or not, and even if they want to avoid the "F-word."

Moreover, in Valenti's view young women, especially, should prize their feminism because it provides them with the orientation and ideas they will need to achieve the kind of lives they desire. And to Valenti, pornography of the right sort can certainly be a part of that life.

On that point Levy and Valenti are far from complete agreement. The logo for Feministing is the same silhouette of a naked woman (famous from truck mud flaps) that appears on the cover of Levy's book as an example of the raunch culture she is concerned about. But the two women are alike in searching for a new approach to feminism that acknowledges women's sexuality, and even the desire to be sexy, while at the same time remembering the fine line between sexiness and objectification.

THE BIG QUESTIONS

Though anti-porn activists have had little long-term success in discouraging the dissemination of pornography, they raised the questions that remain in the public consciousness. Here, we address a number of these questions, with attention to the most current research.

Does pornography cause violence toward women?

This is, of course, the blockbuster question. If it could be proven that pornography causes sexual assault, then censorship would be inevitable. Since the mid-1970s, women's groups, with support from many academics and scientists, have answered the question with a resounding yes. Sociologists and psychologists, however, have offered a more tepid response: pretty much, no.

Recent statistics offer no evidence that porn has spurred violence against women. According to the U.S. Department of Justice, rates of rape and sexual assault dropped 68 percent between 1993 and 2005, a period during which, thanks largely to the Internet, porn boomed. Further, over time the Internet has made available porn of every imaginable stripe, including an increasing amount of porn dedicated to violence and degradation. The fact that specifically violent porn thrived while actual sexual assaults plummeted suggests that for the vast majority of men, at least, pornography does not in any legal or scientific sense *cause* sexual aggression.[4]

But the issue is not quite so easily resolved. Beginning in the 1980s, an enormous amount of research investigated every possible connection between pornography and violence. Here are the results, in brief:

- There is no compelling evidence to suggest that "normal" men (those who have no history of sexual aggression and do not display hypermasculine, aggressive personality traits) become more likely to commit sexual aggression because of exposure to violent or nonviolent pornography. In fact, porn does not appear to change their general attitudes toward women in any long-term way.

- Some studies of men have shown short-term increases in sexual callousness as a result of exposure to images of sexual violence and "rape myth" stories. (Rape myth stories show women experiencing pleasure in being victimized.) But the same change occurs when men watch films that are simply violent, without the element of porn, suggesting that the problem is with the violence rather than the explicit sex.

- There is a strong correlation between sexual aggression and the use of violent pornography. That is, rapists and others who are sexually aggressive tend to be users of violent pornography. Men who commit acts of sexual aggression display a general set of personality traits—such as hostile masculinity, sexual promiscuity, and pornography use—in excess of men who do not commit sexual assault. Indeed, a 2007 study found that pornography was predictive of sexual aggression only in men already at high risk of sexual aggression. The use of pornography, then, may well be a part of the sexually aggressive profile rather than a cause of sexually violent behavior. Research psychologists have been searching for ways to isolate and measure the influence of porn so that they might answer the critical question of just how important pornography is in the eventual turn toward violence.

- One possible connection between porn and sexual aggression is that men so inclined could perhaps be "activated" by their exposure to pornography. Research shows, however, that sexual offenders generally have neither earlier nor more intense exposure to pornography. This suggests that pornography is not, then, a significant cause of the development of their sexual aggression. Rather, something quite different seems to be the case: preexisting hostile sexual attitudes toward women tend to determine how men respond to pornography.[5]

In summation, pornography will not transform a psychologically healthy man into a violent sexual abuser. But porn does play a disturbing, if uncertain, role in the lives of men predisposed toward sexual violence.

Do women watch porn?

Yes. And though dependable precise figures are impossible to come by, women are watching in increasing numbers.

For years, the industry claimed that roughly 20 percent of visitors to porn shops were heterosexual couples, meaning women made up roughly 10 percent of browsers, with a few percent more browsing alone. It has, though, reported the number of couples as high as 50 percent at upscale porn stores increasingly popular in major cities like Las Vegas and Los Angeles.[6]

Porn statistics have always been difficult to come by and harder to trust, for obvious reasons. (Some critics of industry-derived statistics have noted that it is a business that exaggerates the size of *everything*.) Over the last twenty years, though, pornography for couples has become a growing market. *Porn for couples* is often code for "tolerable to women," or "tailored to women's tastes." But how many women watch porn not just to satisfy a partner, but entirely for their own pleasure, or even alone by themselves?

According to a 2007 story in *AVN* (*Adult Video News*, the trade publication of the adult entertainment industry), "No one disputes the fact that the women's market may be small, but just about everyone is convinced it's growing." Nielsen Media Research, in 2003, found that one-third of visitors to porn websites were women, which came out to more than 9 million a month. On the other hand, a 2004 ABC News survey found that only 10 percent of women have visited Internet sex sites (compared to a third of men, and more than half of all men under thirty years old).

Producers of porn for women say that the growing market is driving their success. They are struggling to keep up with demand, they claim, and an increasing number of movies, websites, and retail stores whose primary audience is women backs that up. Playgirl TV and Inpulse TV, the first pay-per-view porn channels for women, have been steadily added to cable systems, and are now in 15 million and 5 million homes, respectively. According to the retail chain Hustler Hollywood, 60 percent of its clientele are women.

Even in our own experience as professors, we have noticed that many young women now speak openly about their use of pornography. For most it's a lark, some version of "We get together with friends, get a pizza, put on some porn, and just laugh at it." It is easy to see, in such gatherings, that "laughing at porn" could become a lighthearted, accessible way for these young women to work out and even conquer some of their uncertainties about sex, as well as uncertainties about how to live as "in charge" young women in a porned culture that sees them first and foremost as sexualized objects.

It should come as no surprise to us that many young women talk openly of watching porn with their friends and lovers. This is, after all, the generation of Facebook and MySpace, and they have been trained to think in terms of personal display. They are familiar with cloaked pornography. Even *AVN* agrees that "the Internet, the relative muting of anti-feminist porn rhetoric—so much in everyone's face back in the day—the popularity of *Sex in the City* and other racy programs" can take much of the responsibility for bringing more women into porn.

This isn't to say that young women who like porn are merely the dupes of a porned culture. The women's porn market is growing for the same reason that all businesses grow, it has begun to produce the kind of product that women want to buy.

What kind of porn do women watch?

Well, lots of different kinds. But much of the most popular porn for men is decidedly *not* on the women's list.

Until the 1980s, even those within the porn industry believed that women just didn't like pornography, and so porn was designed with only men in mind. One woman changed all that. If there is a pioneer of women's pornography, it is Candida Royalle.

A feminist activist in the early 1970s, Royalle (born Candice Vitala) began with nude modeling and then moved into the porn scene, appearing in twenty-five movies. Dissatisfied with the crudeness of the industry, she left the business. But in 1984 she returned, creating her own production company, Femme Productions. Faced with industry resistance, she began distributing her movies as well, and the enterprise became increasingly popular and lucrative. Femme Productions remains one of the top producers of women's porn.

Royalle explained her motivation to *AVN* in 2007: "The most bottom line reason was to put a woman's voice to adult movies. I could sense that women were curious, they were interested, but there was nothing out there for most of them." She has directed most of the films in her oeuvre, though she has hired a few other women directors.

At the core of her corporate philosophy is sexual mutuality, and the exploration of women's fantasies. That is to say, the women do not just service the men. Their own pleasure is every bit as important as their partner's, and women's fantasies, which can be quite different from men's, occupy the center of every film. Royalle, a founding member in the 1970s of the activist organization Feminists for Free Expression, sees her approach to porn as an extension of her early feminism. She even agrees with much of Levy's *Female Chauvinist Pigs*. Like Levy, Royalle believes that women, not men, should create and shape female sexuality, and then find their own ways to express it. For Royalle, giving in to the images of women found in most of the porn made for men is an abdication of women's rights, especially the rights of women to self-possession and sexual pleasure.

Royalle sees her work in porn as a continuation of her female activism in its own right. For instance, mainstream, or high-end, porn generally remains a racially divided genre, with the occasional exception of Asian women. In 2007, however, Royalle launched Femme Chocolat, "Erotica of a Different Flavor," a line of porn intended to be ethnically diverse. *AfroDite Superstar* (2007) is its first release, and the film's star, Simone Valentino, won Best New Star at the Feminist Porn Awards in 2007.

Feminist porn? Well, yes, women in the business use that term and confer that award, though not in a lock step way. Like most commercial enterprises, women's porn is not monolithic, and a good bit of variety does exist. There are, however, several characteristics that express female preferences.

- A lot of porn looks like it was shot with a video camera bought at Wal-Mart twenty years ago. Women, however, want clear images, nice lighting, and, often, beautiful surroundings. A popular convention, usually placed early in the film, is to focus on fashion, often, for instance, setting a sex scene backstage at a fashion show.

- Women tend to be less interested in the mechanics of sex, and more interested in the relationship between the participants. So there are few films with the money shots typical in men's porn of piston-like penises in vaginas, and few cumshots. Rather, women's porn focuses on seduction, on the chemistry between the sex partners.
- Women want to watch real orgasms. Women can tell when female performers are faking it, and they prefer to see other women enjoying real pleasure.
- There is a growing audience for fetish material in women's porn, especially bondage, but it must be obviously about power "play"—that is, about enticing ways to play with sexual power —and not about male dominance and disempowerment of women.
- Women prefer more realistic body types in women performers, as opposed to the pneumatic blonde that still dominates men's porn. Yet women often reverse the poles, focusing on attractive, buff young men (seldom a priority in men's porn).
- While the anthology format is popular in men's porn (a series of sex scenes with no connecting storyline), most women's porn develops a storyline. According to Carol Queen of Good Vibrations, a sex toy company, "Women would like to know just why these people are fucking" (again, not generally a priority in men's porn). Further, the women's porn industry is unanimous about what women especially *do not* want to see, and therefore never show: women mistreated. Shauna Coverdale, an Oregon retailer, explains, "We don't like to see women with their mascara running."

The roadway that Royalle opened has seen a veritable rush hour of traffic. A host of women now hold positions of power in the porn industry as directors, producers, and corporate leaders. Much of their success comes from a closer relationship with their customers. When Susie Bright, one of the most famous pro-porn feminists, convinced the company Good Vibrations to distribute women's porn, the customers "treated the video collection so reverently and offered their opinions about each one. It was like a laboratory that made money."

For women in the business, the connection of women's porn to other sexual products is, well, intimate. Overwhelmingly, they see women's enjoyment of porn as merely a part of their exploration of their sexuality. Online and at brick-and-mortar shops, women tend to spend more money on sex toys and novelties than they do on pornography, but both parts of the industry are growing.

Does pornography harm the women in the business?
This remains a difficult question. Without any doubt, women have achieved a level of prominence within the porn industry they never before commanded. Yet despite porn's mainstream success, the industry remains tarnished, and the mistreatment of women within the business is a principal reason.

The history of pornography is fairly clear on this issue. As the Meese Commission reported, organized crime was intimately involved in the porn industry through the 1980s. The Mafia allegedly bankrolled the making of *Deep Throat* and used the profits for a variety of illegal purposes, including funding drug smuggling. Whether or not a gun was put to her head, it is easy to see why Susan Boreman (Linda Lovelace) would have felt pressured, at the very least, to perform as she was told. Like Boreman, many performers came into porn from prostitution, with their pimps retaining power over them.

The current state of women in pornography is more complex.

The Mafia's influence faded in the same decade, the 1990s, that the industry enjoyed wider freedom from government oversight and gained the Internet as a new venue. Since then, the industry has worked hard to improve its reputation as a legitimate business, which means, for one thing, more transparency regarding the treatment of female performers.

The growth of the porn industry and the mainstreaming of its product have been an important part of the improvement of women's place within porn. While Linda Lovelace achieved national fame and appeared on major magazine covers, she benefited very little from her participation in the most profitable porn film ever made. On the other hand, Jenna Jameson, as we have shown, chartered her own career within porn, becoming the most famous porn star ever and selling her own company, Club Jenna, to Playboy Enterprises for untold millions. While she is easily the most successful woman in porn history, the list of women following her example is large and growing. And she is far from the only woman to achieve real riches from porn. Ever since Danni Ashe in the 1990s modeled the transition from porn movies to the Internet, women who earn porn fame in movies can add further riches online.

Porn performers regularly appear at conferences and scholarly round tables to discuss their business as sex workers. Books like *Naked Ambition: Women Who Are Changing Pornography* create cultural profiles for porn performers and producers that are entirely new. When we hear women like Jameson and others, articulate and obviously in charge, talk about their successful and highly lucrative business enterprises, it's easy to conclude that the tide has changed.

But they are an elite, small portion of the whole industry, and in that sense not representative. The vast majority of female porn performers have a very different kind of career than Jenna Jameson, and produce a different kind of porn. A walk through an average adult video store or an hour spent online browsing the virtual shelves makes the internal class structure of the business of pornography painfully clear.

Most women are in the business for a short time, and this is for a reason. Unlike the porn elites, the run-of-the-mill female performers lack distinction of any kind. They are generic, utterly interchangeable, and usually appear in anthology movies along with other interchangeable performers. Watching their DVDs makes the anti-porn feminists' claims about the degradation of women suddenly convincing, if only until we regain our larger perspective. Unless they quickly leave the porn world, they are whisked along the entire dark highway of its sex acts, always with the same series of stops: as we have seen, they start with girl/girl, then move on to girl/boy with oral and vaginal penetration, then to anal penetration, followed by "double penetration," then on to interracial, and finally they are dumped at the grimy end of the road, "pinkeye" and abuse porn. An entire "career" often lasts less than a year. Six months is not unusual.[7]

Also, the expanding market for degradation porn compromises defenses of pornography as a healthy career choice. In degradation porn, "harm" doesn't happen secondarily, it's the specific point of it all. Harm to women is the very reason men buy such DVDs. The violence in Janet Romano's *Forced Entry* is a mixture of acting and reality. But the women in degradation porn movies are not paid to act at all. All the pain and humiliation is real.

On the other hand, the growth in women's porn is in part a direct response to the ways porn harms women in the business. Candida Royalle explains that she chose to focus on more realistic body types because, first of all, it's good business: women do not want to watch performers who have become virtual cyborgs. But in addition to that, the performers themselves shouldn't have to submit their bodies to a variety of painful surgeries designed to please unrealistic male fantasies. Even worse, Royalle continues to hear from younger performers who elsewhere in the industry have had to submit to the casting couch in order to get work. This may not be the same kind of force that Boreman wrote about in *Ordeal*, but it is coercion nonetheless, which women's porn aims to remedy.

What effect does a porned culture have on women?

Without repeating here the history of the feminist arguments about porn, suffice it to say that we feel women have had good reason to feel personally oppressed by the direct effect pornography has on their lives, or by porn's general power in the culture.

We will focus here, though, on what the country has been learning in the past few years about the way our porned culture is affecting young women. In 2007 the American Psychological Association released "Report of the APA Task Force on the Sexualization of Girls." Through this process of sexualization, girls (the study looked at females ranging in age from seven to college age) are stripped of all value except for the sexual use to which they might be put. They are, to use an old and familiar term, nothing more than sex objects.

The APA panel drew on clinical experience, a survey of cultural influences, and the research of dozens of studies. Their conclusions are chilling, documenting damage to girls ranging from psychological problems such as eating disorders to cognitive impairment.

The panel found that the sexualization of girls and women was indeed pervasive and increasing. Through cartoons, music, magazines, clothing, advertisements, toys, and a host of other products and images, girls are told indirectly and directly, over and over, that their only value is their sexuality. Living with this cultural mantra, girls begin to self-objectify: they begin to see themselves as others see them, as objects of desire. When a girl accepts sexualized images as personal ideals she must live up to, and sees herself always through the eyes of others, she is in trouble.

Sexualized girls and young women face several potential pit-
falls. Some, constantly monitoring their appearance with constant
disappointment, develop depression, low self-esteem, and eating
disorders. Others may come to believe that the cultural stereotypes
about female worth are perfectly natural and right—a highly toxic
idea.

The APA report lists a host of other damaging consequences
of sexualization, some quite surprising. For example, according
to several studies, the process of self-objectification can result in
decreased intellectual performance, specifically in such areas as
mathematics and logic. Also, sexualization at a young age has been
shown to lead to unhealthy sexual behavior during the teen years,
such as sexual passivity and the decreased use of condoms.

Another recent study, titled "Sexy Media Matter" and published in *Pediatrics* in April 2006, gauged the precise impact on
adolescents of sexual content in music, movies, television, and
magazines. Girls, aged twelve to fourteen, with a high consumption of media with sexual content, are 2.2 times more likely to have
sexual intercourse over the next two years than those with a low
diet of the same material.

In Chapter 2 we talked about universal sexualization, and how
in our porned culture everyone—both genders, individuals of all
ages, classes, and professions—is increasingly seen primarily in
sexual terms. We might argue which professions have been most
affected, or which classes. Boys have surely also been sexualized,
and, again, we could argue about how (in the absence of a great
body of research) sexualization affects them.

But research, cultural analysis, and common sense lead to
one indisputable conclusion. It is simple, glaring, and impossible
to avoid: we have created a culture that puts our daughters in grave
danger and leaves them there to fend for themselves.

8. Where We Go from Here

One thing is certain about where we go from here: we do not go *back*. Not to the 1950s, not to the nineteenth century, not to any idealized notion of the good old days.

In the second half of the twentieth century, culminating a struggle that began in the nineteenth, Americans managed to throw off long-standing sexual proscriptions rooted in ignorance, sexism, and bigotry. Our sexual freedom was indeed hard-won, having to prevail on the one hand against religious fanatics who warned, for instance, that masturbation damned one to eternal hellfire, and, on the other, against secular zealots who claimed that all manner of physical and mental debility derived from "self-abuse." In the middle of the nineteenth century, James Caleb Jackson and Dr. John Harvey Kellogg, to cite two such secular zealots, created competing grain-based wafers, or flat biscuits (which Jackson called granula and Kellogg, granola) that were intended to diminish sexual appetite—though Kellogg found the application of carbolic acid to the clitoris, and, for males, circumcision without anesthetic, to be highly effective as well.

In 1856 Walt Whitman was so moved by the needless anguish of young men and women coming into normal sexual maturity that he wrote "Spontaneous Me," the first poem in American literature about masturbation. Notice, in the section below, Whitman's reassurance to his young male and female readers that he himself feels the same natural urges as they, and that indeed so does every-one. That everyone experiences sexual desire seems to us, in 2008, hardly worth stating, but in America's hypocrisy-laden Gilded Age this was news, if not exactly of the earthshaking variety, certainly seismic enough to rattle a few teacups.

> The curious roamer, the hand, roaming all over the body—
>   the bashful withdrawing of flesh where the fingers
>   soothingly pause and edge themselves,
> The limpid liquid within the young man,
> The vexed corrosion, so pensive and so painful,
> The torment—the irritable tide that will not be at rest,
> The like of the same I feel—the like of the same in others,
> The young man that flushes and flushes, and the young
>   woman that flushes and flushes,
> The young man that wakes, deep at night, the hot hand
>   seeking to repress what would master him;
> The mystic amorous night—the strange half-welcome pangs,
>   visions, sweats,
> The pulse pounding through palms and trembling encir-
>   cling fingers—the young man all color'd, red, ashamed,
>   angry. . . .

Who among us does not, on behalf of red-faced adolescents every-where, cheer these lines loudly? More generally, we, the authors of this book, cheer all the writers, artists, feminists, comedians, straight and LGBT activists, researchers, publishers, and others who were part of the long struggle to claim sexuality as a normal, natural part of human experience—and, more than that, as one of life's surpassing joys.

For decades now, certainly since the early 1970s, Americans have enjoyed enormous sexual freedom, which porn played an important part in winning. Pornographers such as Al Goldstein and Russ Meyer were in the legal trenches fighting for First Amendment rights that extended well beyond porn, opening up the topic of sexuality for treatment in mainstream movies and novels as well. Sex, thanks in part to their efforts, became something ordinary people could begin to talk about openly and frankly.

Also, the content of porn, which has remained much the same over vast intervals of time, and much the same in cultures far removed geographically, prods even the reluctant among us to acknowledge a simple fact about ourselves: we are, all of us, sexual beings. Denial of that fact leads only to repression that breeds hypocrisy and sexual dysfunction at the very least.

In extreme cases, such denial gives rise to communities of fanatics, such as that at Wellville, in Battle Creek, Michigan, around the turn of the century. There, treatments such as daily multiple enemas and the wearing of wet diapers were prescribed to heal the sickness of sexual desire. This facility was run by Dr. Kellogg, who as previously noted found that pure carbolic acid applied to the clitoris was an effective depressant of sexual appetite. If such thinking seems safely behind us, consider that today in parts of Africa and the Mideast young girls are commonly forced to undergo the surgical removal of the clitoris and the sewing shut of their labia to ensure chastity.

When conservatives praise the good old days of sexual innocence and restraint, they describe a fantasized and sentimentalized past in which the real suffering caused by ignorance and bigotry are conveniently forgotten. It can also be argued, quite contrary to the view of "lost innocence," that the porning of America has resulted from the surfacing of attitudes and values regarding women and sex that had long been submerged in American life and culture, consigned to locker rooms, neighborhood bars, fraternity houses, and men's clubs of various kinds, and manifesting as innumerable dirty jokes and smutty wisecracks, stifled guffaws and innuendo, the nudge in the ribs exchanged by men when an attractive female walked by in a tight sweater.

Porn today is no longer, as it was in the past, the dirty secret men think they are keeping from the good girls. The secret is out. In becoming mainstream, porn has stepped out from the back rooms of men's smokers and into the light of day. Before this outing, we could look away, culturally speaking, and pretend not only that porn didn't exist, but that the universality of sexual desire, the reduction of women and men to body parts, the no-strings ideal of uncommitted sex—none of this existed. Now we have to face porn, and all that porn carries in tow. We have to deal with what is liberating about porn as well as what is limiting, even damaging.

In dealing with it, however, whereas many on the right sentimentally call for a return to a never-never land past, many on the left, for their own political reasons, fail to look critically at our porned culture and in effect accept without question the current expression of sexual freedom that is based on the styles, values, and behaviors of porn.

In this final chapter, then, we have two main purposes. First, as a way to get our bearings, in a sense, and decide where porned America goes from here, we will undertake just such a critical examination of porn. Because the trend is so disturbing, both in itself and in its rapid growth on the Internet, we will further examine here the dark porn discussed in Chapter 6, the porn of degradation, humiliation, and torture. We will connect it now with the broader, related issue of the devaluation of human life in the media.

Having done that, we will conclude the chapter, and the book, by again turning our attention to one critically important aspect of the porning of America, the problem of sexualization. *Sexualized*, as we have shown, does not mean *hypersexed*. It means, rather, that a person, female or male, young or old, is divested of all other qualities he or she may be said to possess—intelligence, spirituality, sense of humor, athleticism, compassion, talent—and reduced to an outward husk, utterly empty but for a single potential, the ability to satisfy someone else's sexual needs.

Today as in Whitman's time, sex is at the heart of much confusion, emotional turmoil, and anguish. The sexualization of girls, as well as what we have called universal sexualization, is much to blame for that contemporary anguish.

These negative aspects of a porned America must be addressed, but, frankly, it is not clear to us in many cases how to proceed. For, without some kind of censorship (which we would oppose), how can the sheer volume of porn on the Internet—which in itself trivializes sex—be reduced? How (again without resorting to censorship) can the porn of humiliation and torture be kept from slowly seeping into more mainstream porn (as seems already to be happening), and from there into the culture at large?

The tendency for people, in hearing the word *problem*, is to word-associate *solution*. For this reason, dark porn should perhaps not even be called a problem, as it is far too unwieldy and complex to be addressed via any particular solution. Dark porn is perhaps better described as bundles of problems, tied, nailed, and stuck together. The necessary first step in dealing with it, then, is simply to begin to open the bundles, sifting through and describing the contents as clearly as possible. That step in itself might not reveal where we go from here, but it is a start.

Fortunately, not all of the problems we associate with the porning of America are intractable. We in fact see sexualization, despite all the grief it causes, as remediable, and we conclude our book with some specific recommendations.

A CRITIQUE OF THE "FLESHY CATASTROPHE"

We reject the oft-posited "innocence" of eighteenth-, nineteenth-, and early-twentieth-century America because this conception relies on a puritanical denial of the body and of all things sexual. But as we've discussed, we find the same ethic of bodily denial and sin in pornography. Like Puritanism, the world of porn frames or presents sex as evil, bad. The women on Internet porn sites, for instance, are described as "sluts," "bad girls," "whores." Sex itself is described as "nasty," "filthy." Shame, central to Puritanism, appears in porn in acts of sexual humiliation that form the core offering of many websites. The main difference, then, between Puritanism and porn is that instead of fleeing from sex, porn, proceeding from the same premises, indulges in it transgressively and promiscuously.

The sin and shame of both Puritanism and porn are landmines in the sexual landscape we all traverse. But they are not in any sense a necessary or inescapable part of human sexuality. In Nepal, for instance, there exists an ancient tradition called tantra that is earthy, sensual, and uninhibited, but absent the sense of sin and transgression permeating porn.[1] In the ritualistic sexual exercises of tantra, the male partner plays the role of a Hindu deity, Shiva, and the female takes on the role of a Hindu goddess, Shakti. In some of the enactments, for example, the male paints the female's body with various scented oils and colored pastes as a way to highlight and celebrate her beauty and sexuality. The two recite erotic verses to each other that are as explicit as anything found in porn, but rather than a stigmatized, demeaning vocabulary, the language of tantra is joyful, playful, and celebratory. The partners join in yoga-like postures and positions designed to enhance sexual arousal and ecstasy.

Such ritualized tantric sex is not intended to replace the more improvised, spontaneous sex that is typical of our ordinary experience. Rather, tantric practices are meant to carry over into daily life in a broad way, including sex but also extending beyond sex, to sharpen and enliven all perceptions and sensations, thereby infusing ordinary experience in general—sexual and otherwise—with heightened awareness and the spirit of praise. In tantra, then, we see an approach to sexuality that is not only different from but indeed the opposite of Puritanism and porn.

We are not proposing that everyone become a tantric yogi (indeed, we do not make such a claim for ourselves). Rather, we cite tantra as one specific example of what is more generally possible, and much to be desired, in human sexuality: an indulgence in complete sensuality, an abandonment of inhibition, with neither the wallowing in guilt and shame of Puritanism and its modern derivatives nor, in the case of porn, the rebellious sexual transgression that depends on—and thereby holds firmly in place—that same guilt and shame. And tantra models other positive sexual possibilities that ought to be achievable even outside of this formal tradition: an emphasis on giving as well as receiving pleasure, along with an affectionate and playful respect for one's partner.

In a telephone interview with the authors in April 2007, Al Goldstein, one of the exemplars of porn profiled in Chapter 4, reflected on Internet porn: "What streaming porno video does, and the porno I see, it desensitizes us, it makes it more boring, it does not maximize the potential to be better."

Goldstein's point, which he reiterated in various ways throughout our interview, is that with just a few clicks of a mouse, one can surf endlessly from porn site to porn site, deluged with images of sex acts, the sheer quantity of which reduce sex to the point of triviality and boredom. Goldstein concluded—sadly, given his decades of legal battles and the resultant cost to him in dollars and health —that the porn of today is a "fleshy catastrophe." In imitating porn, Goldstein said, people are imitating "the worst possible kind of sex."

When, as is the case in much of contemporary porn, we reduce human sexuality, a universe in itself, to the sex act, and thereby turn it into a kind of glandular aerobics, what results is the shallow, superficial sexuality of the hookup. And shallow, impersonal couplings in the real world may often fall victim to the same problems that beset Internet porn sites featuring exactly such sex: the sheer, repetitive volume can become boring. To quote again from our interview with Goldstein: "The people who make it [Internet porn] are as bored as the people watching it."

Internet sites respond to boredom by raising the shock bar. Instead of mere fellatio, for instance, they move on to something increasingly evident on porn websites: rough oral sex in which the erect member is forced down the female's throat, causing her to gag. And they invent shocking sexual practices designed to provoke the gag reflex by other means.

Since, as we have seen, viewers imitate porn, we then have the strange effect of entertainment imperatives driving sex in the real world.[2] For those so driven in their real lives by the entertainment imperative constantly to outdo what came before, simple male-female couplings begin to seem old-fashioned, quaint, like holding hands on a porch swing. As is abundantly evident if one monitors porn chat rooms, threesomes of various combinations, bondage and domination, sadomasochism, group sex, public sex, and so on, become the new standards of sexual excitement. That is, they become so until repetition dulls them as well, and the shock bar is then necessarily once again raised.

With the exceptions of true amateur porn and some women's porn, it is certainly true, as Goldstein observes, that Internet porn especially reduces sex to what is called in the industry "mechanics": close-ups of genitals in action, culminating in visible ejaculation. The sex is impersonal, and one bit of evidence that ordinary people, especially the young, are indeed imitating porn is found in the postcoital question of the typical hookup: "What did you say your name was again?"

THE DEVALUATION OF HUMAN LIFE

The most disturbing trend in contemporary porn is the growth of porn focusing on abuse, humiliation, and torture. Dark porn is of a piece with a more general media devaluation of human life that has leeched into the populace and seems to be spreading. We see this devaluation of life in the growth of extreme, graphic violence increasingly available on the Internet and on DVDs, and also to a lesser extent on network and cable television, where in fact it began. Like sex, violence has also been driven in recent decades by the entertainment imperative to continually outdo what came before, to go farther, more graphically, into more extreme violence.

Many factors have combined and overlapped to energize the devaluation of human life that manifests as a violent or sexual (and sometimes both) humiliation and debasement of men and women for entertainment purposes. Some are simply too large and complicated in themselves to allow for full examination here, but we will note them nevertheless.

The first is the cultural breakdown of the wall between public and private, or perhaps we should say the wall shielding private events. Everything about a person's life has become public to us, or potentially so. We are quickly losing respect for the very idea of privacy, even for the most elite in society. Paparazzi catch celebrities in every kind of private moment, the photos splashed across tabloids and television screens. Even presidents are not off-limits. President George H. W. Bush was, during his tenure as chief executive, photographed vomiting at a banquet in Japan, and more recently breaking down in tearful sobs as he talked about his love and support for his son, President George W. Bush. President Clinton's sex life was examined publicly in intimate and minute detail, right down to a semen stain on a young intern's blue dress. The privacy of ordinary people is even more under assault.

The practice, however, of keeping some things about ourselves private and protected—perhaps narratives of a personal struggle that we share only with friends and family, perhaps revealing, intimate anecdotes about family members that, again, we share only with family, perhaps our deepest aspirations and insecurities, our religious and spiritual beliefs and doubts, shared only with one or two most trusted friends—the protected privacy of such elements of our personal lives invests them with importance and value.

When that protection disappears, and everything about us becomes public, personal life is emptied of content, or at least of valuable content. The idea of the personal life erodes, and the value of what is left—human life turned inside out, with every debased or trivialized detail exposed—is consequently diminished.

How did this happen? Beginning in the 1970s, countless hours of television talk shows toppled the bricks of the privacy wall. Our traditional cultural sense that the personal is private was undermined by talk shows on which guests revealed the most personal things imaginable. These were led by Phil Donohue, and continued through the 1980s and 1990s with Oprah and a host of lesser luminaries (Geraldo Rivera, Ricki Lake, Montel Williams, Maury Povich, to name a few) and culminated in that parody (intentional or not) of the tabloid talk show, *The Jerry Springer Show*. On *Donohue* and *Oprah*, and on numerous other such shows, tearful guests would talk about, apparently, anything—their childhood sexual abuse, addictions to drugs/alcohol/gambling/sex, affairs with family members or neighbors, guilt over placing an Alzheimer's parent in a poor-quality nursing home, men who liked to dress in women's clothes—whatever. No topic was "too personal." Confessions and revelations in intimate detail were made to studio and television audiences, which is to say, to complete strangers.

To achieve the outrageous in such an environment, a typical *Jerry Springer* show of the 1990s consisted, for instance, of a young woman's boasting that she had taken revenge on an unfaithful boyfriend by having sex with all his friends, including a man's best friend, his dog.[3]

The tumbled bricks of the wall of privacy—as an idea, a cultural ideal—were ground to a powder by the appearance in 1992 of MTV's *The Real World*, in which seven strangers lived together in a house for months with cameras everywhere recording almost everything that happened. The private, or the private turned inside out, was indeed the subject of the show. The show was the first of the popular genre of reality shows in which ordinary people, often strangers to one another, as well as celebrities (Ron Jeremy, Anna Nicole Smith, Paris Hilton have all appeared), lived under the constant surveillance of cameras.

The crossover in 1996 from television to the Internet removed the need to censor the very few still óff-limits private events that happen in the bedroom and bathroom. A Dickinson College student, Jennifer Ringley, then nineteen years old, installed a webcam in her dorm room. What could not be shown on MTV's *Real World* was indeed shown on JenniCam, including Jennifer sleeping nude, masturbating, and having sex with her boyfriend. The webcam phenomenon has so dramatically expanded in the decade since JenniCam that one can choose now from tens of thousands of webcams in a variety of formats and venues, including cameras placed around toilet bowls, known as toiletcams.

In recent years one of the most rapidly expanding areas of porn on the Internet has been amateur porn. As discussed in Chapter 5, there are some decidedly positive aspects to true amateur porn. But there is no question that when ordinary people, many in committed relationships, post video clips on the Internet of themselves having sex, the ideas of "privacy" and "personal life" have significantly eroded.

Increasingly, not only those who choose webcams but all of us, whether we like it or not, are subjected to surveillance that undermines the very notion of the private and personal. Cameras are everywhere in cities and even in small towns, as part of crime prevention and terrorist detection: on light poles, inside and outside public and private buildings, in parking lots. In the U.K., there is now one surveillance camera for every fourteen people in the country. The U.S. seems headed in the same direction. As a *New*

York Times article, "New York Plans Surveillance Veil for Down-
town" (July 9, 2007), reports, "By the end of [2007]...more than
100 cameras will have begun monitoring cars moving through
Lower Manhattan, the beginning phase of a London-style surveillance system that would be the first in the United States. The
Lower Manhattan Security Initiative, as the plan is called, will resemble London's so-called Ring of Steel, an extensive web of cameras and roadblocks designed to detect, track and deter terrorists."

In 2007 Google Earth published on its webpage a photo of
a woman in the front seat of her car. Turning and bending inside
the vehicle, the woman's awkward motion had caused her pants
to be pulled down in back, revealing her thong and buttocks—
photographed, quite unknown to her, from a satellite in space. It
was a photograph not only of this particular woman, but also of
these particular times we live in. Here was a woman on a quiet res-
idential street in her car alone. (Or so she thought.) What could be
more private? But in actuality at the very moment that she turned
and bent over, maybe fussing with something in her purse, a camera in space was recording and broadcasting her every move—and
her ass was ogled and Googled for the world to see! Google Earth
will soon have the technology not only to photograph our homes
in detail from space, but to creep right up, so to speak, and peek in
the windows.

Human death and suffering, also traditionally granted the protection of privacy, have also moved into this public sphere. *Real
TV*, a television show from 1996 to 2001, featured mostly homemade videos of actual accidents (a girl loses a leg in a shark attack,
drag racing teens crash into each other, killing one), along with
surveillance videos of crimes (thieves rob a jewelry store and shoot
some of the clerks), mixed in with a smattering of cute videos for
comic relief (kids sing the "Oscar Meyer wiener" song in tryouts
for a commercial). Later syndicated video-clip shows, *World's Scari-
est Police Chases* in 1997 and *World's Wildest Police Videos*, produced

from 1998 to 2005 (though both shows are still aired), included pursuits and other confrontations that sometimes ended in death, though the actual moment of, say, a criminal's being struck by police bullets was usually (but not always) edited out.

As with sex, the crossover to the Internet meant shaking free of all taboos. Many websites show horrific videos and still photos of every imaginable kind of human suffering and death. Two such videos on many sites, viewed countless millions of times, show the terrorist beheading of Nicholas Berg, a contract worker in Iraq, and the execution by hanging of Saddam Hussein. Some websites, such as Rotten, online since 1996, revel in the morbidly grotesque: a suicide jumper embedded headfirst in the roof of a car, a Taliban soldier shot in the face with a 40 mm round, and so on.

The more mainstream sites YouTube and Breitbart.tv include all sorts of videos in a vast catalog, including some showing graphic violence and death. Still other sites, such as HumorON, mix porn videos with graphically violent film clips.

When privacy goes, the personal life is emptied and left vacant. When personal life is a cipher, human life in general becomes trivial, with formerly distinct, unique individuals reduced to faceless members of abstract categories, as happens in dark porn.

And so it is on the website Pinkeye that young women, all in the "slut" category, are humiliated for our amusement: with the women's apparent consent, men hold back their eyelids and ejaculate into their eyes. There are many such sites on the Internet on which women are humiliated in various ways, and some far worse than what we have described here: websites, and DVDs as well, on which women are brutally beaten and tortured.

History shows that humans are capable of doing anything, no matter how horrible, to people seen as faceless members of abstract categories, "Jews" in Nazi Germany, for example, and "slaves" in the antebellum South. Specialists dealing with kidnappings, terrorist and otherwise, have learned to instruct potential victims to try to get their captives to see them as individuals, as "real people" rather than abstract entities. Experience shows that those victims that manage to be recognized by their captors as distinct individuals—perhaps by calling attention to a medical problem or talking about their children and families—are often spared the most brutal mistreatment, torture, or even death.

How far will porned America go down this path of dark porn? How many more such websites will spring up in coming years? How extreme the violence and degradation? To what degree will more mainstream porn sites be affected? How much of the perverse "fun" of humiliating others will seep out into the culture at large? The prisoner-abuse scandal at Abu Ghraib might have been an anomaly, or it might be—as we think it is—a red flag warning us of the danger that a particular type of porn poses to our very humanity.

At the heart of the human objectification that dark porn depends on is the sexualization of girls and young women, and, more generally, the sexualization of all members of our society, or what we have called in these pages universal sexualization.

It is difficult to argue against sexualization and the trappings of sexualization—such as slutwear—without sounding prudish or anti-sex. The distinction, however, between sexuality and sexualization is crucial and must be understood clearly. One can enjoy sexuality without being sexualized. One can be sexualized and not enjoy one's sexuality. (In fact, we would argue that the sexualized person likely does not enjoy her or his own sexuality, since that sexuality is so much in the service of others—the perceptions of others, the judgments of others, the enjoyment of others, the approval of others.)

In the words of the *Report of the APA Task Force on the Sexualization of Girls,* discussed in Chapter 7, sexualization causes a person to feel that his or her "value comes only from his or her sexual appearance or behavior, to the exclusion of other characteristics."

In a *New York Times* article, "For Girls, It's Be Yourself, and Be Perfect, Too" (April 1, 2007), for instance, Kat Jiang, a student with a perfect 2400 score on her SAT, confesses in a quoted e-mail, "It's out of style to admit it, but it is more important to be hot than smart."

WHERE WE GO FROM HERE

Let us begin by thinking about where girls and women go from here in a porned America, for they are without question the most sexualized groups.

Relatively new to the landscape of porn in America, having appeared in significant numbers only in the past few decades, is the female viewer. Reliable numbers are hard to come by, but *AVN* (*Adult Video Newsletter*), an industry source, cites women's porn, or porn produced specifically for female viewers (as discussed in Chapter 7), as one of the fastest growing segments of porn.

Young women in 2008 are very much of the "anything you can do I can do better" mindset, having heard the incantation "You go, girl!" since childhood. Many are Title Nine athletes who were in soccer leagues and camps at age four, and now excel in soccer, basketball, track and field, lacrosse, and indeed almost every formerly males-only sport. Many are heading for, or are already in, careers in medicine, law, engineering, and other professions that were until recently male dominated. These females are, to understate it, not shrinking violets. It is not surprising, then, that in significant numbers, these young women have responded to the culture of porn by rolling up their sleeves, so to speak, and jumping in. Porn is one more item girls have lined out of the "boys only" playbook.

The reason they have done so has no doubt been in part defensive. A familiar tactic that oppressed groups have long relied on to diminish the arsenal of weapons they face is to co-opt as many of those weapons as possible. In this way, for instance, some African Americans use the word *nigger* in conversation with one another, and gay men the term *queer*. And in this way also some young women in porned America describe themselves, and friends, as "sluts." Some go further and purposefully wear slutty clothes. And some go even further and engage in slutty behavior, such as serial hookups, as a way of battling the sexual double standard.

Joining in, however, for whatever reason, is only at best a partially effective female response to the porned culture. A good deal of research indicates that young women, from preteen to college age and beyond, are not doing well psychologically and emotionally in porned America. In this regard, the *Report of the APA Task Force on the Sexualization of Girls* is of landmark importance. The APA report lists a number of problems related to the sexualization of girls, including body dissatisfaction, eating disorders, low self-esteem, and depression.

And yet, many of the young women that Ariel Levy talked with in connection with her book *Female Chauvinist Pig*, as well as some college women that Laura Sessions Stepp interviewed for her book *Unhooked*, seem to revel in rather than suffer from their own sexualization.[4] They flash their breasts for Girls Gone Wild cameras, for instance, because, as the girls themselves put it, they have such beautiful breasts to flash. Far from feeling exploited or victimized, they say, they positively *enjoy* putting themselves on display in skimpy clothes at bars and clubs. On first consideration, such reveling in the reduction of oneself to an attractive body might seem like the healthy exercise of a newfound freedom, sexualization as empowerment.

NO COUNTRY FOR OLD MEN ... OR WOMEN

When both men and women endorse the cultural ideal of the nineteen-year-old body as not only the highest good, but in effect the *only* good ("to the exclusion of other characteristics"), they effectively undermine themselves. We would call attention to a further inevitability, even for those young women who embrace their own sexualization: No one struts the nineteen-year-old body forever. Or even for very long.

And here is the salt rubbed into the wound of that fact: there is always a new crop of nineteen-year-olds coming along. Soon—too soon—the women who not long ago flaunted their own sexuality stand in the shadow of the up and coming, failing now to measure up to the one-dimensional standard of personal worth that they themselves helped institute. Data from the American Society of Plastic Surgeons cited in the APA report offers a glimpse into the struggles of aging women to remain young looking. Between 2000 and 2005, Botox injections rose from about 750,000 per year to almost 4 million, an increase of 388 percent. Tummy tucks increased from 62,713 to 134,746, an increase of 115 percent. Buttocks lifts rose from 1,356 in the year 2000, to 5,193 in 2005, a 283 percent increase. Most stunningly, in that same five-year period upper arm lifts increased by 3,413 percent, and lower body lifts by 4,010 percent.

The numbers speak volumes, but Plato said it best: "Beauty is a short-lived tyranny." Sexualized women in general go through the same exalted-and-trashed cycle that we see in the careers of sexualized celebrities: elevation to a pinnacle, followed soon by an inevitable and swift descent and crash. In 2005, for example, the Comedy Channel sponsored a roast of the sex symbol Pamela Anderson. The graphic jokes about her (as the roasters would have it) aging, worn body—her drooping breasts and stretched-out vagina —were tasteless and cruel, even by the reversed standards of the roast in which it is understood that the more savagely attacked the guest, the more highly honored.

Baywatch, nicknamed *Babewatch* in its prime, was a hugely popular television show, largely because of Anderson's blond bombshell body, adoringly photographed in revealing swimsuits from every possible angle. No longer in possession of quite so young and gorgeous a body, she was presented in the Comedy

Channel special as the object of ridicule, the roast's obligatory good sport, braving nonstop anatomical and sexual insult.

The spectacle was in some ways stunning, occurring less than a decade after Anderson's last *Baywatch* appearance in 1997. But it was also revealing of our cultural glee in attacking and debasing former sexual icons. The show drew the Comedy Channel's biggest-ever audience, 16 million viewers.

We love our blond bombshells—we love to watch them, we love to watch them age and decline, and then we love to watch them blow up. On a sofa near Pam Anderson sprawled Courtney Love, like a loose assemblage of shrapnel.

As we write, on the heels of the quasi-necrophilia of the televised deathwatch of Anna Nicole Smith, Britney Spears offers the latest evidence of the culture's perverse delight in the dissipation of sexual allure. The Internet is replete with photos of Britney with a flabby belly and shorn head, Britney making out drunk in clubs, "upskirts" of Britney's shaved genitalia. One YouTube video, a typical example, opines in a text lead-in that "Brittney [*sic*] spears is a Has been Skank."

The potent images of the dazzling nineteen-year-old Britney are in a sense the short-fused dynamite blowing up the still young and, by any sensible standards, still very physically attractive mother of two. It is reasonable to speculate that much of our delight in trashing former sexual icons might be rooted in our personal resentment of the ravages time deals each of us. Powerless to do anything about what we see happening to our own bodies, or what we anticipate will happen to our bodies and our sexual attractiveness, we take it out on those celebrated cultural symbols of erotic allure when they, like our own fated flesh, begin to fail us.

In any case, the progression from hottie to skank, from virgin to hag, is just a hop, skip, and a jump if one accepts what sexualization stipulates: that the most important thing about a person— in fact, the only important thing—is sexual attractiveness. Never mind how gifted an athlete—how hot is she? Never mind how smart—how hot is he?

This fact is especially problematic because surveys of young women and men consistently show that marriage and family remain the goals for the overwhelming majority. Even that preeminent party girl Paris Hilton, in an interview with Larry King shortly after her release from jail in June 2007, said that she looked forward to meeting and marrying "the right guy" within a couple of years and having kids. In an otherwise wooden and flat interview, it was one of the few moments when she smiled and appeared animated, with no apparent awareness that the bright prospect she contemplated was completely at odds with everything else about her sexualized life.

Even for ordinary young women and men, having grown up sexualized surely adds layers of difficulty to the already formidable challenges of being a wife, a husband, a mother, a father. For one thing, how does one make the transition from the hookup culture to monogamy? For another, *on what basis* does one make such a transition when relations with the opposite sex have up to this point been deliberately confined to the superficially sexual? (Can marriages made on the basis of superficial sexuality be expected to last?) And how does one continue in the marriage when sexual excitement, the basis of the union, is compromised by the demands of raising kids? Or, as is inevitable over the years, when the sexual attractiveness (defined in totally physical terms) of the partner diminishes? Most of these questions touch on matters that have always been vexing. But the sexualization that marriage partners have grown up with nowadays only adds to the vexation. Research by professors from the University of Southern California and the University of Wisconsin at Madison indicates that recently married couples preserve the happiness of their sexual union for about three years.[5]

Any path to a healthy, worthwhile sexual future, then, must

avoid the desert of sexualization, for males as well as females. Putting aside the problems men face from their own sexualization (as boytoys and studs) they too struggle in many ways with the sexualization of women.

To take just one example: boys and young men mistakenly read the sexualization of young women as a green light for inappropriate behavior. Isn't a girl in slutwear inviting sexual comments and behavior? If not, why is she dressed that way?

In the past few years, the popularity of slutwear, among other concerns, has led many public middle and high schools to consider the adoption of uniforms. One of the authors recently attended a public hearing on school uniforms in a generally conservative district in south central Pennsylvania. A middle school teacher told of often having to send girls home—seventh- and eighth-grade girls—because they showed up in class wearing pajama bottoms (a fad at the time). The sheer bottoms, often silk, were see-through in direct sunlight. Boys in class would stare, make sexual comments and jokes, and sometimes even touch the girls inappropriately or grab them.

The offending boys were disciplined, as they should be. Boys of course need to learn unequivocally that no style of female dress excuses bad behavior. But if what we wear, all of us, signals others in society about how we see ourselves (as discussed in Chapter 2), slutwear (in itself, apart from any behavior) indicates, in the words of the APA report, that girls dressed this way "exist for the sexual use of others." Slutwear does not justify rudeness or sexual assault, but simply punishing the boys for bad behavior does not satisfactorily put the matter to rest. Let's consider a parallel example.

If someone walks the dark streets of a high-crime neighborhood with twenty-dollar bills sticking out of every pocket, whoever mugs that person commits a felony that warrants the full punishment of the law. The victim's display of cash in no way excuses the crime of robbery. Still, it might be a good idea for someone to point out to the victim that he should stop walking around with twenty-dollar bills sticking out of his pockets if he doesn't want to get mugged again.

Of course, the victim might argue that he likes walking around with visible money, that he is within his rights to do so, and that he simply wants potential muggers more closely policed, or better educated about the rights of those who walk around with visible money, so that they don't commit crimes against him. We might at that point think that he is correct about his rights but hopelessly missing the point.

Similarly, the issue of slutwear is often framed in terms of the wrong argument. There is no question that women have the right to wear any style of clothing they choose. But whatever they choose, whether slutwear or a burka, inevitably signals others about who they are, or who they want to be. The question, then, is not "Don't I have the right to wear a micro-miniskirt and belly shirt?" Or, "Can't I wear low-slung pajama bottoms with the top of my thong visible if I want to?" The more precise and pertinent questions are, "What do I want my clothes to say to the world about me? Do my clothes in fact say what I want them to say, so that others will be more likely to treat me as I want to be treated?"

Confusion arises, along with consequent problems, when girls and women choose slutwear without much thought, simply following fashion. Girls so attired who do not believe that they exist "for the sexual use of others" are surprised and upset when, for instance, some boys in school hallways treat them this way. Hearings on the proposed adoption of school uniforms are filled with such stories.

For this reason, the messages murkily implicit in sexualization need to be brought into the light of full consciousness. Boys and girls, especially, need to think clearly about what else, besides sexuality, is important about themselves, and how these qualities might find expression in their personal styles of dress.

Given the universal sexualization that exists in a porned America, we need to think beyond the sexualization of females. What are the effects on all groups—on males and females, children and the elderly—of being treated as if sexuality is the exclusive value of a person? What happens to the very idea of childhood when children are sexualized? What happens to our views of the elderly when they, too, are sexualized but necessarily consigned, since they are the furthest from the nineteen-year-old ideal, to the bottom rung of the ladder of social status? (Porn sites regularly feature elderly men and women, but they do so under headings such as "old pervs," "grannies," and "old hags.")

The pervasive sexualization in our culture is not a hopeless situation, though at times it might seem so when we begin to fathom the enormity of the problem. The kinds of questions we just asked, above, can, as the APA report recommends, be raised in the home, as well as in comprehensive sex education classes that go beyond the biological basics and the need for condoms.

It's to be expected that, as educators, we believe in the power of ideas and rational discussion. But our belief is solidly grounded in empirical evidence that destructive, unhealthy attitudes and values can be reshaped in positive ways. Try, for instance, walking away from a running tap with a school-age child in the bathroom. The child will—we have had this experience with our own kids— almost immediately turn off the faucet with a reprimand about not wasting water. In general, the ecological awareness of the young is very high, thanks largely to education, to classrooms in which the need to respect and protect the environment has, for some years now, been presented clearly and emphatically.

We see similar kinds of change for the better with other social problems that were brought into the classroom, such as racism.

Racism remains a major problem in America, as does protection of the environment, for that matter, but the movement in a positive direction, thanks largely to education, is undeniable. For example, the truly unspeakable word in contemporary America is not a sexual obscenity, the F-word, but a racial obscenity, the N-word. Dr. King's "Letter from Birmingham Jail" has been required reading in middle schools and high schools for decades, along with, for instance, such books as Maya Angelou's *I Know Why the Caged Bird Sings,* and slave narratives, such as Frederick Douglass's *A Narrative of the Life of Frederick Douglass.* In social studies and in history courses the evils of racism have been discussed and exposed.

Political correctness is a term of derision, but the matter is a bit more nuanced than the silly examples usually cited would have us believe. The term often describes educational efforts to undo racial, ethnic, gender, sexual orientation, and other negative stereotypes that our culture is unquestionably better off without. As a result of such political correctness, the young know, even better than their elders, that it is not cool, for instance, to tell jokes making fun of African Americans, Jews, Italians, Poles, and others, or to use insulting slang terms for ethnic, racial, and LGBT groups.

Along formal and informal educational lines, the problems of sexualization can similarly be confronted. For example, parents need to watch television shows with their kids and comment on, let's say, ads for Bratz dolls, and other examples of sexualization, whether in ads or in the shows themselves. Even very little girls, three, four, or five years old, can be guided in ways to countervail the messages of such ads. We, the authors, tell our own five-year-old daughters, for instance, that we don't like the way the Bratz dolls dress. And that we don't like the makeup they wear—makeup is for much older girls. Simple as that. There is usually no need for explanation or justification at the age levels to which the Bratz ads, and others like them, are pitched. After all, the ads themselves do not in any way explain why the dolls are supposed to be cool, or argue for their coolness. They simply present the dolls, and drawing on the persuasive power inherent in the medium of television itself, in effect tell kids, "Bratz are cool." Parents, then, using the equally potent persuasive power inherent in being that child's mom or dad, can simply tell their young daughters, "Bratz are not cool."

At later ages, these kinds of discussions will of course be more intellectualized, for instance, in terms of how girls and boys are harmed when the clothes they wear reduce them to just their sexuality. But the sexualization of children begins very early in the lives of the kids themselves, and so must be counteracted very early.

Through formal instruction in the classroom as well, girls and boys need to gain what the APA report on sexualization calls "media literacy." The report focuses on girls, but boys as well need to develop skills enabling them not merely to view ads passively and naively, but to *see through* them—to see the underlying assumptions, the implicit and encoded messages, in commercials on television as well as in Internet and magazine ads.

Ads that might otherwise successfully shape the attitudes and values of passive, naive viewers can be openly, clearly discussed and challenged. Is it really, for instance, more important to be hot than smart? Can you be smart and still be sexy and attractive? If you have to be stupid to be attractive (we're thinking of Pink's song "Stupid Girls" here), is that a trade-off worth making? Can you be sexy and attractive even if you are not stick thin? Is it more important that *you* be pleased with the way you look or that others be pleased? And so on. Many of the messages implicit in sexualized advertisements and television shows are utterly flimsy and even transparently foolish when made explicit.

Clearly, we think that sexualization is an unmitigated harm to all. Yet that is not our position on porn. Porn, as we have shown, is not one thing, but a wide spectrum of possibilities. Some porn is toxic, beyond offensive, most especially violent porn, but also porn in which women ("sluts") exist only to service the sexual needs of men. Some porn, however—what Larry Flynt calls "vanilla sex"—is more or less unobjectionable, except perhaps from the point of view that a glut of it may trivialize sex. And still some other porn, such as women's porn and true amateur porn, may in fact offer viewers something positive and affirming about sexuality.

Again, to be clear about this, we are not in any sense champions of porn. Rather, we are making a realistic, practical point: porn has been so thoroughly absorbed into our culture that it is not going away any time soon, no matter how ardently thoughtful anti-porn crusaders might wish it to disappear. Therefore, rather than quixotically and indiscriminately campaigning against it, as if porn were monolithic, we intend to instigate a cultural dialogue on the subject of porn and the choices that confront us. We want to point out directions in porn that are absolutely poisonous, such as torture porn, or gorno. We also want to point out that other directions, however, are not only "less bad," but may actually in tangible ways offer something positive for our collective sexual values and behavior.

Most women's porn and true amateur porn, for instance, minimalizes, even eliminates, sexualization. Personal appearance is a critical part of sexualization: having a slender, toned, tanned body, and showing it off in revealing clothes. But in women's porn we often find "realistic" bodies, and in true amateur porn we find all adult ages and body types represented, often far indeed from the "porn star" ideal.

Another defining characteristic of sexualization is nearly anonymous, impersonal, unfeeling sex, which mirrors the sex in the male-oriented "anthology" porn movie—a disconnected series of sex scenes, each with no, or almost no, plot. On the other hand, in women's porn the storyline is crucial. Women want to know why a particular couple is having sex, what their relationship is, why they are so attracted. In true amateur porn, the partners usually know and at the very least seem to like each other, as is evident in the eye gazing, grins, and other gestures of affection we sometimes see there (and almost never see in professional porn). Many are in committed relationships, even married, which suggests regard for the other beyond their momentary sexual utility.

We should point out that these categories of women's porn and true amateur porn are in themselves enormous, so generalizations need qualification. To be more precise: we find that the kind of porn we are praising here is available within these categories, though not consistently, not uniformly. (There are, for instance, true amateur sites with names like "slut wives," and so on.) Perhaps the kind of women's porn and true amateur porn we have described above should be extracted and, to distinguish it from the rest of porn, be labeled differently. Perhaps it is best termed *erotica*.[6]

In any case, what we see on true amateur sites, especially, is sensual enjoyment and real pleasure—again, generally absent from professional porn and for that matter probably from most sexualized sex (the hookup) as well. The partners might be older, they might be overweight or out of shape, but they are enjoying great sex!

And that genuine enjoyment is enormously appealing, attractive, and arousing—exceeding, even, the appeal of the anatomical perfection of highly sexualized porn. What else but the attraction of real enjoyment can account for the astonishing growth of true amateur sites on the Internet?

And so, true amateur and most women's porn return sexual pleasure to the real lives of most people, many of whom felt that glamorous porn had co-opted it. Rather than watch physically per-fect specimens go through the motions, an enormous number of viewers would rather see ordinary-looking men and women, persons as flawed as themselves, truly excite one another to real orgasms.

Acknowledgments

Our thanks to Elizabethtown College for supporting our research and writing. Specifically, we thank Chris Bucher, dean of the faculty, and Louis Martin, chair of the English Department, who were supportive and helpful with money and time to complete this project. We have been lucky to work with an extraordinary editor, Gayatri Patnaik, who believed in this book from the outset. She always knew when to leave us alone to do our work, and when to step in and steer us back on course, and she made these shifts adroitly. Thanks to our research assistants, Molly Campbell and Katie Blackman, and to our wives, friends, and innumerable students who discussed some of these issues with us openly and frankly and gave us important insights.

Notes

INTRODUCTION

1. We realize that *sex worker* may be considered preferable to *prostitute* as a less stigmatized term, but in its traditional associations, *prostitute* more effectively calls to mind the specific style of dress and makeup characteristic of the Bratz dolls. In this book we use the term *prostitute* when the intention is to convey such associations, as well as in historical context.

I. NORMALIZING THE MARGINAL

1. The following books, from which we draw in this chapter, provide a detailed examination of the early history of pornography in the West: Walter Kendrick's *The Secret Museum: Pornography in Modern Culture* (New York: Viking, 1987); Isabel Tang's *Pornography: The Secret History of Civilization* (London: Channel 4 Books, 1999); and Julie Peakman's *Mighty Lewd Books: The Development of Pornography in Eighteenth-Century England* (Houndmills, Basingstoke, U.K., and New York: Palgrave Macmillan, 2003).

2. Certainly these facts have a social and historical underpinning. A Puritan couple typically observed a long betrothal, and so were in effect "married" before the formal ceremony. And life in the colonies was so tenuous, and death rates so high, that survival itself required speedy remarriage to maintain the necessary production rate of offspring. Our point here is simply that the Puritans had undeniably active sex lives.

3. The original "girl gone wild" in America (at least from the point of view of the earliest settlers) was Pocahontas. When she visited the settle-

ment at Jamestown (which was not a Puritan community) as a young girl, she shocked the colonists by turning cartwheels in a scanty leather skirt.

4. The best study of prostitution and pornography in the Civil War, from which we have drawn some examples of period pornography, is Thomas P. Lowry's *The Story the Soldiers Wouldn't Tell: Sex in the Civil War* (Mechanicsburg, Pa.: Stackpole Books, 1994). Lowry, an MD, also has some chilling descriptions of venereal diseases and their often ghastly treatments.

5. The word *hooker* has been traced to General Joseph "Fighting Joe" Hooker, who permitted prostitutes to encamp near the soldiers on the theory that it was better for soldiers to deal with boredom and release pent-up energy with prostitutes than to get drunk, fight, and gamble. Another theory on the origin of the term is that prostitutes used to fall into step with prospective clients and "hook" an arm through the arm of the male.

2. A NATION OF PORN STARS

1. In the summer of 2005, Yahoo shut down the user rooms because of allegations that the sites were being used for child pornography. Initially, they were unclear about whether such rooms might be reopened, with some corrective modifications, but as of this writing they have not reappeared.

2. Tom Wolfe, *Hooking Up* (New York: Farrar, Straus, and Giroux, 2000), 7.

3. Ibid, 8.

3. POPPING ROSIE'S RIVETS: PORN IN THE GOOD OLD DAYS

1. Scholars have created a rich trove of histories of women in postwar America. Two of the best are Sherna Berger Gluck, *Rosie the Riveter Revisited: Women, the War, and Social Change* (Boston: Twayne, 1987), and Maureen Honey, *Creating Rosie the Riveter: Class, Gender, and Propaganda during World War II* (Amherst: University of Massachusetts Press, 1984). Postwar labor statistics can be found in Howard N. Fullerton, "Labor Force Participation: 75 Years of Change, 1950–98 and 1998–2025," *Monthly Labor Review* 122, no. 12 (December 1999), 3–12.

2. Much like our understanding of Puritanism, our glossy view of sex-

ual relations during the World War II and Cold War eras is not always consistent with reality. See Jane Mersky Leder, *Thanks for the Memories: Love, Sex, and World War II* (Westport, Conn: Praeger, 2006).

3. For discussions of modern porn's Cold War forebears, see Al Di Lauro and Gerald Rabkin, *Dirty Movies: An Illustrated History of the Stag Film: 1915–1970* (New York: Chelsea House, 1976); Liz Goldwyn, *Pretty Things: The Last Generation of American Burlesque Queens* (New York: Regan Books, 2006); and Richard Foster, *The Real Bettie Page: The Truth About the Queen of the Pinups* (New York: Citadel, 2005).

4. Two very different but excellent histories of the comics are Mike Benton, *The Comic Book in America: An Illustrated History* (Dallas: Taylor, 1989), and Bradford W. Wright, *Comic Book Nation: The Transformation of Youth Culture in America* (Baltimore: Johns Hopkins University Press, 2001).

5. See Trina Robbins and Catherine Yronwode, *Women and the Comics* (Sonoma County, Calif.: Eclipse, 1985).

6. As a result of such efforts, EC is widely regarded by historians as the producer of the most complex explorations of American culture and the human psyche in comics of the golden age. Of course, sometimes a zombie is just a zombie, and the writers and artists of horror comics competed to produce the most extreme images. One artist described it as a "contest to see how many running sores you could get on a guy's body before you lost your lunch" (Howard Nostrand, quoted in Benton, *The Comic Book in America,* 47).

7. Vintage men's adventure magazines have grown in popularity in recent years, thanks in part to eBay, and a site search using the terms "Nazi bondage" will turn up dozens of old copies for sale. For information on the MAM phenomenon, see Max Allan Collins and George Hagenauer, *Men's Adventure Magazines in Postwar America* (Cologne, Germany: Taschen, 2004), and Adam Parfrey, ed., *It's a Man's World: Men's Adventure Magazines, the Postwar Pulps* (Los Angeles: Feral House, 2003).

4. PORN EXEMPLARS: ADVANCING THE FRONT LINES OF PORN

1. Al Goldstein is, however, the subject of an excellent documentary, *Porn King: The Trials of Al Goldstein* (Lancaster Associates, 2005), directed

by James Guardino. Goldstein's autobiography, *I, Goldstein: My Screwed Life*, written with Josh Alan Friedman, was published in 2006 (New York: Thunder's Mouth Press).

2. There are a number of good biographies of Russ Meyer, the best of which is Jimmy McDonough's *Big Bosoms and Square Jaws: The Biography of Russ Meyer, King of the Sex Film* (New York: Crown, 2005).

3. Ibid., 111.

4. Goldstein made a copy of the article, "An Al Goldstein History Lesson: The Wichita Trials," available to the authors.

5. Al Goldstein and Josh Alan Friedman, *I, Goldstein: My Screwed Life* (New York: Thunder's Mouth Press, 2006), 30.

6. Telephone interview with the authors, April 2007.

7. After his Pyrrhic victories in federal courts in 1974 and 1975, many costly lawsuits, including several divorce settlements, lay ahead for Goldstein throughout the 1980s and 1990s. *Screw* folded in 2003 and, soon after, Goldstein declared bankruptcy. Deteriorating health problems, along with arrests for harassment (for which he spent prison time on Rikers Island) and for shoplifting sped a general decline that left him wandering the streets of Manhattan, homeless. The performer Penn Jillette (of Penn and Teller fame) began paying Goldstein's rent for an apartment in Howard Beach, New York, and in 2007 Goldstein had returned to porn as a blogger on the website Booble.

8. Camille Paglia, "Madonna—Finally, a Real Feminist," *New York Times*, December 14, 1990.

9. Madonna, *SEX*, edited by Glenn O'Brien (New York: Warner Books, 1992), 40.

10. Madonna also found success in the 1990s reaching outside of her earlier, bubblegum, image, with cover stories in several mainstream, status-conferring magazines, such as *Vogue* and *Vanity Fair*. No profile, however, had more long-term impact on her career than a two-part interview, in 1991, for the *Advocate*, the most popular gay magazine.

11. Snoop Dogg, with Davin Seay, *Tha Doggfather: The Times, Trials, and Hardcore Truths of Snoop Dogg* (New York: William Morrow, 1999), 77.

12. This is not to suggest that interracial pairings in porn are never presented in a positive light. But the degradation theme has been utilized

so frequently in porn featuring black male/white female sex that it has become almost a given within the industry. Within women's porn and in true amateur porn, this trend is changing.

13. On March 3, 2007, addressing the Conservative Political Action Conference in Washington, D.C., Coulter also called John Edwards, former senator from North Carolina and a 2008 presidential contender, a faggot. The Huffington Post website the next day featured perhaps a harbinger of things to come. The Huffington Post is a generally liberal site favoring the Democratic Party, and among the readers' comments on the article reporting Coulter's insult was this post: "Every year Coulter raises millions of dollars for the Repiglican Party by happily serving as a bukakke centerpiece at their private fund-raisers. Repiglican insiders say she's never happier than when she has dozens of 'deposits' on her face."

Bukakke is a group sex act in which masturbating males surround a female and together ejaculate on her face. Publicly calling a vice president or a U.S. senator a faggot only skims the surface, we fear, of the dark waters yet to be plumbed in porned political commentary.

14. As a cultural metaphor, porning extends beyond politics, also describing the direction of many professional sports, perhaps following the example of pro wrestling— never a legitimate sporting event in America —which is porned in both literal and metaphorical senses. Pro wrestling is, of course, pure entertainment, but increasingly the main attraction involves watching gorgeous women rip off one another's clothes down to thong and bra, and prematch interviews replete not only with the familiar vulgar insults, but with explicit and extremely graphic sexual taunts and put-downs.

Boxing is becoming more and more a porned entertainment, beginning with Muhammad Ali's rap-like taunts before, during, and after his fights, which often got as much attention as the bouts themselves (and which, of course, have nothing to do with the sport of boxing itself). Prefight trash-talking soon became a regular feature of impending bouts. In recent years, the prefight weigh-in, traditionally simply a ritual, has become an entertainment event in itself, progressing from "stare-downs" with muttered insults and tentative shoves to (sometimes scripted, one suspects) screaming matches and brawls.

Professional football, too, has gradually been surrendering the ideals of sportsmanship and fair play that elevated it above mere entertainment and invested it with culturally important values (such as team play, character-building persistence in the face of setbacks, and so on) and, like pro wrestling and boxing, has degenerated into pregame, game, and postgame trash-talking. Increasingly common and increasingly theatrical sack and touchdown "celebrations" have nothing whatsoever to do with the sport of football and exist simply to humiliate opponents and entertain viewers.

5. WOULD YOU LIKE PORN WITH THAT BURGER?

1. In 2004 Indiana University at Bloomington was back in the news when "Kiera," a freshman, launched a website, Teenkiera, featuring nude photos in her dorm room and shower. She was quoted in the *Indiana Daily Student,* the student newspaper at IU, "It kind of helps pay for school and living next year."

2. In an article in Conde Nast's *Portfolio* (November 2007), Claire Hoffman reports on a meeting between Stephen Paul Jones, from YouPorn, and Steve Hirsch, founder of Vivid Entertainment Group, the largest producer of porn videos in the world. Jones offered to sell YouPorn to Hirsch for $20 million, a proposition whose feasibility rested on the skyrocketing growth of Internet amateur porn, and the decline of professional porn DVDs. The article reports that professional porn DVD sales have dropped by 50 percent since 2004, and industry insiders believe that the worst is yet to come. On the other hand, YouPorn went online in September 2006, and just nine months later, in May 2007, had logged more than 15 million visitors. Jones claims that its growth is a phenomenonal 37.5 percent per month. (At the time of the publication of Hoffman's article, however, YouPorn had not been sold.)

6. THE NEXUS OF PORN AND VIOLENCE: ABU GHRAIB AND BEYOND

1. The list of news reports and commentaries that discussed the Abu Ghraib photographs and the culture that led to them in terms of pornography is too long to include here, but nearly every major news outlet is

represented: the *New York Times,* the *National Review,* Salon.com, the *Chronicle Review,* CBS News, *Newsweek,* and the *Christian Science Monitor.* A simple Lexis/Nexis search reveals that media outlets of every political philosophy and purpose weighed in on the issue.

2. That insurgents used the events at Abu Ghraib as a public excuse for terrorist activity and justification for the accusation that America is an immoral society is to be expected. The fact, however, that the American occupation opened up Iraqi culture to porn, now sold on street corners, lends an unfortunate credibility to their complaints. See "A Glimmering of Hope—Iraq, a Year On," in the *Economist,* March 20, 2004.

3. Hersh's reporting is perhaps more responsible than any other source for keeping the investigations—both journalistic and governmental—of the Abu Ghraib scandal going. This chapter owes most of its details of the events at the prison to Hersh's work. In 2004 the *New Yorker* published his articles on the prison on May 10, 17, and 24, and it published his profile of General Taguba on June 25, 2007. Also see his *Chain of Command: The Road from 9/11 to Abu Ghraib* (New York: HarperCollins, 2004).

4. Though we feel like curmudgeons for pointing it out, the military has long promoted a similar kind of sexual distancing from objectified women in its famous USO shows, which have regularly featured Hollywood starlets and such iconic symbols of male fantasy as the Dallas Cowboy cheerleaders. In March 2005, female military personnel complained about the Purrfect Angelz, a review show that toured Kuwait and Iraq. The Angelz show is essentially a series of provocative dances, with the performers wearing bikinis, lingerie, or similar gear. We do not mean to insult or belittle the performers (who are usually motivated by a patriotic desire to entertain the troops) when we say that they encourage their audience to see them as sexual objects. And, clearly, neither the USO shows nor any of the Purrfect Angelz should be identified as causes of what happened at Abu Ghraib. Their presence does demonstrate, however, that despite the fact that 15 percent of the armed forces are women, the military remains a traditionally masculine environment.

5. For the most complete description of all the materials collected from Abu Ghraib, see Mark Benjamin, "Salon Exclusive: The Abu Ghraib

Files," salon.com, February 16, 2006, www.salon.com/news/feature/ 2006/02/16/abu_ghraib/index.html.

6. Oddly, though the videos available on such sites are cheaply produced, the acting of the female performers is far more convincing than we find in high-end, more mainstream, porn. This may suggest that it is easier to convey pain and terror when making violent porn than to convey ecstasy when making professional heterosexual porn.

7. WOMEN AND PORN

1. Susan Brownmiller, *Against Our Will: Men, Women, and Rape* (New York: Simon and Schuster, 1975), 443.

2. Boreman's accusations have been contradicted by several associates who worked with her on *Deep Throat* and other porn films. The 2005 documentary *Inside Deep Throat* includes refutations by Harry Reems, who costarred in the role of the doctor, and Gerard Damiano, who directed the film. For the major statements on pornography from Andrea Dworkin, see *Intercourse: The Twentieth Anniversary Edition* (New York: Basic, 2007), and *Pornography: Men Possessing Women* (New York: Perigee, 1981). Also see Dworkin's coauthored work with Catharine MacKinnon, *Pornography and Civil Rights: A New Day for Women's Equality* (Minneapolis, Minn.: Organizing against Pornography, 1988), and *In Harm's Way: The Pornography Civil Rights Hearings* (Cambridge, Mass.: Harvard University Press, 1998).

3. Many anti-pornography activists resent the use of the term *pro-sex,* because it implies that they are anti-sex. It should be said, however, that those who self-identify as pro-sex generally have a significantly broader notion of what constitutes healthy or acceptable sex and sexual material— including fetishism—than do anti-pornography activists.

4. See the U.S. Department of Justice Bulletin, *Bureau of Justice Statistics: Criminal Victimization, 2005* (Washington, D.C.: U.S. Department of Justice, September 2006), www.ojp.gov/bjs/pub/pdf/cv05.pdf.

5. Pornography, and its effects, has long been of particular interest to research psychologists and sociologists. Studies used in this chapter include Robert Bauserman, "Sexual Aggression and Pornography: A Review of Correlational Research," *Basic and Applied Social Psychology* 18, no. 4 (1996), 405–27; Kimberly A. Davies, "Voluntary Exposure to Pornography

and Men's Attitudes toward Feminism and Rape," *Journal of Sex Research* 34 (1997); Jeffrey A. Golde et al., "Attitudinal Effects of Degrading Themes and Sexual Explicitness in Video Materials," *Sexual Abuse: A Journal of Research and Treatment* 12, no. 3 (July 2000), 223–32; P. A. Lopez, W. H. George, and K. C. Davis, "Do Hostile Sexual Beliefs Affect Men's Perceptions of Sexual-Interest Messages?" *Violence and Victims* 22, no. 2 (2007), 226–42; Neil M. Malamuth, Tamara Addison, and Mary Koss, "Pornography and Sexual Aggression: Are There Reliable Effects?" *Annual Review of Sex Research* 11 (2000), 26–91; Esau Tovar, James E. Elias, and Joy Chang, "Effects of Pornography on Sexual Offending," in *Porn 101: Eroticism, Pornography, and the First Amendment,* edited by James Elias et al. (Amherst, N.Y.: Prometheus, 1999), 261–78; and V. Vega and Edward Malamuth, "Predicting Sexual Aggression: the Role of Pornography in the Context of General and Specific Risk Factors," *Aggressive Behavior* 33, no. 2 (March–April 2007), 104–17. Many more such studies are available.

6. As stated, trustworthy statistics regarding porn usage and about the porn industry are difficult to find. In 2007, however, *Adult Video News* attempted to determine women's level of porn consumption in their report by Jared Rutter, "The Women's Porn Market," *AVN* (February 2007), 56–67. The quotations in this section from women's porn producers and distributors derive from this article.

7. Many porn insiders (performers, producers, directors) have Internet blogs in which they discuss their experiences in the industry. For a discussion of the short career of porn stars, see Sam Sugar's (Sugarbank .com) blog for February 5, 2007, "The Short Life of a Porn Star."

8. WHERE WE GO FROM HERE

1. *The Tantric Way: Art, Science, Ritual,* by Ajit Mookerjee (London: Thames and Hudson, 1977), is a thorough and scholarly exploration of the philosophy and artistic expressions of tantra. It is not a guide for practitioners, but in avoiding an undue focus on sexuality, it offers a broad perspective on this ancient yogic practice and approach to life.

2. For an insightful examination of the imperatives of the world of entertainment, and a devastating assessment of the effect of electronic media on our lives, including public discourse, see Neil Postman, *Amusing Our-*

selves to Death: Public Discourse in the Age of Show Business (New York: Viking, 1985).

3. *The Jerry Springer Show* is still running, featuring women in the audience flashing their breasts to earn "Jerry beads," audience members (both female and male) pole dancing, and, of course—one of its most long-standing features—fistfights among guests, audience members, and sometimes between guests and audience members.

4. See *Unhooked: How Young Women Pursue Sex, Delay Love, and Lose at Both*, by Laura Sessions Stepp (New York: Riverhead, 2007), for a critical analysis of the culture of the hookup, derived mainly from interviews with outspoken young women. Also, *Female Chauvinist Pigs: Women and the Rise of Raunch Culture*, by Ariel Levy (New York: Free Press, 2006), is particularly good on young women who flaunt their sexualization, especially in such venues as Girls Gone Wild videos.

5. Sam Roberts, in "The Shelf Life of Bliss," *New York Times*, July 1, 2007, notes, regarding this research, that the "analysis, which included unmarried, cohabitating partners but not gay couples, was based on the National Survey of Families and Households, a national sample of 9,637 racially diverse households conducted by the University of Wisconsin Center for Demography and Ecology."

6. Some writers on porn are contemptuous of the term *erotica*, believing it to indicate nothing more than elitism. Material that would otherwise be deemed porn, the argument goes, becomes "erotica" in the hands of elites. Class does figure in the story of porn, but we think there is a substantive difference separating women's porn and true amateur porn from most professional porn.

Index

Abbott, Richie, 102
Abercrombie & Fitch, 28, 125
abjection process, 158–59
abortion, 172, 179
Abu Ghraib prisoner-abuse
  scandal: and culture of porn,
  145–50; and "female" role of
  prisoners, 147–48, 157; Google
  searches on, 152; and guards'
  role confusion, 156–57; Hersh's
  reports on, 137, 140–41, 143;
  hoax photos of, 150; and Internet violent porn sites, 150–60;
  Limbaugh on, 139; list of
  abuses, 142–43; newspaper
  coverage of, 150–51; and othering, 145; photos from, 137–39,
  145–48; and porn as language
  of control, 139–44; Sontag on,
  138; and strategies of military
  intelligence (MI) personnel,
  140–41; Taguba's investigation
  of, 140, 142–43, 146, 152; and
  turning crime into porn, 144–
  50; and violent porn, 150–60,
  162

adulthood, disappearance of,
  34–44
adventure magazines. *See* men's
  adventure magazines (MAMs)
advertising: by Abercrombie &
  Fitch, 28, 125; of Bratz dolls,
  217–18; Calvin Klein ads, 22,
  23, 119, 125; by Carl's Jr. fast
  food chain, x, xvii, 123–24; children as sex objects in, 22, 23;
  Clinique ad, 117–20; and com-
  modification of bodies and
  sexuality, 124–26, 130–31;
  and Craigslist, 126–27, 130–31;
  education to counteract, 218;
  effectiveness of, 123–24; and
  Facebook, 126, 187; in men's
  magazines, xvii; and MySpace,
  xvii, 126, 127–30, 187; nudity in,
  125; Old Spice ad, 119–21, 122;
  Orbit gum ad, 121–23; by prostitutes, 131; and Rosie the Riveter
  image, 51–52; of sexually
  charged products for children,
  28–29; and slutwear, 124–25;
  Snoop Dogg in GM commer-